Law and Justice in Post-British Nigeria

Recent Titles in
Contributions in Comparative Colonial Studies

The Man on the Spot: Essays on British Empire History
Roger D. Long, editor

Imperialism and Colonialism: Essays on the History of European Expansion
H. L. Wesseling

The Racial Dimension of American Overseas Colonial Policy
Hazel M. McFerson

Meeting Technology's Advance: Social Change in China and Zimbabwe in the Railway Age
James Zheng Gao

U.S. Imperialism in Latin America: Bryan's Challenges and Contributions, 1900–1920
Edward S. Kaplan

The Kingdom of Swaziland: Studies in Political History
D. Hugh Gillis

The Bringing of Wonder: Trade and the Indians of the Southeast, 1700–1783
Michael P. Morris

Policing Islam: The British Occupation of Egypt and the Anglo-Egyptian Struggle over Control of the Police, 1882–1914
Harold Tollefson

India: The Seductive and Seduced "Other" of German Orientalism
Kamakshi P. Murti

The Betrothed of Death: The Spanish Foreign Legion During the Rif Rebellion, 1920–1927
José E. Álvarez

Britain's Sterling Colonial Policy and Decolonization, 1939–1958
Allister Hinds

Mixed Blessing: The Impact of the American Colonial Experience on Politics and Society in the Philippines
Hazel M. McFerson, editor

Law and Justice in Post-British Nigeria

Conflicts and Interactions Between Native and Foreign Systems of Social Control in Igbo

Nọnso Okereafọezeke

Contributions in Comparative Colonial Studies, Number 43

GREENWOOD PRESS
Westport, Connecticut · London

Library of Congress Cataloging-in-Publication Data

Okereafọezeke, Nọnso, 1963–
Law and justice in post-British Nigeria : conflicts and interactions between native and foreign systems of social control in Igbo / Nọnso Okereafọezeke.
p. cm.—(Contributions in comparative colonial studies, ISSN 0163-3813 ; no. 43)
Includes bibliographical references and index.
ISBN 0-313-31308-3 (alk. paper)
1. Justice, Administration of—Nigeria. 2. Customary law—Nigeria. 3. Law, Igbo. I. Title. II. Series.
KTA3409.O39 2002
347.669—dc21 2001023853

British Library Cataloguing in Publication Data is available.

Library of Congress Catalog Card Number: 2001023853
ISBN: 0-313-31308-3
ISSN: 0163-3813

First published in 2002

Greenwood Press, 88 Post Road West, Westport, CT 06881
An imprint of Greenwood Publishing Group, Inc.
www.greenwood.com

Printed in the United States of America

The paper used in this book complies with the Permanent Paper Standard issued by the National Information Standards Organization (Z39.48–1984).

10 9 8 7 6 5 4 3 2 1

To my wife, Ezii, and son, Chinedumụ, with love

Contents

Illustrations

FIGURES

PHOTOGRAPHS

TABLES

Preface

> *Maka ọdị n'ihu omenala na iwu Igbo, ya na ndị n'ile asụsụ, omenala, na iwu Igbo na adị mma–omenala nne nne na nna nna anyị ha ji wee bikaa nka.*
> [For the future of Igbo traditions, customs, and laws, as well as all those who appreciate the Igbo language, traditions, customs, and laws–the traditions and customs according to which our parents, grandparents, and their forebears lived and grew old.]

Law and Justice in Post-British Nigeria explores the relationship between Nigeria's native and foreign justice systems. This book critically examines the promises and contradictions of Nigeria's native, foreign, plural, hierarchical, unofficial and official justice systems, as well as the origins and sources of the different justice models, and offers suggestions for reconciling the existing plural–often multi–systems or methods of justice in Nigeria. The Igbo system is used to illustrate the confused justice situation in Nigeria. The plurality resulting from a mix of native and foreign justice systems often leads to confused, inadequate, and unsatisfactory justice. This book advocates strategies for advancing the cause of justice in Nigeria's pluralistic setting through the effective and efficient utilization of the existing justice systems.

Nigeria is an enormously complex country with some 120 million citizens, over 250 nations and ethnic groups, diverse religions, cultures, social lifestyles, languages, and native justice systems, among other differences. Nigeria–a British colony until October 1, 1960–continues to struggle with the additional elements of plural justice injected into the country's life by its former colonizer. Plural justice refers to a condition in which there are two or more justice models operating concurrently in the same jurisdiction (Creel, 1988; Black, 1990; Garland, 1990; Smandych, 1991a, b, c; Hazlehurst, 1995; Thompson, 1996). For instance, justice in Igbo (one of Nigeria's nations) is based partly on the native Igbo system and partly on the imported English system. The native Igbo system of justice is based on the pre-existing philosophies, traditions, customs, and laws (customary laws) of the Igbo communities. Nigeria's English-style justice system is based on the English philosophies, principles of law, and justice as introduced into Nigeria by the British colonialists. The native Igbo system of justice and the English justice system differ procedurally and substantively in many respects. Those differences, the resulting problems, and solutions for post-colonial Nigeria are the foci of this book.

I studied and practiced law in Nigeria before traveling to the United States of America, where I obtained a Master's degree in criminal justice and a Ph.D. in criminology. Although I teach in the United States, I have maintained close ties with relevant sources in Nigeria, and these sources have helped tremendously in the data collection for this book. In the five years preceding the completion of the manuscript for this book, I completed several research projects on "the Nigerian government criminalization of the citizenry" (Okereafọezeke, 1999a; 2000e), "informal/formal justice techniques" (Okereafọezeke, 1996; 2000a, d; Okereafọezeke and Austin, 1996), and "the need to fashion an acceptable justice system for Nigeria" (Okereafọezeke, 2000b). Among other things, this book builds upon the earlier projects.

This book is divided into three parts. Each part is made up of three chapters. Part I examines the British colonial legacy as the basis of Nigeria's contemporary justice, law, and social control problems. Case studies from Nigeria's Igbo are studied, which demonstrate the efficacy of the native Igbo justice system as an instrument of social control. The elements of informal and formal justice are analyzed by scrutinizing the case studies. Part II presents three main aspects of justice in contemporary Igbo: law making, law application (case processing), and enforcement of judicial decisions (law enforcement). In each of these areas, discussions of the methods, steps, and procedures followed in the relevant area are included. Part III deals with the future of justice and traditions, customs, and laws as instruments of social control in Nigeria. The origins, present circumstances, and future of the native/foreign systems interface are examined. Suggestions are offered for repositioning Nigeria's native justice systems. Throughout this book, the reader may encounter words and phrases whose meanings are not familiar. To assist the reader with such situations, a glossary is provided, which defines many such terms.

Several people deserve thanks for the different ways in which they have contributed to the success of this book. In Nigeria, the invaluable efforts of *Eze* C. O. Nwosu (*Eze* VI of Ajallị), Madam Mgborie Okereke, Mazị Noel Obu, Mazị Jerry Nwankwọ, and Engr. Onyeka C. Okafọ toward the data collection are very much appreciated. Special appreciation, love, and thanks to my mother, Mrs. Bessie Nwagboro Okafọ, for guiding and encouraging me before, during, and since the preparation of this book. Even without having the *opportunity* of any formal education, she appreciates its great value. In the United States, my deep appreciation goes to Dr. W. Timothy Austin at Indiana University of Pennsylvania. Dr. Austin has offered numerous suggestions on ways to improve the original manuscript. His suggestions have certainly helped to make this book what it is. At Greenwood Publishing Group, thanks especially to Dr. Heather Staines, acquisitions editor, for her patience and encouragement through the process of preparing the manuscript. At Western Carolina University, thanks to Alicia Estes, Pipa Klubb, and Martha Robinson for helping to set up some of the illustrations and formats. My wife, Ezii, deserves a lot of credit, appreciation, and love for being so supportive especially through the preparation of the manuscript. My seven-month-old son, Chinedumụ, has–without knowing it–made me value time and opportunity much more than before he arrived. This book is for the past, the present, as well as the future. Chinedumụ is a part of the present and the future. I am alone responsible for the contents of this book.

Introduction

For many readers, it is necessary to provide an outline of the research population used in this book, which identifies and explains the relevant native structures. A reader who knows the research population sufficiently to follow the discussions may skip this introduction.

THE SETTING

Nigeria, a former British colony, is a country of more than 110 million citizens. The National Population Commission of Nigeria (NPCN) has estimated the country's population at 108.5 million.[1] Other estimates place Nigeria's population at about 120 million, and it is growing rapidly. The Igbos[2] are one of some 300 ethnic nationalities living in Nigeria's thirty-six states and national capital territory, Abuja. The Igbos are found mainly in Abịa, Anambra, Ebọnyị, Enugu, and Imo states, and the eastern fringes of Delta state, parts of Akwa Ibom, Bayelsa, Benue, Cross River, Kogi, and Rivers states (in the area shown in figure I.1).

STRUCTURE OF A CONTEMPORARY IGBO COMMUNITY – AJALLỊ

The town of Ajallị serves as a community case study for portions of this book to illustrate, among other things, the contemporary, traditional law-making practices, traditions, customs, and law applications to cases and enforcement of judicial decisions in Igbo. The data obtained from Ajallị consists noticeably of written, typed, and printed records derived from an array of organs

Figure I.1
Igbo Area of Nigeria (approx. 24,141 sq. kilometers or 15,000 sq. miles)

for law making, case management, and social control. The records are unsolicited (see Berg, 1998). In this book, the original records from Ajallị are called "Record of Proceedings." An identifier, for example, "Case Number 21," distinguishes each case in the records. Identifying each case by a number rather than by the names of the parties keeps each person or group anonymous in view of the fact that most of the Record of Proceedings and the cases contained in it are unpublished. Other data types from Ajallị are in the forms of photographs (for example, see those in this chapter), personal interview statements, and the author's personal observations during field trips to Nigeria.

Considering its land area, Ajallị is an average Igbo town, with a population of about 5,000, excluding those Ajallị natives living in other parts of Nigeria and outside the country. It is said that in Ajallị formal education is the main industry–see photo I.2. As a result, a great percentage of the population resides outside the town where they engage in their educational and occupational dreams. However, most natives that reside outside the town continue their strong ties to the community typically by returning home frequently and, even if

Figure I.2
Hierarchical Structure of Socio-Cultural and Political Organization of a Contemporary Igbo Town – Ajallị

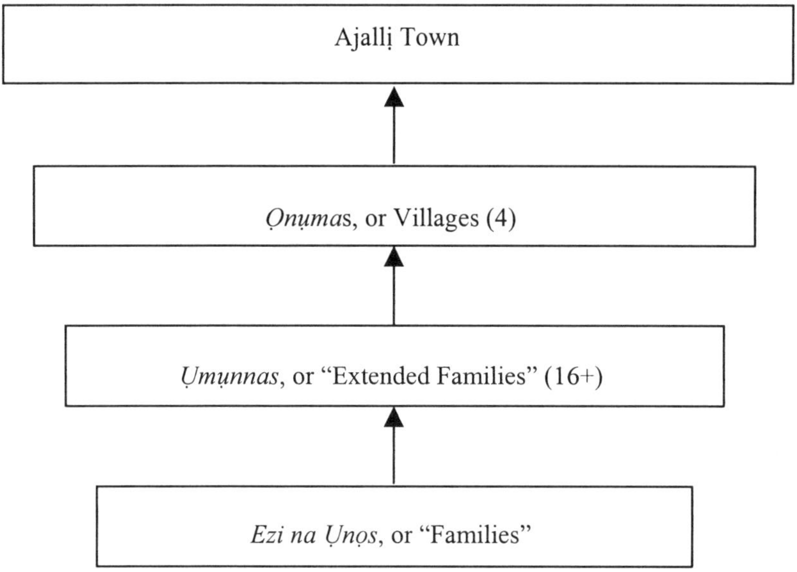

they are away from the town, they usually participate in the Ajallị community life and endeavors through their relatives at home who represent them whenever necessary. This is similar to what takes place in other Igbo towns.

Like all Igbo towns, Ajallị maintains several levels of social control (see figure I.2). The levels and organs of social control are independent of the official governments. The lowest social, structural level of control in Ajallị is the *ezi na ụnọ* or *ngwuru*. This may be the nuclear family made up of the husband, wife (or wives), and their children, or a number of nuclear families sharing a common residential compound. Two or more brothers living together in the same compound with their respective wives and children is an example of *ezi na ụnọ*. Apart from its position as a social entity, this structural level may also be used to advance religious and economic endeavors. However, it is not usually regarded as a political group.

Immediately above the *ezi na ụnọ* or *ngwuru* is the *ụmụnna*. The *ụmụnna* is a group of nuclear families and *ngwuru*'s. The members of this group have a common ancestor from whom they descended. However, an individual, a nuclear family, or an *ngwuru* may be permitted to join a particular *ụmụnna* even though their ancestor is different from that of the *ụmụnna* they seek to join. The *ụmụnna* could be a social, political, religious, as well as an economic group. Each *ụmụnna* has a male leader that may or may not be the oldest person in that

Photograph I.1. Entrance to the Orumba North Local Government Secretariat, which houses the Ajallị Customary Court. Picture shows *mmanwụ mgbadike* and its human guide painted on the wall.

Photograph I.2. Local Government Secretariat entrance showing paintings of very young and young adult students in school outfits. These paintings illustrate the Ajallị community's commitment to education.

Photograph I.3. The Ajallị Customary Court Building.

Photograph I.4. Another view of the Ajallị Customary Court Building.

ụmụnna. Where an *ụmụnna* leader is not the oldest male in the *ụmụnna*, he may be an elected leader of the group. Election to the leadership of an *ụmụnna* could take place as often as once a year.

Higher on the hierarchy than the *ụmụnna* is the *ọnụma*, or village. Each village contains a number of *ụmụnna*'s. There are four villages that make up Ajallị Town, namely: *Amagụ*, *Obinịkpa*, *Ụmụabịama*, and *Ụmụeve*. Unlike the *ụmụnna*, the *ọnụmạ* does not have a standing leadership. Individuals and groups are appointed to lead the villagers on an *ad hoc* basis. Even then, each village has some persons who are very highly regarded by the other villagers. The high regard enjoyed by such persons places them in unique positions to play important roles in the management of the village affairs. Social control is an important aspect of village affairs in Igbo.

The *Eze* (literally, "king")–a male community member–leads Ajallị Town. He is the "chief" (or "traditional ruler") of the town. The *di ọkpala* (first surviving son) of the *Eze* who passes on inherits the position of *Eze* Ajallị. Since the passing of *Eze* Nwosu Nwafo, *Eze* V Ajallị, in 1978, succession to the stool has become disputed with more Ajallị families demanding to be included in the process of selecting a successor to a passing *Eze*. However, a successor to the position of *Eze* Ajallị needs the consensus of other community leaders. A reigning *Eze* is expected to hold office for the rest of his life. However, an *Eze* could be forced from office. Apart from voluntary resignation, an *Eze* could be forced to leave office if he loses his support among the key members of the community. An *Eze* will lose the support base if, for instance, the *Eze* is seen as favoring one part of the community at the expense of the others.

The *Eze* Ajallị, like the leader of any Igbo community before the advent of colonial rule, was an important political figure. However, since the creation of superior political entities in Nigeria (local government authority, state government, and the federal government of Nigeria), the political clout of the *Eze* has been substantially diminished. The *Eze* nevertheless continues to wield some influence on religious and economic issues. He remains particularly influential on social and cultural issues.

Despite the structural emphasis on the male leadership, the sociocultural and political organization of Ajallị Town recognizes several female and male groups. Some of the groups are exclusively female or male, as the case may be, while the genders make up the memberships of the other groups. However, Ajallị, being a patriarchal society like most Igbo societies, the male groups are generally more visible and probably more influential than their female counterparts. Nonetheless, it is important to recognize that some female groups, such as the *Ụmụ Ada* (daughters of the community), are very powerful and influential in Igbo. Thus, some female groups may wield as much power and influence as the male groups. The *Ụmụ Ada* played key roles in the management of several of the cases studied for this book.

NOTES

1. "Nigeria's Population Tops 108 Million," in Cable News Network (CNN), October 23, 1998. Available from *http://cnn.com/WORLD/africa/9810/23/RB000959.reut.html*. However, there have been reports of undercounting in various parts of the country – see "Headcount" (1990); "The Missing 20 Million" (1992).

2. "Igbo" and "Ibo" were used to refer to the people and their language, respectively. However, it has become more fashionable to use "Igbo" for these and other purposes. "Today, 'Igbo' is used in three senses: to refer to the Igbo territory, to the domestic speakers of the language, and to the language spoken by them" (Uchendu, 1966, at p. 3).

Part I

Nature of Native Versus Colonially Imposed Justice in Nigeria: Dimensions of Informal and Formal Justice

1

Colonial Rule, Justice Issues, and Postcolonial Problems

INTRODUCTION

In the contemporary world, there are well-known justice issues and problems arising from the colonization of different peoples. The summary of these fundamental issues and problems are conflicts of justice and laws between the native (or indigenous) systems and the imposed foreign systems, as well as confusion between the opposing systems of justice and laws. However, the degrees of such conflicts vary from one population to another. There is significant confusion resulting from the British colonial legacy of plural justice in Nigeria. The confusion exists in every aspect of justice, tradition, custom, law, and social control in the country, including homicide, land, and marriage issues (Salamone, 1980; Ebbe, 1985; Jones, 1993). This chapter identifies, discusses, and illustrates the conflicts and confusion in Nigerian justice and law between native and foreign (English or English-style) law and justice.

BRITISH COLONIAL LEGACY AND PROBLEMS OF JUSTICE IN CONTEMPORARY NIGERIA

The problems of Nigeria's native justice systems, such as the Igbo system, are twofold. First, each native system operates as a part of a pluralistic justice structure. Second, it is the neglected part in the plural arrangement. The plurality of justice in Igbo and in all of Nigeria means that there are two or more justice systems operating at the same time in the same jurisdiction (see Creel, 1988; Black, 1990; Garland, 1990; Smandych, 1991a; Hazlehurst, 1995; Thompson, 1996; Austin, 1999). Justice in Igbo is based partly on the native

Igbo system and partly on the imported English system. The native Igbo system of justice is based on the pre-colonial and contemporary philosophies, traditions, customs, and laws of the Igbo communities, often called "customary law." The English justice system in Nigeria is based on the English philosophies and principles of law and justice as introduced into Nigeria by the British colonialists. The native Igbo system of justice and the English justice system differ procedurally and substantively in many respects.

Nigeria's pluralistic justice systems have caused four main problems in the country. First, social, cultural, political, and economic problems and difficulties arise from the simultaneous maintenance and attempted management of the competing justice systems. Second, the average Nigerian does not nor is he or she given an opportunity to appreciate the conflicts and interactions between the competing systems of law and justice. Third, because of the often unnecessary duplication and competition between the native and foreign justice systems, each system tends to produce neutralizing effects on the alternative methods of justice processing and social control. Fourth, most Nigerians are alienated from the English justice system, which is the dominant system in Nigeria, because its origin, history, experiences, and contextual roots differ from those of most Nigerians. Conversely, a Nigerian is able to identify with the country's native justice systems, particularly the native system in his or her ethnic home. Another form of alienation is that created by the officially imposed "repugnancy test," which denies official enforcement of a tradition, custom, or native law that conflicts with an official (English) law.[1]

The word *dominant*, in reference to the English justice system, is used to characterize the status of the English justice system in Nigeria as the official, general justice system, which is made even more powerful because it is backed by the enforcement powers and resources of the country's official governments. The English justice system's dominance in Nigeria does not mean that it is the most widely used system in the country. It is apparent that Nigerians use their native justice systems more commonly than the English justice system in the management of grievances, conflicts, and disputes. The variety of cases examined in this book support this assertion. However, the official governments and their agents continue to emphasize the English justice system over the native systems.

In writing on a similar condition of justice in the aboriginal populations of Canada, Ross (1992) notes the diversity of the pre-existing modes of dispute resolution among the aborigines. He points out that there were general rules and values that regulated conduct among the aborigines before colonial rule. The rules and values were (a) noninterference in the lives of others, including relationships between parents and children; (b) decision making based on consensus; (c) the repression of anger or other feelings, which might disturb or provoke; and (d) the importance of the interests of the community over the rights or interests of the individual. In various forms, these rules and values remain present in contemporary aboriginal populations.

Levi's case, a 1996 case out of Miramichi, New Brunswick, Canada (see *Miramichi Weekend*, volume 31, number 38, July 12, 1996), illustrates several aspects of the aboriginal social control rules and values as noted by Ross (1992). In the case, the Royal Canadian Mounted Police (RCMP), one of Canada's official law enforcement outfits, arrests a twenty-four-year old man of the Red Bank First Nation (RBFN). He is charged with arson and breach of probation at Miramichi official, provincial court. The arson charge stems from the burning of the community lodge, which is intended to serve as a healing center. There is little, if any, challenge to the arson charge. The accused is reported to have admitted the arson charge, while insisting that others not charged have participated in the arson. He states: "I'm going to jail anyway. I'm sorry about it. And I'm not going down alone. It wasn't just me." A RBFN community leader explains the need to consider a native "sentencing circle" rather than adhere to the strict rules and regulations of the official criminal laws and procedures. The leader explains the native "sentencing circle" as follows (at p. 1):

> The native community gets together and the guilty person listens to how his or her actions have affected others and how they feel about it. Each person takes their turn talking to the person. A judge is present to take recommendations from those people into consideration before sentencing [because] a number of natives don't feel it's up to one person to judge another.

To support his position, the community leader points out that "[official] jail sentencing has not been successful for many native individuals and it may be time to explore other methods of healing, such as the sentencing circle. Putting [Levi] in jail will not bring back the lodge and it won't make him better (at p. 1)."

Analysis of the RBFN's position in *Levi's case* (as reflected by the community leader's statements) reveals the currency of at least three of the four aboriginal values and rules of social control as identified by Ross (1992). The RBFN's leader's statements clearly demonstrate that the "sentencing circle" is built on the following: decision making based on consensus; assuaging and repressing the community anger or other feelings, which might disturb or provoke; and ensuring the importance of the community interests over the rights or interests of the individual.

A review of the literature on Igbo affairs before the advent of the British shows that the four characteristics observed by Ross (1992) were present in various forms in Igbo social control and community affairs. The British colonialists forcibly changed the face of social control in Igbo and the other parts of Nigeria by imposing English law and justice on Nigerians. However, Ross's aboriginal values and rules of social control remain visible in the native Igbo justice system. During colonial rule and since independence, the native Igbo justice system has remained efficient, effective, and widely used in Igbo social control even though it has received little or no support from the successive official governments in Nigeria. The governments have consistently emphasized the British-imposed English justice system.

The question has been asked whether or not the British mode of justice as introduced into Nigeria has been an efficient means of social control among Nigerians (Okafor, 1978; Ebbe, 1985; Oli, 1994; Okereafọezeke, 1996). This question is worth asking because of the obvious cultural, social, religious, political, and economic conflicts that were brought about by the British colonization of Nigeria. Among the Igbos, civil and criminal cases, which could be settled more quickly and satisfactorily in an unofficial, informal atmosphere, are nevertheless often taken through the formal processes of the official courts. It is common for the official criminal justice system to incarcerate convicts who could have been more useful to themselves and the society if they had been processed through a community-based, informal system of case management such as the native Igbo justice system provides.

Jurisdictions throughout the world rely more or less on informal and formal justice methods for case management and social control. An overdependence on the formal process could create problems for a society (Hazlehurst, 1995). In examining the patterns of dispute management in ten societies, Nader and Todd (1978), in reference to the United States justice system *vis-à-vis* other less formal systems, state as follows (at p. 3):

> Within one of the most professionalized systems of law in the world we have voices crying out that the legal system is overburdened, that extrajudicial systems must be developed. We have come full circle; there has been overdependence upon the law, some say. In this context it is crucial that we look at smaller societies to see how things as a whole work. In particular, it is important to see how things work in societies where the boundaries between formal and informal systems are often blurred, and can be crossed when convenient by participants who understand and use the total system for specific ends, and where law often plays a secondary role in the management of disputes.

The dilemma recounted by Nader and Todd still exists, both in the United States and in Nigeria.

Nigeria's official, English justice system is in many ways similar to the official justice systems in other "common law" countries, including Britain and the United States. It is based almost exclusively on statutes and the English common law, and it is highly formalized. The criminal justice division of Nigeria's official justice system includes the police, courts,[2] and prisons subsystems. The official system focuses on crime control through fines, incarceration, and execution of convicts. There are few, if any, alternative means of trying to correct the behaviors of convicts. Unlike the United States justice system, for example, Nigeria's official justice system has no provision for probation or parole. Therefore, every person who is convicted of a crime is almost certain to be incarcerated.[3] This is problematic for the criminal justice system because the system is compelled to manage more clients than it can handle. This situation contrasts with the central pivot of Nigeria's native justice systems, which is reconciliation (see Adeyemi, 1990, July).

Black's (1976) theories of social control and Oli's (1994) research findings have guided parts of this book. The relationship between law and other means of social control in Igbo is one of the concerns of this book. Writing on the role of law as a means of social control, Black (1976, at pp. 6-7, 107-111), states as follows: "Law varies inversely with other social control." Thus, law is stronger as a means of social control where the other means are weaker, and *vice versa*. Usually, laws are backed by *official* sanctions. This is not necessarily so with other means of social control, such as customs and traditions. Persons to whom the customs and traditions apply abide by them mostly because those persons are convinced that it is the right thing to do. They do not need the threat of official, government-imposed punishment to conduct themselves as required by the customs and traditions. In a community where customs and traditions are stronger than law, the powers of group opinion combined perhaps with the fear of the supernatural affect a person's conduct.

Traditional Igbos commonly believe in the omniscience of the supernatural and the powers of the supernatural to punish a wrongdoer (including a criminal). Also, traditional Igbos generally bear in mind that the traditions and customs of their ancestors must be followed, whether or not there are punishments attached to those traditions and customs (Achebe, 1959; Ogbalu, 1979). David and Brierley (1978), writing on the importance of a variety of customs in "the parts of Africa south of the Sahara," have concluded similarly: "Obedience to custom [is] generally spontaneous since it [is] thought that one [is] obliged to live as one's ancestors [have]" (at p. 505). Thus, the following question is relevant: What should be done to change the evident modern over-reliance on the official governments' laws at the expense of traditions, customs, and native laws in social control efforts in contemporary Nigeria?

David and Brierley point out that each African community was prior to foreign intervention capable of dealing with the issues that faced it, however complex the issues might be: "The fairly complex social system had means for the resolution of disputes or the creation of new rules of conduct when new circumstances created fresh problems for the community in question" (at p. 505). The other relevant question for this book is as follows: Are the native justice mechanisms in the Nigerian communities still capable of dealing with the grievances, conflicts, and disputes that have become more complex and diverse as a result of Nigeria's colonial and postcolonial experiences and the changing world? None of the Nigerian communities can continue to function without interacting with the rest of the country, indeed the rest of the world. Such interaction exerts many demands on every modern community. Thus, questions are now being raised about those practices that in times past were certain. Such questions or challenges of societal norms would be some of the elements of Black's (1976) heterogeneous, diverse, and unorganized society.

From a theoretical perspective, this book amplifies some of Oli's (1994) findings and conclusions. Oli studies patterns of criminality and the rates of crime between *Traditional Igbos* and *Christianized Igbos*. In Oli's study, there are 360 participants, all of Igbo origin. Face-to-face interviews, direct observation, and mailed survey questionnaires are used to collect data in the study. Also, data is obtained from the Nigerian police, the Nigerian Prison Services, the official courts in the cities of *Enugwu* (Enugu), *Ọnịcha* (Onitsha), and *Ọka* (Awka), and the Federal Office of Statistics.

Oli's (1994) study examines three major questions (at p. 30): (1) Why was crime so insignificant during the early days in Igbo communities when traditional social institutions were intact? (2) Why are the Igbos presently over-represented in the criminal population in Nigeria? (3) Why are Christianized Igbos over-represented in the population of incarcerated criminals in Nigeria? From the research report, the conclusion that can be drawn in answer to the first question is that prior to the British intervention in Igbo, traditional institutions were cared for and maintained. They played important parts in the socialization of the Igbos. With regard to the second question, Oli presents statistics showing that Igbos are over-represented in the population of incarcerated persons in Nigeria (*Annual Abstract of Statistics, 1990*). His answer is that the over-representation is the result of an increasing number of Igbos abandoning their cultural and social institutions for foreign alternatives. According to Oli, the answer to the third question is that the Christianized Igbos have lost interest in the Igbo traditional religion, laws, and customs. Ogbalu (1979) supports this finding.

In the absence of a comprehensive social control mechanism such as the Igbo traditional system provided prior to British colonization of Nigeria, crime is likely to increase among the Christianized Igbos (Okafor, 1978). As Oli (1994) puts it:

> The fear of spirits is gradually replaced by belief in expiation of sins, and an increased resort to devious means for achieving greatness. Control by tradition is replaced by police control. The English legal system notion that one is presumed innocent until detected and proven guilty, replaces fear of the omnipresence of spirits, admission of guilt and certainty of punishment. (at p. 26)

Oli concludes: "Information tends to support the original hypothesis that traditional Igbo social control systems are more compelling [than Christian social control systems] on behavior" (at p. 29).

Oli (at pp. 26-27) points out that he has identified a participant as either *Traditional* or *Christianized* based on the person's name. According to him, a participant is identified as Christianized if he or she bears a Christian name (usually European name), or the participant's name, although Igbo, has not been derived from any of the four market days in an Igbo week (*Afọ*, *Nkwọ*, *Eke*, and *Orie* or *Oye*). Although many Igbos who bear European names claim the Christian religion, identifying as Christianized those Igbos whose Igbo names are not derived from any of the Igbo four market days tends to categorize as Christianized persons who in fact hold traditional beliefs. It is increasingly fashionable for contemporary Igbo parents to give such names as *Tābụgbo*, *Obinanị*, *Nneka*, *Ifeanyịchukwu*, and *Chukwunọnso* to their children. None of such names is derived from any of the Igbo four market days. A person that bears such a name may be Traditional, Christianized, or something else. It is therefore misleading to categorize as Christianized those research participants whose names have not been derived from the Igbo four market days. A much more accurate and reliable way to determine whether a person is a Traditional, Christianized, or other Igbo is to ask the individual. Where this is impossible, some other trustworthy procedure should be utilized to ascertain the person's religious belief.

Despite the procedural concern about Oli (1994), the conclusions from the study have helped in shaping the issues for this book. If Oli's conclusion that "traditional Igbo social control systems are more compelling [than Christian social control systems] on behavior" (at p. 29) is correct, then it means that Nigeria's official social control agencies have, since independence from Britain, emphasized a less effective social control system (the English system) over Nigeria's native, more effective social control systems. Thus, the emphasis in Nigeria on social control by means of English processes is misplaced. The emphasis creates significant complications and problems for the country's criminal and civil justice systems because of the fundamentally alien nature of the English processes to most Nigerians.

SIGNIFICANCE OF THE ISSUES AND PROBLEMS

The effects of British intervention in the lives and affairs of the nationalities of the present Nigeria are undeniable and consequences of this phenomenon endure to the present time. Thus, the contemporary social, cultural, religious, political, and economic lives of the Igbos and other Nigerians are colored by British conceptions of life and ways of life, which tends to compound the lives of Nigerians who are constantly required by their circumstances, particularly by the official governments, to abandon Nigerian native lifestyles for "enlightened," foreign lifestyles (Okereafọezeke, 1998a). It is encouraging to note that even against the official odds, many Nigerians continue to devise unofficial, innovative ways of blending the native and foreign ways of life, wherever appropriate, in such a way that the native systems are retained at both the unofficial and official levels as the basis of the Nigerian society. Adeyemi (1990, July, at p. 138) describes such a situation facing Africans as "cultural anomie," which he finds transcends cultural and political fields. He states: "African societies have undergone and are still rapidly undergoing considerable cultural changes in a process which is producing a blending of the traditional systems and outlook[s] with modern European/American systems and approaches in the various facets of life" (at p. 135). Based on Adeyemi's description, cultural anomie should be read to include social, religious, political, and social control anomie, each of which is abundant in Nigeria.

The anomic (or confused) lifestyles among contemporary Nigerians are very pronounced on the issue of social control. However, Nigeria is not the only African country that lives in this anomic condition. African countries' official justice systems unduly emphasize foreign laws and justice systems (usually those of the African countries' ex-colonizers) at the expense of the native African systems. The official governments' personnel, official court judges, law teachers, and law practitioners share the blame for this situation. The African emphasis on foreign legal and justice systems has attracted condemnation even from outside Africa. Gower, cited in Onyechi (1975), describes the situation as follows (at p. 270):

> Lawyers and law teachers in Anglo-phonic Africa [are] even more traditional than their English Brethren. The besetting sin of secondary education in Africa is that too few children are taught the need for original thought. Furthermore, the besetting sin of *the British trained African lawyer* is complacency. He appears to believe that English law is the embodiment of everything that is excellent even when applied to totally different social and economic conditions. Certain it is that no one who studies criminal law from Mr. Seidman's Casebook is likely to continue to believe that English criminal law makes complete sense when applied to African conditions. [African lawyers] merely substitute for a study of English law, a study of Nigerian, Ghanaian, Tanzanian, Zambian or Malawi law. The received criminal law of all these countries is basically English criminal law. The statutory provisions in any of them closely resemble those in others. Yet at present relevant decisions in one are rarely cited in the others because the lawyers know English decisions best, their local decisions next best, and those of African states not at all.[4]

Even though Gower's English system is the system copied by many African countries, he resents the idea and prefers that the African countries develop their native systems. On the complacency mentioned by Gower, many locally trained African lawyers are even more complacent. The author, in studying and practicing law in Nigeria, has encountered many native-born Nigerians in and out of the Nigerian Law School, who hold the view that Nigerian traditions, customs, and native laws are irrelevant to social control in the modern era. To such Nigerian-trained lawyers, effective social control necessarily means what the British and the Western world do. Nigeria's law teachers, judges, and older practitioners are to blame for this. Most of them are too loyal to the British legal system at the expense of Nigeria's native systems of justice and traditions, customs, and laws. These teachers, judges, and practitioners, in turn, inculcate this undue allegiance into the Nigerian lawyer-in-training.

There is much to gain from interactions among different societies. However, three levels of interaction may be distinguished, the first level being the least intrusive and the third being the most intrusive.

Level 1 (Cooperative Interaction): In this kind of interaction, a society shares ideas and experiences with other societies. Nevertheless, each society preserves its native systems and learns from the others to improve on what already exists. Thus, the cooperating societies interact on an equal basis. The question that is foremost in the mind of each of the cooperating societies is: "What can we learn from other societies to improve on what we have?"

Level 2 (Pluralistic Interaction): A society interacting with another on this level maintains its native systems, but also establishes alternative systems based on foreign ideas. The society then has two or more alternative systems operating simultaneously. The simultaneity is prone to create an anomic, or confused, population. Also, there is the danger that the authorities will unjustifiably favor one of the alternative systems.

Level 3 (Substitutive Interaction): Interaction at this level results in a society abandoning its native systems and replacing them with foreign alternatives. The abandonment may be internally or externally engineered. However, Substitutive Interaction is the most intrusive form of interaction because it compels the natives who are already used to living their lives according to the native rules and regulations to change course and begin to live differently. Substitutive Interaction fails to realize that what is officially emphasized may be at variance with societal traditions, customs, and norms.

Since the end of colonialism, Nigeria and other African countries have had ample opportunities to emphasize native-based, relevant justice and legal systems over the colonially imposed systems. The Nigerian state in particular has failed on this issue. The country's official governments since independence have consistently pursued policies or no-policies that have emphasized or reinforced English law and justice as the basis of Nigerian justice. Thus, these governments have, with or without intending to do so, pursued *Substitutive Interaction* policies, which seek to replace Nigeria's native justice systems with the English system imposed on Nigerians by the British colonialists.

The contemporary position of masquerades in Igbo further illustrates the anomic dilemma that the Igbos and other Nigerians face. Prior to the British intervention, masquerades served important purposes among the Igbos. The masquerades provided entertainment for the people and added prestige to some ceremonies. They were involved in honoring notable citizens who had died. Masquerades were also agents of social control. Those were the days when all Igbos were *Traditional*, as opposed to *Christianized* (see Oli, 1994). In contemporary times, some Igbos identify themselves as Christianized. They believe that masquerading is sinful because it amounts to devil worship. However, rather than reject everything about masquerades, the Christianized Igbos reject only some elements of the tradition while accepting others. A Christianized Igbo accepts masquerades for entertainment on some occasions only. But he or she rejects the use of masquerades to honor a respectable community member, or for the purposes of honoring the dead by way of *ịkwa ozu*, or to celebrate a cultural festival. Nor does a Christianized Igbo accept masquerades as community agents of law, order, and justice. A Christianized Igbo–who views traditional institutions as backward and satanic–is more likely than a Traditional Igbo to reject the role of masquerades in Igbo life and culture. This confused attitude of the Christianized Igbo erodes an important means of social control among the Igbos.

The plurality and confusion concerning marriage, divorce, and social control further illustrate the quandary of the Igbos. Most Christianized Igbos believe that a marriage celebrated outside the church is no marriage. The problem is that these Igbos are unwilling to embrace church marriage exclusively. Instead, a Christianized Igbo insists on celebrating marriage in both the church and according to the Igbo customs and traditions. It is very common for Igbo Christians who marry according to the Igbo tradition to celebrate the same marriage again, the second time usually in the church (see Mann, 1985, particularly at pp. 54-76). The social control problem that this confusion creates becomes patent later. If a dispute should arise as to the validity of the marriage, the key question will be: Which marriage is at issue? If either of the parties to the marriage should want a divorce, it must be asked: Which marriage is to be dissolved? Ultimately, if a dispute arises on the death of either party, the following questions must be asked: Which custom or law should be applied to determine the rights of the disputing parties? Should the native customary law or the English law be applied? Even if the native customary law is applied, should the application be subjected to the rules of the English law? These questions continue to arise in case management in Nigeria.

SUMMARY

The problems of justice and law in post-colonial Nigeria are manifold. They range from the retention of the British-created plural justice in Nigeria, the subjugation of the country's native justice systems to the English justice system, to official neglect of Nigeria's native systems. Whereas Nigeria's native justice and legal systems have been popular among Nigerians, and are the preferred means of case management in most circumstances, the country's official governments emphasize the imposed English system. The result is that Nigeria's official governments before and since independence from Britain have elevated the imposed English law and justice over Nigeria's native justice and legal systems. Thus, there is a confused and largely inefficient official justice system in the country. What is lacking is the official acknowledgment of this situation (Okereafọezeke, 1996).

NOTES

1. See the discussions on the repugnancy test in chapters 7 and 8.

2. There are no jury trials in Nigeria. All cases (civil as well as criminal) are decided by the judge or magistrate sitting alone.

3. The following exception may apply: If a judge convicts *A* of criminal contempt because *A* fails to do an act mandated by the court, the judge may decide not to send *A* to prison. The judge may instead order *A* to specifically perform the act in question.

4. Italics added for emphasis.

2

Informal Versus Formal Justice

INTRODUCTION

This chapter is based on literature searches on informal/formal social control, and the application of the identified variables (themes) and their operational definitions (descriptors) to the judicial processes in the cases obtained from Nigeria. The themes and descriptors constitute the criteria for measuring the relative informality (or formality) of a judicial process. The literature on informal social control is examined, and twelve relevant themes are identified. Each theme is operationalized to include a number of descriptors. There are forty-nine descriptors altogether. The following five categories can be reasonably created in the informality-formality continuum: "Very Informal," "Informal," "Semi-Formal," "Formal," and "Very Formal." In presenting and discussing the resulting measuring instrument, it is recognized that some themes may have slightly different meanings between research populations. To accommodate such differences, the themes may be operationalized to recognize the local circumstances of each setting, but without losing the spirit of the themes. Table 2.1 provides help in studying the Igbo justice processes. The measuring instrument has been successfully used to assess the informal/formal characteristics of Igbo justice (see Okereafọezeke, 1996). Some of the findings are presented in this chapter to demonstrate the informal and formal characteristics of Igbo (and Nigerian) justice.

ASSESSING THE INFORMAL AND FORMAL CHARACTERISTICS OF JUSTICE

Based on the literature on informal/formal social control, the criteria used to measure the informal (or formal) character of a judicial process are presented. The criteria are presented in the forms of themes and their operational definitions, called descriptors. A descriptor is an identifying characteristic of an aspect of the culture (language, court procedure, use of third parties, etc.) that illustrates the formality or informality of justice processing.

Procedures

The literature on informal/formal social control contains words and phrases that describe the nature and characteristics of justice and justice processing. See as examples, Nader and Todd (1978); Gulliver (1979); Eckert and Newark (1980); Abel (1982); Black (1993); Nettheim (1995); Pratt (1995); Stafford (1995); Fang, et al. (1996); Austin (1999). The words and phrases are collated into twelve general categories (themes). Each theme represents an aspect of justice or case processing. The twelve themes are further detailed by the provision of selected cultural identities (descriptors) – see table 2.1. The use of table 2.1 to test the relative informality (or formality) of a judicial process involves thematic content analysis of the process (see Berg, 1998). In addition to field research strategies and face-to-face interviews in Igbo, archival records of unofficial and official court cases from Nigeria are scrutinized for the themes and descriptors in table 2.1. The themes and descriptors are organized to allow for measurements of the informality as well as the formality of judicial processes.

To test the quality of table 2.1 as a measure of judicial processes, available records of decided cases were obtained from Igbo villages and towns. The records deal with grievances, conflicts, and disputes (cases) processed in official courts as well as those processed in unofficial tribunals mainly from 1987 to 1995. Other cases were processed in the period 1996-2000. The records are analyzed to determine the presence or absence of the twelve themes and their forty-nine descriptors. The continuum between informality and formality is divided into five categories: "Very Informal," "Informal," "Semi-Formal," "Formal," and "Very Formal." Every case studied is put in one of the categories depending on the number of themes and descriptors identified in its recorded process. The test is successful because the measuring instrument satisfactorily establishes the different degrees of informal and formal judicial processes in Igbo.

Findings

Table 2.1 contains the twelve themes and forty-nine descriptors used to test the relative informality of the judicial process in each case study. An examination of each process entails scrutinizing the process, as reflected in the case, to uncover express and implied references to informal or formal procedures of managing the civil or criminal grievance, conflict, or dispute. Table 2.1 shows the columns in which each case would fall regarding the themes and descriptors. Each case would fall in one or the other of the following response categories: "Clearly identifiable," "Somewhat identifiable," and "Not identifiable."

The "appropriate response" was determined for each descriptor in table 2.1. The appropriate response to a descriptor is the response expected of an informal judicial process. Thus, based on the literature on informal/formal social control, the appropriate responses have been identified as shown in table 2.1. Every descriptor under each of the twelve themes in table 2.1 is marked with one or more asterisks. The *primary descriptor* is marked with one asterisk (*). Each of the other descriptors is marked with two or more asterisks, depending on the number of descriptors under the theme. These other descriptors are regarded as *secondary descriptors*. The "appropriate response" category is marked with the same number of asterisks for each descriptor that falls in that category. Where the correct response to a descriptor could be in two or more response categories, the applicable response categories are each marked with the applicable number of asterisks. The asterisk(s) for each descriptor are marked in the same box as the letter of the alphabet representing that descriptor. To ascertain the appropriate response category for a descriptor (based on informal judicial processes), simply count the asterisks marked against the descriptor. Find out which of the three response options contains the same number of asterisks arranged in a single column (note that each column of the asterisks in the response categories applies to a different descriptor). The response category that contains the same number of asterisks in a single column as the number of asterisks contained in the same box as the alphabet representing a descriptor is the appropriate response category for that descriptor.

The decision as to which descriptor would be regarded as the primary descriptor for a theme is a decision based on the author's reasonable judgment. The main focus is to identify as the primary descriptor the descriptor that best captures the essence of the theme regarding informal justice and case processing. Thus, a judicial process that correctly responds to the descriptor marked with one asterisk (the primary descriptor) is regarded as having satisfied the relevant theme of informal justice. The responses to the other, secondary, descriptors are considered to determine the relative strength of a process regarding the theme at issue. To illustrate, consider theme 1 (Officialism). Descriptor (a) is the primary descriptor for the theme. Thus, descriptor (a) is marked with one asterisk (*). Also, with one asterisk (*), "Not identifiable" is the appropriate response category for the Officialism theme concerning informal

Table 2.1
Analysis Indices for Assessing Relative Informality/Formality Regarding Specific Processes

	Characteristic/Theme and its Descriptors:	Presence of theme in a particular process:		
		Clearly Identifiable	Somewhat Identifiable	Not Identifiable
1.	[Officialism] Specific descriptors:			
		* * * * * * *	* * * * * * *	* *
a. *	Process set up by the Constitution or other law, or established by the state			
b. * *	Indication in report showing that dispute was settled in "court," or *uno ikpe*			
c. * * *	Any reference to *omenala*, "custom or tradition"			
d. * * * *	Reliance on the supernatural–any mention of a shrine, cult, etc.			
e. * * * * *	Specific locales of state authority: police stations, court houses, etc.			
f. *** ***	Authority figures of state			
g. *** ****	Uniforms/badges or other credentials			

Table 2.1 continued

	Characteris-tic/Theme and its Descriptors:	Presence of theme in a particular process:		
		Clearly Identifiable	Somewhat Identifiable	Not Identifiable
2.	[Mediation] Specific descriptors:			
		* * * * * * * * * *	* * * * * * * * *	* * *
a. * *	Reconciliatory–reference(s) to "making amends," "settlement," etc.			
b. *	Non-adversarial procedure–whether each party states case without being cross-examined			
c. * * *	Mention of 3rd party ("go-between") involved in resolving the case			
d. * * * *	Reference to order-maintenance in the community			

Table 2.1 continued

	Characteris-tic/Theme and its Descriptors:	Presence of theme in a particular process:		
		Clearly Identifiable	Somewhat Identifiable	Not Identifiable
3.	[Lawyer Involve-ment] Specific descriptors:			
				*
a. *	Suggestion(s) of need for lawyers			
b. *	Indication of attempt to secure lawyer			
c. *	Involvement of lawyers in case processing			

Table 2.1 continued

	Characteris-tic/Theme and its Descriptors:	Presence of theme in a particular process:		
		Clearly Identifiable	Somewhat Identifiable	Not Identifiable
4.	[Litigiousness or Argumentativeness in a Legal Sense] Involvement of lawyers in:			
				*
a. *	Bickering			
b. *	Debating			
c. *	Contentiousness			
d. *	Disagreement			
e. *	Altercation			
f. *	Challenge			

Table 2.1 continued

	Characteris-tic/Theme and its Descriptors:	Presence of theme in a particular process:		
		Clearly Identifiable	Somewhat Identifiable	Not Identifiable
5.	[Punitiveness] Specific descriptors:			
				* * * * * *
a. * *	Emphasis on guilt			
b. *	Emphasis on placing blame			
c. * * *	Focus on proof			

Table 2.1 continued

	Characteristic/Theme and its Descriptors:	Presence of theme in a particular process:		
		Clearly Identifiable	Somewhat Identifiable	Not Identifiable
6.	[Stigmatization] Specific descriptors:			
		* * * * * *	* * * * *	* * * * * * * * * * * * * *
a. *	Loss of dignity by a party–any indication that a party has lost the respect of other community members; or any indication that party is no longer to be looked up to; or denying or stripping party of position or honor			
b. * *	Loss of autonomy by party–is a party's freedom of movement, freedom of association, or freedom of speech curtailed such as by pre-trial detention or incarceration?			
c. * * *	Loss of wealth by a party			

Theme 6, Table 2.1 continued

	Characteris- tic/Theme and its Descriptors:	Presence of theme in a particular process:		
		Clearly Identifiable	Somewhat Identifiable	Not Identifiable
		* * * * * *	* * * * *	* * * * * * * * * * * * * *
6 d. * * * *	Loss of time by a party in the process			
6 e. * * * * *	Loss of face by party–any indication that a party was shamed or humiliated by members of the community			

Table 2.1 continued

	Characteris-tic/Theme and its Descriptors:	Presence of theme in a particular process:		
		Clearly Identifiable	Somewhat Identifiable	Not Identifiable
7.	[Individualization] Specific descriptors:			
		* * * *		* *
a. * *	Existence of rules barring an individual holding a position in the process from exercising discretion on an issue			
b. * * *	Flexible rules and procedures			
c. *	Persons holding positions in the process bend rules and procedures to suit individual cases			

Table 2.1 continued

	Characteris-tic/Theme and its Descriptors:	Presence of theme in a particular process:		
		Clearly Identifiable	Somewhat Identifiable	Not Identifiable
8.	[Proscriptiveness of Norms] Specific descriptor:			
				*
*	Codification of laws, rules, regulations, or customs			

Table 2.1 continued

	Characteris-tic/Theme and its Descriptors:	Presence of theme in a particular process:		
		Clearly Identifiable	Somewhat Identifiable	Not Identifiable
9.	[Record Manage-ment] Specific descriptors:			
		*		* * * * * * * * * * * * * * *
a. * *	Sketchy, handwrit-ten files of the proceedings kept			
b. * * *	Complete, handwritten files kept			
c. * * * *	Complete, typed files kept			
d. * * * * *	Complete, verbatim transcription of proceedings kept			
e. *	Memory only (oral history)			

Table 2.1 continued

	Characteristic/Theme and its Descriptors:	Presence of theme in a particular process:		
		Clearly Identifiable	Somewhat Identifiable	Not Identifiable
10.	[Simplicity of Process] Specific descriptors:			
		* * * * * *		
a. *	Procedure for initiating and conducting a case–spoken words may be sufficient			
b. * *	Non-contractual procedure–little or no need for signatures in the process			
c. * * *	An individual holding a given position in the process may play two or more roles in the process			

Table 2.1 continued

	Characteris-tic/Theme and its Descriptors:	Presence of theme in a particular process:		
		Clearly Identifiable	Somewhat Identifiable	Not Identifiable
11.	[Cost of Invoking Process] Specific descriptors:			
		* * * * * * *		* * * * * * * *
a. *	No cost			
b. * *	Minor gifts			
c. * * *	Major gifts			
d. * * * *	Small amount of money			
e. * * * * *	Large amount of money			

Table 2.1 continued

	Characteris- tic/Theme and its Descriptors:	Presence of theme in a particular process:		
		Clearly Identifiable	Somewhat Identifiable	Not Identifiable
12.	[Peacemaking Emphasis] Specific descriptors:			
		* * * * * * * * * *	* *	
a. *	Parties encouraged to integrate and cooperate with each other and the others in the community			
b. * *	Reference to the community's interest in peace, progress of the community, etc.			
c. * * *	Presence of altruistic qualities – party does not stand against the system			
d. * * * *	Absence of self-help–party involves family relations, friends, volunteers, and neighbors in the efforts to resolve the case			

justice processing. Any case that is processed according to descriptor (a) and the appropriate response category is categorized as having met the "Officialism" requirement. Whether or not the process also meets the requirements of one or more of the other descriptors impacts on the relative strength of the process in the case on the "Officialism" theme.

The eighth theme (Proscriptiveness of Norms) has only one descriptor, which is marked with an asterisk. Therefore, a judicial process must satisfy this descriptor before the process could be regarded as having met the "Proscriptiveness of Norms" condition for informal justice. The third theme (Lawyer Involvement) and the fourth theme (Litigiousness or Argumentativeness in a Legal Sense) have three and six descriptors, respectively. A process must respond correctly to each of the descriptors to be characterized as informal. Thus, the only descriptor under theme 8 is the primary descriptor. The three descriptors under theme 3 and the six descriptors under theme 4 are primary descriptors. The reason for insisting on the satisfaction of all the descriptors under themes 3 and 4 is that any form of lawyer involvement (in a professional capacity) in case management sufficiently gives rise to questions about the informality of the process.

Every judicial process used in the management of a case is individually examined to determine the extent to which it possesses the predicted themes and descriptors of informal justice. The meanings of the themes and descriptors are presented next. It is necessary to bear in mind that for the purposes of the research discussed here, the themes are operationalized against the background of the Igbo judicial processes (Okereafọezeke, 1996).

The primary concern of theme 1 (Officialism) is whether or not the official government or its agency created the person or body that manages a case. Where the person or body is thus created, it is regarded as official. Otherwise, it is classified as unofficial. The theme is also intended to determine if the person or body is maintained by, or under the influence of, the state or any of its agencies. A state-run or state-influenced judicial body would be official. Conversely, a person or body, which is neither run by, nor under the influence of, the state would be unofficial. Based on theme 1, nine major case management avenues are found in Igbo: five of the avenues are created and managed by the official governments, while the other four are independent of the official governments – see chapter 5, figure 5.1.

Theme 2 (Mediation) predicts that informal case processing would be non-adversarial in nature. An informal process would be directed toward reconciling the parties to the case. The efforts toward reconciling the disputants and maintaining order in the community may include a third party as a middleman (or go-between) between the parties. Based on theme 2, if a judicial process is not focused on reconciliation, it is not informal. The essence of theme 3 (Lawyer Involvement) and theme 4 (Litigiousness or Argumentativeness in a Legal Sense) is that no lawyer would play a role in an informal processing of a case. A lawyer involved in a professional capacity in the management of a case usually pursues the client's rights vigorously. This results in conflicts between the opposing parties. If a party to a case has secured or attempted to secure a lawyer for the case, that is viewed as an indication of the party's intention to manage the case in a way that would give rise to conflicts between the parties. Conflicts and arguments are central to formal, rather than informal, judicial processes.

Theme 5 (Punitiveness) predicts that informal case processing would neither emphasize guilt nor put emphasis on placing blame. Similarly, the process would not focus on proof. The primary descriptor for theme 5, identified as "Emphasis on placing blame" [theme 5 (b)], predicts that an informal judicial process would not emphasize blame. It is, however, noted that a judicial process could be informal but purely punitive. One of the criminal case studies discussed in this book is processed informally, yet the guilty parties are punished for criminal violations of the community's laws on masquerading. Thus, informality cannot be reasonably measured solely based on theme 5 (b). The other descriptors and themes should also be considered.

Under theme 6 (Stigmatization), either party or parties to a case processed informally would be discredited in some way by the process. Theme 6 predicts that the denunciation would be clearly shown through any of the five descriptors (see theme 6 a-e). Of the five descriptors, (a) is identified as the primary descriptor. Thus, for a case to satisfy the informal expectations of theme 6, its process must accord with the appropriate response to theme 6 (a) (Clearly identifiable). By theme 7 (Individualization), an informal judicial process is expected to include the exercise of discretion and the bending of the rules and procedures to suit the unique needs of each case. The more discretion exercised in a judicial process, the more informal the process. Theme 8 (Proscriptiveness of Norms) predicts that the customs, traditions, laws, rules, or regulations applied in an informal case processing would be uncodified, that is unwritten. Codified laws are key features of formal justice.[1]

The operationalization of theme 9 (Record Management) is based on the conclusion that written records are attributes of formal, rather than informal, justice. Under theme 9, the author expects the proceedings in a purely informal judicial process to be recorded in "memory only (oral history)" [see theme 9 (e)]. However, because of the relative nature of informal and formal judicial processes, a process that is recorded other than in memory only could be informal, albeit less informal than a process recorded in memory only. As an example, a process that is recorded by hand, in summary form, and on scraps of paper is less formal than a process in a printed, verbatim record of proceedings [see theme 9 (a)-(d)]. Theme 10 (Simplicity of Process) projects that the procedures used in initiating and conducting a case in an informal process would be simple and that the rigors associated with a formal process, for example, signing Court Summons, would be absent or minimal. Further, a person holding a position in an informal process is assumed to be able to play two or more roles in the process.

Under theme 11 (Cost of Invoking Process), it is predicted that an informal judicial process would be invoked at no cost. Thus, a party who wishes to involve the process in the management of a case will not incur any monetary or material expense. *Cost* under theme 11 should be distinguished from the types of losses enumerated under theme 6 [Stigmatization, particularly theme 6 (c)]. Theme 6 concerns the losses suffered in the course of a judicial process, that is, during the proceedings. On the other hand, theme 11 deals with the expenses needed to invoke or initiate a judicial process to manage a case. Theme 12 (Peacemaking Emphasis) predicts that an informal judicial process would stress the importance of peace to the parties and that it would encourage them to integrate with each other and with other members of the community in the interest of peace and the progress of the community. Further, it is predicted that a party in an informal process would cooperate with the process by not challenging it. The party would also avoid the use of self-help to resolve a case. A party that avoids self-help would refrain from individual or private revenge. Rather than use self-help, theme 12 expects the party to involve family relations, friends, volunteers, and neighbors in the efforts to resolve the case.

Table 2.2 is a summary of the cases studied to determine whether or not the processes employed in the case management satisfy the author's predictions of judicial informality based on the twelve themes identified in table 2.1. A theme is either "satisfied" or "not satisfied." Thus, table 2.2 includes the identification numbers (ID #s) of the cases that satisfy each theme in one column and the ID #s of the cases that do not satisfy the theme in the other column. Note that the applicable theme descriptors are not included in table 2.2, even though the descriptors have been considered in deciding whether or not a process satisfies a theme.

The judicial process employed to manage a case is expected to fall in one of the five categories created in the informality-formality continuum as follows: "Very Informal," "Informal," "Semi-Formal," "Formal," and "Very Formal" (see table 2.3).

In creating the five categories in table 2.3, it is recognized that the relationship between informality and formality is a continuum. Therefore, in measuring the informality or formality of a judicial process, the more the number of categories reasonably created in the continuum, the more precise the measurement. Against this background, five categories of informality and formality are regarded as better than fewer categories.

The "Very Informal" category is the most extreme form of informality, whereas the "Very Formal" category is the most extreme form of formality. The following considerations have guided the creation of the five categories in table 2.3. On a distribution of numbers from 0 through 12 (1-12 for the themes), 0 represents the absence of all the twelve predicted themes (Very Formal category). The number 12 at the other extreme represents the presence of all the predicted themes (Very Informal category). Of the remaining numbers 1-11, 5, 6, and 7 in the middle represent the "Semi-Formal" category. The numbers stand for the middle ground in the informality-formality continuum. The numbers 8, 9, 10, and 11 represent the "Informal" category, and the numbers 1, 2, 3, and 4 stand for the "Formal" category. The category into which the process in a case falls depends on the number of themes of informal justice found in the process.

Table 2.2
Data Summary Showing Whether or Not a Case Satisfies a Characteristic/Theme

Characteristic/Theme	ID #s of Cases Satisfying Theme	ID #s of Cases Not Satisfying Theme
1. Officialism	1-28, 31	29, 30, 32-42
2. Mediation	1, 2, 4, 6, 9, 10, 13, 20, 21, 25, 26, 35, 36, 40, 41, 42	3, 5, 7, 8, 11, 12, 14-19, 22-24, 27-34, 37-39
3. Lawyer Involvement	1-34	35-42
4. Litigiousness or Argumentativeness in a Legal Sense	1-34	35-42
5. Punitiveness	1-3, 8-10, 12, 14, 16, 17, 19, 22, 23, 25, 27, 28	4-7, 11, 13, 15, 18, 20, 21, 24, 26, 29-42
6. Stigmatization	4, 6, 13, 18, 20, 21, 24, 26, 31, 40	1-3, 5, 7-12, 14-17, 19, 22, 23, 25, 27-30, 32-39, 41, 42
7. Individualization	1-28, 33, 35, 36, 38-42	29-32, 34, 37
8. Proscriptiveness of Norms	1-31, 33-35	32, 36-42
9. Record Management	None	1-42
10. Simplicity of Process	1-25, 27, 28	26, 29-42
11. Cost of Invoking Process	4, 6, 13, 18, 20, 21, 24-26, 28	1-3, 5, 7-12, 14-17, 19, 22, 23, 27, 29-42
12. Peacemaking Emphasis	2, 3, 5-10, 12, 14-17, 19, 20, 22, 25, 31	1, 4, 11, 13, 18, 21, 23, 24, 26-30, 32-42

The bracketed number(s) in the middle column of table 2.3 is the number of informal justice themes that the process in a case must satisfy before the case could be put in the relevant category. Where there is a range between one number and another, a process is put in that category if it satisfies a number of themes within the range. Consideration has been given to the possibility of weighting the themes differently. The idea is rejected because differential weighting would present a misleading image of degrees of importance among the themes. Thus, none of the twelve themes is considered more important than the other. The literature on informal/formal social control makes obvious that all

Table 2.3
Distribution of Judicial Processes in the "Very Informal"-"Very Formal" Continuum

Category	*Number of Themes a Judicial Process Needs to Be Categorized*	*ID #s of Cases Found*
Very Informal	(12)	None
Informal	(8-11)	1-4, 6, 8-10, 12-14, 16-22, 24-26, 28
Semi-Formal	(5-7)	5, 7, 11, 15, 23, 27, 31
Formal	(1-4)	29, 30, 32-36, 38-42
Very Formal	(0)	37

twelve themes must be present in a judicial process for the process to be regarded as "Very Informal." Notwithstanding the position against differential weighting of the themes, in determining the informality (or formality) of a judicial process, theme 1 (Officialism) may be considered first. If a judicial process is an official state creation or if it is run by the state, that would be an indication that the process is formal rather than informal. On the other hand, a judicial process that exists independently of the state would strongly suggest the presence of an informal process. The decision to consider theme 1 first does not make it more or less important than any of the other themes.

Table 2.4 is an analysis plan or checklist of indices used to scrutinize each of the cases to determine the issue(s) involved ("content"). Regarding table 2.1 (for measuring "process") and table 2.4 (for measuring "content"), in a tradition of grounded research (Glaser and Strauss, 1967), the author recognizes that some research findings, which might become theoretically relevant, could not always be anticipated or predicted. Thus, the door is left open for the data to generate, at least in part, its own direction. Some themes, descriptors, and case contents should therefore be expected to emerge as important to the overall categories of research questions only after data analysis has begun.

Table 2.4
Index of Igbo Judicial Cases Studied Regarding the Content of Rule Breaking or Crimes

Established Legal Classification	Kinds of Infractions Processed		
	None/Unclear	*Civil/Tort*	*Criminal*
Dispute concerning insult/ disrespect for one's elder			
Matrimonial dispute –			
marriage			
divorce			
Dispute over succession to title (royalty, chieftaincy, *ụmụnna*, or village headship, etc.)			
Property oriented dispute –			
(a) over inheritance			
(b) over land (to include squatting)			
(c) over structure – [building (farm house, shed, etc.)]			
(d) over contractual obligation (contract to sell goods, contract to perform services, etc.)			
(e) stealing by –			
taking			
conversion			
(f) breaking and entering			
(g) burglary			
Violence oriented dispute –			
(a) assault			
(b) battery			
(c) homicide –			
justifiable death			
excusable death			
manslaughter			
murder			

Application of the Themes and Descriptors to Igbo Cases

Some of the cases studied in the research leading to this book are used here to illustrate the application of the twelve themes and forty-nine descriptors in table 2.1, as well as the predicted contents in table 2.4. Many of the case studies in this book have been processed in the period 1987-1995. The other cases were processed between 1996 and 2000. Some of the cases are derived from official, governmental courts, while the others are obtained from unofficial, non-governmental case management tribunals. The judicial process in each case is examined to identify the characteristics that qualify it as "Very Informal," "Informal," "Semi-Formal," "Formal," or "Very Formal" (see table 2.3). Five of the case studies (three from unofficial case management tribunals, two from official courts) are presented here to illustrate the application of the themes and descriptors. The judicial processes in Case Numbers 4, 8, and 20 are "Informal" because each process contains 8-11 of the predicted themes of informal justice. Case Number 32 is "Formal" because its process includes 1-4 of the themes. Case Number 37 is "Very Infotmal," since its process contains none of the themes (table 2.3).

Case Numbers 4 (1988), 8 (1990), and 20 (1994) involve disputes over disobedience of *iwu mmanwụ* (rules and regulations on masquerading),[2] battery, street fighting, harassment, and assault. Case Numbers 4 and 20 are criminal cases. Their processes are examined jointly. Case Number 8 is a civil case. Its process is examined separately. The Record of Proceedings on Case Number 4 details the handling of several misconducts by seven young men of Ajallị Town. The accused persons are tried together. The alleged misconducts are three incidents of battery, five incidents of assault, two incidents of street fighting, and a disobedience of an order against masquerading on a Sunday. All the misconducts involved in this case result from *otute* (annual yam festival) celebrations.[3]

Case Number 4 includes ten crimes under the *Criminal Code Law of Anambra State*. Each of the ten incidents involved in the case is a ground for criminal prosecution of the alleged offenders in the official courts. Also, each of the incidents is a sufficient ground for a civil claim in the official court. The accused persons are, however, tried before the *Eze*-in-Council (an unofficial, non-governmental case management tribunal in Ajallị town). If the accused were tried in an official court, such trial would go on for a much longer time (one year or more) than it takes the *Eze*-in-Council to dispose of all the cases. Moreover, a conviction in an official court would attract a punishment of imprisonment or, at a minimum, a fine. However, in dealing with Case Number 4, the *Eze*-in-Council has applied the customary laws and traditions of Ajallị community. The infractions are treated as crimes against the community. The accused are convicted and fined between one and seven goats each, depending on the gravity of the convict's offense.

In Case Number 20, a masquerade and an accomplice[4] have allegedly assaulted the complainant. As in Case Number 4, the assault in Case Number 20 is a ground for criminal prosecution and civil claim in the official court. However, the complainant decides to have the case handled by the *Eze*-in-Council. The records actually refer to the second disputants (the parties complained against before the *Eze*-in-Council) as the "accused." They are held responsible for the misconduct at issue. The seriousness of the misconduct causes the *Eze*-in-Council to ban them from taking part in any masquerading in the town for two years. The *Eze*-in-Council processes Case Number 20 as a criminal case because of the general community interest in order maintenance.

The process in Case Number 4 includes nine of the twelve themes of informal case processing. Case Number 20 complies with ten of those themes. Each of the two cases fails to meet themes 5 (Punitiveness) and 9 (Record Management) (see table 2.1). Theme 9 is intended to ascertain the method of recording and preserving the proceedings in a case. The options range from "Memory only (oral history)"–the most informal type of record keeping–to "Complete, verbatim transcription of proceedings kept"–the most formal option. Since the "Memory only (oral history)" option is the most informal of all, it is identified as the primary descriptor for the "Record Management" theme. The fact that the records of some of the cases studied in the research already existed in written form before the author requested them effectively disqualifies the judicial processes involved in the cases from satisfying the "Record Management" theme. This sufficiently disqualifies the cases from the "Very Informal" category.

The process in Case Number 4 does not meet the requirements of theme 12 (Peacemaking Emphasis) because the *Eze*-in-Council is primarily interested in protecting the Ajallị community from the transgressors, rather than making peace with them. Case Numbers 4 and 20 include theme 1 in their processes, since the accused persons are tried before the *Eze*-in-Council (an unofficial, non-governmental tribunal). In Case Number 4, the council makes a clear reference to the *omenala* (customs, traditions) that apply to Ajallị town when it states that women are not to partake of the goat meat collected as fines from the offenders[5] [see theme 1 (c)]. The proceedings in both cases are non-adversarial because there is no confrontation of the opponent. This is in line with the expectation under theme 2 (Mediation). As a matter of fact, the accused persons are tried summarily. No witnesses are called. Themes 3 (Lawyer Involvement) and 4 (Litigiousness or Argumentativeness in a Legal Sense) are clearly identifiable in the cases because the accused are tried without the involvement of lawyers. The records of proceedings show an emphasis on placing blame. This means that neither Case Number 4 nor Case Number 20 complies with theme 5 (Punitiveness).

The processes in Case Numbers 4 and 20 stigmatize the accused persons by the fact of their convictions (see theme 6). In Ajallị community, his peers no longer trust a person convicted of breaking the laws and regulations on masquerading. The offender is denied some sensitive offices in the community relating to the secrets of masquerading (Cf. Becker, 1963, for the untrustworthiness of a person labeled "criminal"). In Case Number 20, the *Eze*-in-Council decides to ban the offenders from *otiti mmanwụ* and following *mmanwụ* (any active involvement in masquerade displays) for two years.

The processes in Case Numbers 4 and 20 meet the predictions under themes 7 (Individualization), 8 (Proscriptiveness of Norms), 10 (Simplicity of Process), and 11 (Cost of Invoking Process). In addition, Case Number 20 meets the conditions of theme 12 (Peacemaking Emphasis). Consistently with theme 7, the punishment imposed on each offender in Case Number 4 depends on the seriousness of the offense in the community. Also, in line with theme 8, the laws and customs relied upon in both cases are uncodified. Neither case satisfies the "memory only (oral history)" predicted under theme 9. Both cases meet the "simplicity of process" expected under theme 10 because the proceedings in the cases are initiated orally. Also, there is "no cost" in the invocation of the legal process in either case. This accords with theme 11. Further, in Case Number 20, the tribunal members encourage the disputants to maintain peace and to cooperate with other community members.

In Case Number 8 (1990), the second disputant has allegedly been "haunted and harassed" (at p. 125 of the Record of Proceedings) by the members of his former *ụmụnna* (extended family). The haunting and harassment leads to fights between him and the first disputant. Part of the issue is a land dispute between the parties. One of the disputants has taken the land case to the official court.[6] Subsequent to that, the first disputant brings the case before the *Eze*-in-Council. The council concludes that the dispute before it deals with different issues from those involved in the case in the official court.[7] The present dispute is treated as a civil dispute.[8] As the council members see it, the responsibility of the council is that of "restoring peace among the disputants" (at p. 125). In recognition of this, the council decides that "both parties are hereby bound over from fighting or any behaviour calculated or likely to cause any breach of the peace. But their case in the [official] court is not the concern of the *Eze*-in-Council" (at p. 129). The judicial process in Case Number 8 meets eight of the twelve predicted themes of informal case processing. The case is tried before the *Eze*-in-Council. Theme 12 (Peacemaking Emphasis) is clearly identifiable in the process. The Record of Proceedings contains the following entry based on a resolution of the council: "The two families [are] accordingly to be informed to keep the peace among their members" (at p. 126). The case is initiated by the *ịtụnye mmanya*[9] procedure contrary to the predicted "no cost" of invoking an informal judicial process [see theme 11 (Cost of Invoking Process)].

The record of proceedings on Case Number 8 is complete and handwritten. This differs from the prediction under theme 9 (Record Management). The fact that neither of the disputants loses dignity [theme 6 (a)] leads to the conclusion that theme 6 (Stigmatization) is absent in the processing of Case Number 8. However, both disputants have lost autonomy as a consequence of the council's interim injunction, which bars the disputants from entering the disputed land. They are also directed to be of good behavior. The injunction and the binding over curtail the disputants' freedoms of movement, speech, and association contrary to theme 6 (b). Theme 2 (Mediation) is not identifiable in the case, since the proceedings are adversarial. Case Numbers 4, 8, and 20 deal with assaults. The proceedings in Case Numbers 4 and 20 (criminal cases) are non-adversarial. On the other hand, the proceedings in Case Number 8 (a civil case) are adversarial.

The relative informality of the judicial processes in the official court cases is also examined. Case Numbers 32 and 37 are discussed here to illustrate the processes in these cases. In Case Number 32 (Charge No. CCA/53C/89, October 1989), a criminal charge is brought against two persons for contempt of the order of the Customary Court.[10] The court has previously issued an order restraining all parties to a pending case from plucking pears from a certain pear tree. The two accused persons allegedly plucked and sold the pears contrary to the order. They are charged under *Sections 39 and 59 (i) & (e) of the Anambra State Edict No. 6 of 1984*. The official law empowers the Customary Court to punish for contempt inside and outside the court. The case report lists the court as the prosecutor. Thus, the court, in this case, plays two roles at the same time: prosecutor and judge [see theme 10 (c)].[11] However, the dual roles are not sufficient to satisfy the requirements of theme 10 (Simplicity of Process) because the primary descriptor under the theme (that spoken words may be sufficient to initiate and conduct the case) is not identifiable in the process.

The process in Case Number 32 clearly satisfies the informal justice expectations of themes 3 and 4 because the accused persons are tried without lawyers. Regarding theme 5 (Punitiveness), the court clearly shows that the proceedings are focused on proof (contrary to the expectations of the theme) when it states (at pp. 8-9 of the case report):

> In the absence of [corroboration], and in the absence of either yam or pear, tendered before the Court as Exhibits, [the] Court has no doubt that the complainant merely based his complaint on hearsay. With lapses such as these, [the] Court is left without any doubt that the complainant has not proved his case beyond all reasonable doubts. In the light of these circumstances [the] Court has found both 1st and 2nd accused not guilty on both counts and therefore are discharged and acquitted.[12]

In Case Number 32, the accused persons are prosecuted in the Customary Court (an official court). Thus, it is mandatory that they have to be prosecuted under a written law. Under Nigeria's official laws, an accused person cannot be prosecuted or convicted of a crime in any official court unless the crime is defined and the punishment therefor prescribed in writing by an Act of the National Assembly, the Law of a state or any subsidiary legislation or instrument under the provisions of a law [*section 36 (12), 1999 Constitution*]. This constitutional requirement does not apply to criminal cases processed unofficially, for example, by the *Eze*-in-Council

The other case from an official court is Case Number 37 [Suit No. AB/CC/8A/91 (1992)], a civil case. The issue before the High Court is whether or not the procedure followed in filing an appeal in the court against the judgment of a Customary Court accords with the prescribed procedure. The respondent in the appeal claims that because the appellant's attorney–rather than the appellant himself as mentioned by the *Customary Court Rules*–signed the Notice of Appeal, the appeal is incompetent (invalid, ineffectual). He asks the High Court to dismiss the appeal for that reason. The High Court rejects the argument, ruling that the appellant or his attorney may sign the Notice of Appeal.

The issue involved in Case Number 37 is very technical. Therefore, the processing of the case would also be very technical. This accounts for the absence of all the twelve themes predicted for informal case processing. What actually puts this case in the extremely formal category is that the issue before the High Court is not the merits (or demerits) of the Customary Court's decision. Rather, the issue before the High Court is the usually complex appeals procedure. In interpreting the process in Case Number 37, it is thus important to bear in mind that the High Court has not gone into the merits of the dispute between the parties. Among the Igbos, case processing in the official courts is highly structured. As Case Number 37 shows, the process is even more structured in appeals. The official rules regulating appeals do not apply to unofficial tribunals.

The case studies on the relative informality of the Igbo judicial processes show that the informality or formality of the process adopted in a case is a function of two factors: the issues involved in the case and the avenue where the case is managed. The processes used in the criminal and civil cases in the unofficial tribunals are more informal than those used in the official courts. In the unofficial tribunals, the relatively minor crimes, such as assault, are processed more informally than the more serious crimes, such as incest. However, even among unofficial judicial tribunals, the more serious crimes involve more formal processes to manage the cases. This is in apparent recognition of the severe punishment that awaits the accused person should there be a conviction. In the unofficial tribunals, the processes for civil cases are more formal than those for the relatively minor criminal cases (assault, public nuisance, etc.). In the official courts, the processes in the criminal cases are more formal than those in the civil cases.

SUMMARY

Based on the literature on informal/formal social control, this chapter identified and discussed the criteria for measuring the informal (or formal) qualities of a judicial process. The criteria are presented in the forms of themes and their operational definitions (see table 2.1). Table 2.1 was then applied to the available case studies from Nigeria's Igbo to assess the relative informality or formality of the judicial processes in the cases. This application process is continued in chapter 3. The result shows degrees of informality and formality in the Igbo judicial processes. The variations depend on the issues under consideration and the case management body involved. However, in sum, the cases show that the judicial processes are not exclusively informal or formal between unofficial and official case management organs. For example, although the unofficial tribunals maintain their traditional case management strategies, they have in many instances incorporated features of formal justice, such as recording and preserving the records of their proceedings.

NOTES

1. The features of law making in contemporary traditional Igbo are discussed in chapter 4.

2. *Iwu mmanwụ* refers to the customary rules, regulations, and laws that guide masquerade displays in an Igbo community. The rulers and elders of the community regard a breach of any of the rules, regulations, and laws seriously. Such a breach is a crime in the native Igbo justice system. A series of punishments, including fines, destruction of the offender's home and other property, and exiling the offender from the community, may be imposed.

3. The annual yam festival (*otute*) is celebrated to herald the beginning of the new harvesting season and to thank God for the yield from the farmlands.

4. The "accomplice" is the person(s), young or adult male, who is initiated into the secrets, rules, and regulations of masquerading and who is the masquerade's partner on a particular occasion. This individual criss-crosses the community with the masquerade entertaining people. He is the person who announces the masquerade's approach so that the uninitiated males and females may avoid the masquerade. He does this through his metal gong. A person who has a complaint concerning a masquerade must proceed against the masquerade's partner(s), since the Igbo regard masquerades as the spirits of the dead and so beyond human reach – see photo I.1, this volume, for a painting of *mmanwụ mgbadike* and partner.

5. This is one of the laws governing masquerading activities among the Igbos. With the very few exceptions of elderly and well-respected women (probably title-holders), masquerading is exclusively a male enterprise. No woman may eat any food associated with masquerades.

6. The records are not clear about which of the disputants initiated the case pending in the official court.

7. This ruling resulted from some kind of "preliminary objection" raised by the second disputant to the council's competence to hear the present case in view of the suit pending in the official court.

8. This is the key distinguishing characteristic between Case Number 8 and Case Numbers 4 and 20.

9. *Ịtụnye mmanya* (filing a suit) is a procedure for formally bringing a civil complaint against a person. The complaining party is required to plead with the unofficial, non-governmental case management body, for example, the *Eze*-in-Council, to hear and determine the case between the complainant and the other party. The plea has to be made with certain prescribed gift items, including palm wine and Igbo kola nuts. A

token amount of money may also be required.

10. A Customary Court is an official, governmental court in southern Nigeria established by state law to hear and determine cases based on the native customs, traditions, and laws of the respective communities in the court's jurisdiction. The equivalent court in northern Nigeria is the Native Court. A decision by the Customary Court may be appealed to a higher official tribunal.

11. In Nigeria, it is usual for any court (including the Customary Court) to be the judge and also act as the prosecutor in the consideration of an alleged act or omission of contempt committed "in the face of the court" (before the court). If, however, the alleged contempt occurred outside the court, the prosecution is left to the state's attorneys. Since the alleged contemptuous act in Case Number 32 occurred outside the court, it is unusual that the same court is prosecuting and trying it.

12. In the Nigerian official justice system, if an accused person is "discharged" in criminal proceedings, he or she may be tried again for the same or similar offense. If, however, the accused is "acquitted" or "discharged and acquitted," he or she may not be tried again for the same offense or for an offense having the same ingredients as that offense except on the order of a superior court [*section 36 (9), Constitution of the Federal Republic of Nigeria, 1999* (*1999 Constitution*)]. The amended *Constitution of the Federal Republic of Nigeria, 1979* (*1979 Constitution*) that was in force at the time the cases were processed had equivalent provisions.

3

Survey of Cases and Application of Themes and Descriptors

INTRODUCTION

This chapter provides further examination of the sample cases against the background of the predictions in tables 2.1 and 2.4 and ensures that the wide array of case contents and judicial processes studied in the sample cases (including Case Numbers 4, 8, 20, 32, and 37 used as illustrations in chapter 2) are completely presented to the reader.

To appreciate the processes of Igbo justice, it is essential to understand the different socio-cultural and political layers that play various roles in the administration of justice. Before the advent of British colonialism, the town was the largest political unit in most parts of Igbo land (Obi, 1963; Uchendu, 1966; Ogbalu, 1981). Today, the lives of the Igbos are no longer limited to what happens in their respective towns. Since the creation of Nigeria, whatever happens in other Igbo towns and other parts of Nigeria have their effects on each Igbo town. This is due to the removal of pre-existing barriers to communication and interaction with other towns and ethnic groups, and the British imposition of the officially superior Nigerian state. The Igbo town has greatly dwindled in political significance and is now only a small part of the powerful Nigerian state (see Adeyemi, 1990; Anene, 1991). The diminished role of the Igbo town in politics notwithstanding, the town plays a significant role in the Igbo justice system. This is shown in the discussion of justice processing at the Igbo community level.

Among the Igbos, a grievance, conflict, or dispute may be managed in an unofficial tribunal or in an official court. The decision as to whether to take a case before an official court or manage it out of the official system is mostly for the parties to make. In the example of Ajallị Town, if parties decide to manage a case unofficially, they may take it before the *Eze*'s Cabinet (*Eze*-in-Council). The council has little control over where the parties may take their case for management. However, the council tries to discourage the town's people from going to official law enforcement agencies (police, courts, etc.) to settle their disagreements. The record of one of the council's meetings contains the following entry (at p. 14 of the Record of Proceedings, vol. 3, 1994): "On frequent visits to the police station by litigants on the slightest provocation, the *Eze*-in-Council condemned the idea and promised to re-echo this. However, criminal cases should be reported to [a] law enforcement agency for appropriate attention/action." Despite the statement that criminal cases should be reported to official law enforcement agencies, the data shows that the range of grievances, conflicts, and disputes that the *Eze*-in-Council hears and adjudicates is open ended. The council could, and does, manage civil as well as criminal cases.

The community members frown on, and sometimes react adversely to, conduct aimed at diverting certain grievances, conflicts, or disputes from the native processes to the official, governmental processes (Case Number 47A, Record of Proceedings, vol. 3, 1995). In this case, the accused person has reported certain members of the town to the official police regarding an ongoing dispute between the town and a neighboring town. The accused person (that is, the person who made the report to the police) is arraigned before the town's leaders for reporting the matter to the official law enforcement agency. A substantial fine is imposed upon him for making the report. He pleads for forgiveness. A few other persons also plead on his behalf. The fine is reduced. In addition to the fine, he is warned against calling the police to arrest any member of the town.

CASE CONTENTS AND PROCESSES

This section continues the discussion on the nature and kinds of grievances, conflicts, and disputes found in the case studies (table 2.4). The section also examines how far the methods and procedures used in processing the cases comply with the twelve themes and the forty-nine descriptors predicted for informal case processing (table 2.1). The "process" issue (table 2.1) is answered on three levels: on a case-by-case basis, on a category-by-category basis, and on the level of all the case studies collectively. Both the Igbo customary law and the official government law prohibit some of the misconducts in the cases. In some other circumstances, only the native laws prohibit the misconducts. Thus, in discussing the contents and processes in the cases, the relevant legal authority is identified.

Based on the examination of the cases, there is no relationship between the category in which a case is found (Very Informal, Informal, Semi-Formal, Formal, or Very Formal – see table 2.3) and the contents and processes that emerge from that category. Similarly, the observed contents and processes are not necessarily based on the subcategories (subject matters)[1] into which the cases have been sorted. Therefore, every case–no matter the category or subcategory into which it falls–is examined individually to determine the extent to which it possesses the predicted themes and descriptors of informal case processing. The individual examination is necessitated by the need to ensure that the peculiar characteristics of each case are clearly shown. This also avoids confusing the unique elements of one case with those of another. However, wherever feasible, two or more cases in the same subcategory (i.e., cases on similar subject matters) are examined together.

Consistently with the technique used to present the few illustrative cases in chapter 2, in discussing the first case in the "Informal" category (Case Number 1), the meanings of the themes and their descriptors are examined in some detail. Thereafter, the other cases are discussed with a view to ascertaining the extent of each case's compliance with the predicted themes and descriptors. The five categories of informal/formal justice processes (see table 2.3) guide this discussion.

VERY INFORMAL CATEGORY

None of the completed forty-two case studies in the data has all the twelve themes of informal case processing predicted in table 2.1. Therefore, none of the cases falls in this category (see table 2.3).

Nature and Kinds of Cases

The most extreme level of informality used to assess the processing of the case studies is the "Very Informal" category. A case falls in this category if it meets all the twelve predicted themes of informal case processing. In addition to falling in this category, a case that meets all the twelve themes is assessed for its relative strength to the other cases in the same category. This relative strength is determined by ascertaining whether or not a case that satisfies the primary descriptors of the twelve themes also satisfies other descriptors. If it does, the next issue is to determine "how many?" Examination of the forty-two completed case studies shows that none of them meets the requirements of this category.

Why No Cases Are Found in This Category

Three cases (Case Numbers 6, 20, and 25) come closest to satisfying the requirements of this category. Each of these cases has ten of the twelve required themes of informal case processing. Case Numbers 6 and 20 lack the "Punitiveness" and "Record Management" themes, while Case Number 25 lacks "Stigmatization" and "Record Management." The three cases are discussed further in their category.

Some of the data for this book is archival in nature. The unsolicited archives (Berg, 1998) contain the completed forty-two case studies. The unsolicited archival character of the forty-two cases makes it less likely that any of them will meet the requirements of the "Very Informal" category. Theme 9 of informal case processing (Record Management) seeks to ascertain the method of recording and preserving the records of proceedings on a case. The options range from "Memory only (oral history)," which is the most informal method of record keeping, to "Complete, verbatim transcription of proceedings kept," which is the least informal method. Since the "Memory only (oral history)" option is the most informal of all, it is identified as the primary descriptor for the "Record management" theme. The fact that all the records of the cases already existed in writing before the author requested them effectively disqualifies the cases from satisfying this theme and disqualifies them from the "Very Informal" category.

INFORMAL CATEGORY

This category is made up of the case studies that possess eight to eleven of the twelve themes predicted for informal case processing. Twenty-two of the cases fall in this category (see table 2.3). Among the twenty-two cases, three cases meet ten of the twelve themes, six cases meet nine of the themes, while the remaining thirteen cases satisfy eight of the themes. In other words, there is some variation within category, thus the proccsses in some cases are more informal than others.

Nature and Kinds of Cases

There are eleven subcategories (subheadings based on subject matter) of the "Informal" category. The subcategories and the twenty-two cases found in them (see table 2.3) are used to illustrate informal case processing.

Dispute over Contract to Perform Services and Sell Product

Case Number 1 (Record of Proceedings, vol. 1, at p. 24, 1987) involves a dispute over an oral agreement to make and sell a new palm oil processing machine. The first disputant introduces the second disputant for the job. As a result of the introduction, the second disputant and the prospective buyer of the machine agree that the second disputant will make the machine and sell it to the prospective buyer. The second disputant is eventually paid in full for the machine. The machine is made as agreed in the contract. However, just before the prospective buyer takes away his machine, the second disputant carries it away.

Although the contract at issue is unwritten, the aggrieved persons have the option of taking their complaint to the official court. The aggrieved persons may institute civil proceedings in the official court for a breach of contract. The circumstances of the case in fact justify a criminal prosecution for stealing by conversion, fraud, or obtaining property by false pretences.[2] However, the first disputant, a native of Ajallị Town, and the prospective buyer, a non-native, take the case to the *Eze*-in-Council for settlement. The council treats the case as a civil dispute.

The record of proceedings on Case Number 1 shows that the processing of the case meets eight of the twelve themes predicted for informal case processing (except themes 6, 9, 11, and 12) (see table 2.1). The constitution or other law does not set up the *Eze*-in-Council, nor is it established by the state. Additionally, the council is not run by, nor is it under the influence of, the state or any of its agencies. This accords with the correct response to the primary descriptor under theme 1 (Officialism) (see also Appendix A). Thus, Case Number 1 satisfies theme 1. However, the case also accords with the remaining six descriptors under theme 1.

The process in Case Number 1 also satisfies theme 2 (Mediation). The primary descriptor under this theme predicts that informal case processing would be non-adversarial [theme 2 (b)]. That is clearly the situation in Case Number 1. There is no confrontation between the disputants, nor are there witnesses to be confronted. The second disputant admits before the council that the first disputant's claim is true, thus avoiding adversarial proceedings in the case. The second disputant sends his younger brother[3] to inform the council members that he has no defense to the claim, adding that he is doing everything he could to deliver the machine in the shortest possible time (at pp. 30-31). This case further contains an attempt to involve a third party in the resolution of the dispute [theme 2 (c)]. When the *Eze*-in-Council does not receive the cooperation it needs to finally settle the case, it sends two of its members to the second disputant's father to report his son's misbehavior to him. However, the father does not cooperate with the council members.

Case Number 1 satisfies theme 3 (Lawyer Involvement) and theme 4 (Litigiousness or Argumentativeness in a Legal Sense). Both of these themes predict that no lawyer would be involved in informal case processing. Thus, the non-involvement of lawyers in the settlement of this case means that the process followed in the case satisfies these two themes. The processing of the case also satisfies theme 5 (Punitiveness). This theme predicts that an informal case process would not emphasize guilt nor would it put emphasis on placing blame. Also, that the process would not focus on proof. The primary descriptor under theme 5 predicts that an informal judicial process would not place emphasis on blame. There is no such emphasis in Case Number 1. As already stated, the second disputant admits the first disputant's claim. Thus, it is unnecessary for the council to go into the merits of the case.[4]

The sixth theme (Stigmatization) is only "somewhat identifiable" in Case Number 1. The essence of this theme is that in informal case processing, either disputant (or both) would be denounced in some way by the process. Theme 6 predicts that the denunciation would be clearly shown primarily by loss of dignity by either party – see table 2.1. Thus, in an informal judicial process, loss of dignity would be "clearly identifiable" (see also Appendix A). In the processing of Case Number 1, loss of dignity is only "somewhat identifiable." The council members' mention of the second disputant's "failure to honour" the agreement between him and the first disputant (at p. 35 of the Record of Proceedings, vol. 1) is a vague indication that the second disputant has lost the respect of other community members. Due to vagueness, this case fails to meet the requirements of theme 6. Additionally, however, there is some loss of time in the processing of this case–a two-month period (September-November 1987). In that time period, the case is adjourned four times before it is disposed of.

Under theme 7 (Individualization), the processing of a case, to be regarded as informal, must include the exercise of discretion and the bending of the rules and procedures to suit the unique needs of the individual case. This is clearly identifiable in Case Number 1. Although the parties to the case are the first and second disputants, the council allows a third party (the prospective buyer of the contracted machine) to participate in the proceedings as if he is the person bringing the suit. In taking this step, the council attempts to assure the prospective buyer, a non-native of Ajallị Town, that it is doing what it can to resolve the dispute fairly.[5]

Theme 8 (Proscriptiveness of Norms) predicts that the laws, rules, regulations, or customs applied in an informal case processing would be uncodified. Case Number 1 satisfies this theme because none of the customary laws or traditions applied by the *Eze*-in-Council in the management of this case is written. Under the "Record Management" theme (theme 9), it is expected that the proceedings in an informal process would be recorded in "memory only (oral history)" [theme 9 (e)]. That is not the situation in Case Number 1. It should be noted that even in an exclusively archival research situation, a case report could meet theme 9 (e) if a written record of proceedings were developed for the first time at the request of the researcher ("solicited archive") – see Berg (1998).

Theme 10 (Simplicity of Process) projects that the procedures used in initiating and conducting a case would be simple. Also, that the rigors associated with a formal process, for example, signing of documents, would be absent or minimal. Further, that a person holding a position in an informal justice process may play two or more roles therein. Case Number 1 satisfies theme 10 because the case is initiated before the *Eze*-in-Council by spoken words. Even though theme 10 refers to "initiating *and* conducting" a case, the author, after thoroughly studying all the methods and procedures used by the locals in case processing, decides that a case, which satisfies only the condition of "initiating by word of mouth," will be regarded as having met theme 10. Insisting on the satisfaction of both "initiating *and* conducting" conditions will result in the anomaly of excluding cases whose processes accord with the spirit of the prediction under theme 10. In Case Number 2, for example, "[the first disputant] gave [oral] notice against [the second disputant]. He was advised to meet the *Eze* for necessary directives accordingly" (at p. 42 of the Record of Proceedings, vol. 1). The oral notice against the second disputant *initiates* the case. On the other hand, a case cannot be initiated orally in an official court. After the oral initiation of the case, however, the first disputant completes and signs the form attached hereto as Appendix B. Completing and signing Appendix B is consistent with the prediction under theme 10 because the form should be viewed as "little" need for signature as expected by the theme.

The costs of invoking the process in Case Number 1 are minor gifts and a small amount of money.[6] These costs are contrary to the prediction that there would be "no cost" to invoke an informal case management process. Therefore, Case Number 1 does not meet theme 11. Under theme 12 (Peace-making Emphasis), it is predicted that informal case processing would stress the importance of peace to the disputants and encourage them to integrate with each other and with other members of the community in the interest of *udo* (peace) and *ọga n'iru obodo* (community progress). Further, it is predicted that a disputant would cooperate with the process by not challenging it and by avoiding the use of self-help in managing the case. Rather than use self-help, theme 12 expects a party to involve family relations, friends, volunteers, and neighbors in efforts to resolve the case. However, Case Number 1 does not meet this expectation.

Case Number 1–the only case study in this subcategory–shows the ability of the unofficial case management processes in Ajallị Town to successfully handle a case based on a contract.

Disputes over Land, Economic Trees,[7] and Destruction of Property

Eight case studies (Case Numbers 2, 3, 12, 16, 19, 22, 28, and 14) deal with these issues. Case Number 2 meets nine of the twelve predicted themes of informal case processing. Each of the other seven cases meets eight of the themes. However, the cases differ on the particular themes that they meet. Since these cases deal with similar subject matters and are in the same subcategory, their processes are examined jointly, although the unique distinctions in their "contents" are recognized.

The issues in Case Number 2 (Record of Proceedings, vol. 1, p. 42, 1988) are ownership, possession, and use of land, as well as the palm wine trees and coconut trees on the land. The disputants are two brothers living adjacent to each other. Either disputant could file a civil suit in the official court for declaration of title to the disputed land and recovery of possession. However, the first disputant chooses to complain to the *Eze*-in-Council, claiming that the land "belongs to him and not to both of them" (at p. 45, Record of Proceedings, vol. 1). At the council, the case is treated as a civil dispute. The council advises the younger of the disputing brothers to allow the elder to use the land in dispute because "[the elder] deserves all respect, and he is the eldest (*Aka kpa ọfọ*) in the family still alive" (at p. 47).[8]

The processing of Case Number 2 meets nine of the twelve themes of informal case processing (see table 2.2). With the exceptions of themes 6 (Stigmatization), 9 (Record Management), and 11 (Cost of Invoking Process), all the other themes are clearly identifiable in the case. Theme 1 is present in the process, since the case is managed before the *Eze*-in-Council (an unofficial body). Theme 2 is clearly identifiable in the case because of its non-adversarial proceedings. There is neither cross-examination nor any form of confrontation in the proceedings. In accordance with the predictions under themes 3 and 4, lawyers are not involved in the process. There is no indication on the record that the process puts emphasis on placing blame. This agrees with theme 5. However, the absence of "Stigmatization" in the process runs counter to theme 6. But "Individualization" (theme 7) is clearly identifiable in the case because of the *Eze*-in-Council members' visit and inspection of the disputed land before rendering a decision. The council concludes that the visit and inspection are necessary because of the need to accommodate the specific requirements of the case.

Theme 8 is clearly identifiable in Case Number 2 because none of the customary laws and traditions applied to the case is codified. However, the records on this case are "complete handwritten files" contrary to the "memory only (oral history)" predicted under theme 9. Therefore, this case docs not satisfy theme 9. The procedure that allows the first disputant to initiate the case orally (at p. 42) illustrates the presence of theme 10 (Simplicity of Process). Theme 11 (Cost of Invoking Process) is not identifiable in the case. Contrary to the prediction that there would be "no cost" in an informal justice process, bringing the action by the *ịtụnye mmanya* procedure includes some minor gifts and a small amount of money. The process in Case Number 2 clearly includes "Peacemaking Emphasis" (theme 12). The council encourages the disputants to be cooperative: "*Eze* C. O. Nwosu [the council chairman] appealed to [both disputants] and also advised both parties to maintain peace, tranquility, and mutual love among themselves as relatives" (at p. 49).

In Case Number 3 (Record of Proceedings, vol. 1, at p. 43, 1988), the first disputant (the eldest male member of their *ụmụnna*) claims before the *Eze*-in-Council that "[the second disputant] denied him [the first disputant] of his land rights by force" (at p. 45). The first disputant contends that as the eldest male member of the *ụmụnna*, he is entitled to hold the *ụmụnna* land in trust for all the members. This contention is justified under the Igbo customary law. Under this system of laws, a person who holds family property does so in trust for all the members and may not use or dispose of it as if it belonged to him alone (*Ekpendu v. Erika*, 1959; Elias, 1961; *Nezianya v. Okagbue*, 1963; *Nzekwu and Others v. Nzekwu and Others*, 1989).

The customary law rights of the first disputant in Case Number 3 are enforceable both in and out of the official courts. Further, if the first disputant's allegation that the second disputant denied the former of his land rights "by force" is true, then there is probably a ground for a criminal charge against the second disputant. Such a charge could be for assault or battery under the *Criminal Code Laws of Anambra State*. However, the first disputant takes the dispute before the *Eze*-in-Council for settlement. The case includes eight of the twelve predicted themes of informal case processing. The process in the case accords with the prediction under theme 1 because the case is settled before the *Eze*-in-Council. Theme 2 (Mediation) is not identifiable in the case because the proceedings include the cross-examination of the witnesses. This is contrary to the non-adversarial procedure expected by theme 2. Themes 3 and 4 are present in the case because it is settled without lawyer involvement. Further, consistent with the prediction under theme 5 (Punitiveness), the proceedings do not emphasize placing blame. However, contrary to theme 6 (Stigmatization), there is no loss of dignity by either disputant. Therefore, the case does not satisfy theme 6.

Themes 7 and 8 are clearly identifiable in Case Number 3. The process satisfies theme 7 because of the flexible procedure adopted by the council. Theme 8 is satisfied because none of the laws and customs applied to the case is in written form. Theme 9 (Record Management) is not identifiable in the case, since the record of the proceedings is not based on oral history as predicted. The record of proceedings is in "complete, handwritten files." Theme 10 (Simplicity of Process) is present in the case because the simple procedure makes it possible for the first disputant to initiate the case orally. However, the case does not satisfy the "no cost" expected under theme 11. The case is brought through the *ịtụnye mmanya* procedure. The following statement on the record shows the clear presence of theme 12 (Peacemaking Emphasis) in the proceedings: "To avoid any future breach of peace, both [disputants] were asked and cautioned to keep the peace " (at p. 66).

In Case Number 12 (Record of Proceedings, vol. 2, at p. 4, 1991), the disputes concern land and lack of respect for an elderly person, among other things. The first disputant, who is the second disputant's uncle, claims before the *Eze*-in-Council that the second disputant has prevented the first disputant from using a part of the *ụmụnna* land. On the second issue between the disputing relatives, the second disputant claims that the first disputant has falsely accused the former of stealing. It is alleged that the first disputant has told the town's head of the Federal Government's War Against Indiscipline (WAI)[9] to include the second disputant's name "among known thieves of Ajallị [town]" (at p. 6). There are also allegations of poisoning. The first disputant also claims that the second disputant smokes marijuana and keeps "questionable associations" (at p. 4). Along with these accusations, there are other alleged acts of disrespect that have resulted in the misunderstanding between the disputants.

Most of the issues identified in Case Number 12 (land dispute, false accusations, and defamation) could be litigated civilly in the official court as torts. The *Anambra State Torts Law*, which applies to Ajallị, is the applicable official law in such actions in tort. The first disputant complains instead to the *Eze*-in-Council. The record of proceedings before the council shows that the complaints are treated as civil complaints. The alleged disrespectful conducts in this dispute do not provide bases for actions in the official civil or criminal laws of Anambra State. Under the official laws of the state, *disrespectful* behavior, without more, toward a person does not incur legal liability.

Issues such as those involved in Case Number 12 are taken before the *Eze*-in-Council, rather than before the official court, because the council manages grievances, conflicts, and disputes such as disrespectful behaviors even though the official legal structure does not entertain legal actions based on such behaviors. The fact that the official justice structure does not recognize such behaviors as actionable does not assuage the genuine feelings of hurt among the locals who feel injured by such conducts. The importance of an early resolution of a "grievance" lies in the advantage of nipping it in the bud before it grows into a "dispute" (Cf. Lowy, 1978, at p. 187).

The processing of Case Number 12 includes eight of the twelve themes predicted for informal case management. The process satisfies themes 1, 3, 4, 5, 7, 8, 10, and 12 (table 2.2). It does not satisfy themes 2, 6, 9, and 11. The first disputant's allegations that the second disputant smokes marijuana, consumes alcohol excessively, and keeps questionable company (at p. 14 of the Record of Proceedings, vol. 2) lead to the conclusion that theme 6 (Stigmatization) is only somewhat identifiable in the case. In Ajallị Town, any of those allegations gives the impression to the community members that the person so accused is a loafer, a never-do-well, and should not be taken seriously.[10] However, there is nothing in this case that shows exactly how the locals have reacted to the allegations against the second disputant.

Case Number 12, which is heard and determined by the *Eze*-in-Council (theme 1), does not involve any lawyer (themes 3 and 4). The council does not place any emphasis on punishing the responsible party (theme 5). Instead, it is concerned with bringing the disputing relations together (theme 12). At the proceedings, having heard the disputants' cases, the council asks the disputants to leave the meeting room for the council members to deliberate on the case before reaching a decision (*ịchị izu*). Because of the nature of the issues in the case, the council thinks that the exclusion of the parties at that stage of the proceedings is appropriate (theme 7). The laws and customs applied by the council are unwritten (theme 8). Also, the flexible process allows the first disputant to initiate the case orally (theme 10).

The next four cases in this subcategory are based on land disputes. To avoid unnecessary repetition, the examination of their contents and processes focuses on the factors that distinguish the cases from one another. In Case Number 16 (Record of Proceedings, vol. 2, at p. 55, 1992), the second disputant, a non-native of Ajallị town, attempts to give away to a third party a part of the land that the first disputant's father has allowed the second disputant to use. The third party is to build a home on the land. The first disputant complains to the *Eze*-in-Council, claiming that the second disputant's conduct entitles him (the first disputant) to take back the land in the absence of his father.

In Igbo, a customary tenant (the second disputant) may not do anything that challenges the rights of the customary landlord (the first disputant). If the tenant does, the landlord has the right to recover possession of the land at issue (*Ezeokafor v. Otaluka*, 1964; *Nzekwu and Others v. Nzekwu and Others*, 1989). The *Eze*-in-Council finds that the second disputant has indeed challenged the first disputant's landlord rights. According to the council (at p. 76), "the *Eze*-in-Council decided that [the second disputant] had no right to sell or give out or sublet the area in question as he then lived in the house of [the first disputant's father]. In the event of [the second disputant] leaving Ajalli, the area in question would customarily revert to his landlord or his descendants." In the official court, this finding would have resulted in the second disputant being forced to forfeit the land as claimed by the first disputant. But the *Eze*-in-Council, being more concerned with settling the dispute than pronouncing a judgment based on the law (at p. 64), allows the second disputant to continue to use the land on the condition that he never conducts himself in a similar manner in the future.

The dispute in Case Number 19 (Record of Proceedings, vol. 2, at p. 127, 1993) stems from disagreements between two members of Ajallị Town over the ownership of a piece of land in the town. The dispute is taken before the *Eze*-in-Council. At the end of the proceedings, the council easily concludes that "the ownership of the piece of land is not disputable; it belongs to the [second disputant]" (at p. 163). Having reached this conclusion, the next logical statement would have been that the first disputant should give up the disputed land to the second disputant. But the *Eze*-in-Council, being concerned with more than merely applying the customary laws, recognizes that the first disputant has already begun to build on the land. If the council advises the first disputant to leave the land for the second disputant, the first disputant would likely lose everything he has invested in the building under construction on the land. Under the Igbo customary law, what is attached to land is distinct from the land.[11] Thus, the council could advise the first disputant to remove his partially completed building from the disputed land. However, in an attempt to find a more convenient and satisfactory solution, the council recommends as follows (at pp. 163-164):

> In view of the structural developments already made by [the first disputant] on this disputed land, we recommend that he approaches [the first disputant's family] *in a customary manner* to allow him complete work on the said building which has reached a reasonable height. We sincerely believe that if this very line of action has [*sic*] been adopted earlier, this dispute would not have arisen.[12]

Approaching a person for land *in a customary manner* entails going to the person (usually, an adult male since a female or juvenile male does not negotiate for land in Ajallị) with small gifts, such as a gallon of palm wine and some Igbo kola nuts, and requesting the landowner's permission to use his land. Such a request is usually made for the owner to allow the person making the request to use the land for farming purposes. Where the purpose for which the land is requested is permanent as in the case of erecting a building on the land, more items are presented and the ceremonies surrounding the request are more elaborate. In any case, it is always desirable for the person requesting the land to go with witnesses, usually elderly male members of the community. This adds to the prestige of the person making the request before the landowner.

In Case Number 22 (Record of Proceedings, vol. 3, at p. 23, 1994), the first disputant (the stepmother of the second disputant) complains to the *Eze*-in-Council that the second disputant has prevented her from using her own piece of the family land. The second disputant is the eldest son of his late father's polygamous family. The first disputant requests the *Eze*-in-Council to, among other things, direct the second disputant to give the first disputant's son his own share of the late father's property. The issues involved in this case could be litigated in the official courts in which the customary law rights of the disputants are recognized and would be enforced. The dispute is however taken before the *Eze*-in-Council. Unlike in the official courts, the application of the Igbo customary laws and traditions before the council is done primarily to maintain harmony and peaceful coexistence in the community rather than to allocate legal rights between the disputants (for example, Case Numbers 2, 16; see also Abel, 1982; Black, 1993). Thus, the council decides "in the interest of the family" that the second disputant must hold the family land in trust for all the members of the family "according to the tradition[s] and custom[s] of Ajallị" (at p. 33), and not as personal land (see also *Ekpendu v. Erika*, 1959; *Nzekwu and Others v. Nzekwu and Others*, 1989). The council, however, directs the first disputant and her son to acknowledge the headship of the second disputant and to respect him.

The Ajallị Welfare Union (AWU) processed Case Number 28 (1995).[13] The issue in the case is the ownership of a parcel of land situated in Ajallị Town. The task of the panel set up to consider the case is, according to the members of the panel, "to determine the true owner of the contested piece of land situated at [the location]" (at p. 1 of the Case Report). The first disputant claims that the late *Eze* Ajallị gave the land to the first disputant. The second disputant claims that the land belongs to her through her late husband, and thus the late *Eze* would have given out someone else's land. The members of the panel, observing that the late ruler was a man of integrity and, in reliance on other evidence, conclude that the land belongs to the first disputant.

The processing of each of Case Numbers 16, 19, 22, and 28 meets eight of the twelve predicted themes of informal case processing (see table 2.2). As stated, Case Numbers 16, 19, 22, and 28 are similar because they deal with land and land-related disputes. Case Numbers 16, 19, and 22 each includes the predicted themes except themes 2, 6, 9, and 11. The process in Case Number 28 does not include themes 2, 6, 9, and 12. The processes in the four cases meet theme 1 because the hearing bodies are unofficial tribunals. However, none of the cases includes the requirements of an informal case processing under theme

2 (Mediation). Contrary to the prediction, the proceedings in each case are adversarial. In fact, the record of proceedings on Case Number 19 expressly describes what takes place during the proceedings as an interrogation of the opposing party: "[The first disputant] having closed his case, it was [the second disputant's] turn to interrogate him" (Record of Proceedings, vol. 2, 1993, at p. 128). The four cases satisfy themes 3 and 4 because no lawyer is involved in the case management. Theme 5 (Punitiveness) is also clearly identifiable in these cases because, as predicted, none of the cases emphasizes placing blame. However, in three of the four cases, there is clearly a focus on proof contrary to a secondary descriptor under theme 5 (c). As an example, in Case Number 28, the arbitration panel states as follows (at p. 3 of the Case Report): "We therefore have no hesitations whatsoever to declare the contested piece of land the property of [the first disputant]. Our decision is arrived at through the evidence of the witnesses, the exhibits in our possession (and attached herewith) and [after] interrogating the disputants."

None of Case Numbers 16, 19, 22, and 28 meets the prediction under theme 6 (Stigmatization). The expectation that a disputant in an informal process would lose the respect of other community members, or would no longer be looked up to, or would be denied or stripped of a position or honor does not materialize in any of the four cases. Each of the four cases meets the prediction under theme 7 (Individualization) that steps would be taken in the process to address the individual needs of each case. For instance, in Case Number 19, the *Eze*-in-Council goes and inspects the land in dispute to be in a better position to address the issues brought before the council. Theme 8 is clearly present in the four cases since none of the customs and traditions applied to them is codified. The records of Case Numbers 16, 19, and 22 are "complete, handwritten files." The record of Case Number 28 is a "complete, typed file." However, both record types contradict the prediction that the record of a case processed informally would be based on "memory only (oral history)" (theme 9). Therefore, none of Case Numbers 16, 19, 22, and 28 satisfies theme 9.

The "Simplicity of Process" predicted under theme 10 is clearly identifiable in Case Numbers 16, 19, 22, and 28. Each case is initiated orally. The required completion of Appendix B in Case Numbers 16, 19, and 22 is regarded as little need for signatures. These cases are heard by the *Eze*-in-Council. There is no need for signature in Case Number 28, which is heard by a different arbitration panel. In each of Case Numbers 22 and 28, a person holding a position in the process plays two or more roles. In Case Number 22, a member of the council doubles as the bailiff when he goes and gives a message to the second disputant because the latter is absent from one of the proceedings (Record of Proceedings, vol. 3, 1994, at p. 58). In Case Number 28, a member of the arbitration panel (judge) serves also as the recorder of the proceedings. Case Numbers 16, 19, and 22 fail to meet the requirements of theme 11. The *ịtụnye mmanya* procedure initiates each case. This means that the disputants have made minor gifts and paid small amounts of money to the *Eze*-in-Council contrary to the "no cost" predicted under the theme. Case Number 28 meets the requirements of theme 11 because it is initiated at no cost. Theme 12 (Peacemaking Emphasis) is clearly identifiable in Case Numbers 16, 19, and 22. The council encourages the disputants in each case to integrate and cooperate with each other and with others in the community. However, Case Number 28, which is heard by the AWU, does not contain any emphasis on peacemaking.

The last case in this subcategory is Case Number 14. It is a land-related case. However, it is discussed apart from Case Numbers 16, 19, 22, and 28 because of some interruption in its processing. Case Number 14 (Record of Proceedings, vol. 2, at p. 19, 1991) deals with disputes over the ownership of a breadfruit tree and the alleged demolition by the second disputant of the first disputant's three bedrooms. Both parties' desire "to settle the matter between [them]" (at p. 70) results in their taking the dispute before the *Eze*-in-Council. However, the council later discontinues the civil case because of a letter written by some persons from the disputants' *ụmụnna* to the council suggesting that the *ụmụnna*'s representative on the council is not given opportunity to make contributions to the resolution of the dispute. The council, after considering the whole situation, including the fact that it is almost ready to render a decision in the case, decides to discontinue deliberations on it. The council explains its decision as follows (at p. 90):

> In view of the fact that the *Eze*-in-Council does not want trouble in the town [nor] among ourselves in the Cabinet, the matter [is] still in progress and we are being castigated, the Cabinet hereby discontinues with the matter with immediate effect. The disputants are at liberty to take their case to wherever they have confidence in for adjudication.[14]

The *Eze*-in-Council's statement in Case Number 14 illustrates the fundamental need for consent and cooperation in unofficial case management. The disputants' consent and cooperation are always crucial for an unofficial justice process to work. On the contrary, in the Nigerian official justice system, parties to a civil or criminal case in a court do not have the choice as to whether or not to consent to the proceedings before the court. Such a party may apply for a change of venue or for the presiding judge or magistrate to be changed on grounds of bias or reasonable suspicion of bias. The application may succeed or fail. Regardless, the party must abide by the court's final decision. If not, the authority of the official government would be invoked to enforce the decision. Under the native Igbo justice system, the enforcement of the decision of an unofficial judicial tribunal–particularly in a civil case–depends on the consent and cooperation of the parties. Other community members are likely to have unfavorable opinions about someone who *stands against the system* by rejecting a decision of an unofficial tribunal. But they may not overtly enforce the decision without his or her consent.

The processing of Case Number 14 satisfies eight of the twelve predicted themes of informal case processing (table 2.2). The themes not satisfied are themes 2 (Mediation), 6 (Stigmatization), 9 (Record Management), and 11 (Cost of Invoking Process). The process in the case fully satisfies the other eight themes, including theme 7 (Individualization). The circumstances of the case lead the council members to go and inspect the disputed land. While on the visit, they draw a detailed sketch of the land to be used later in reaching a decision in the case.

The eight cases examined in this subcategory (land and land-related cases) of the "Informal" category illustrate the capability of the out-of-court judicial processes in Ajallị Town to resolve cases dealing with real property. In Nigeria, a real property case in an official court usually goes on for many years. The cases discussed in this subcategory are managed within much shorter time periods.

Disputes over Disobedience of Iwu Mmanwụ[15] (Rules and Regulations on Masquerading), Battery, Street Fighting, Harassment, and Cases of Assault

There are three cases in this subcategory (Case Numbers 4, 20, and 8). Case Numbers 4 and 20 are criminal cases. Their processes are examined jointly. Case Number 8 is a civil case. Its process is examined separately. Case Number 4 (Record of Proceedings, vol. 1, at p. 60, 1988) records the processing of several misconducts by seven young Ajallị men. The accused are tried jointly. Their misconducts are: three incidents of battery, five incidents of assault, two incidents of street fighting, and a disobedience of an order against masquerading on a Sunday. All the misconducts involved in the case result from *otute* (annual yam festival) celebrations.[16]

Each of the first ten misconducts in Case Number 4 is a ground for criminal prosecution in an official court (see *Criminal Code Law of Anambra State*). Also, each of the misconducts is sufficient basis for a civil claim in the official court. A trial of each offender in an official court would last for a much longer time (one year or more) than it takes the *Eze*-in-Council to dispose of all the cases. Moreover, a conviction in an official court would attract punishment of imprisonment or, at a minimum, a fine. However, the *Eze*-in-Council, an unofficial, non-governmental body, processes the case. The council applies the customary laws and traditions of the community. The infractions are treated as community crimes. Each offender is fined between one and seven goats, depending on the gravity of his offense.

The fact that a case such as Case Number 4 is processed at the community level rather than in the official court provides the community the added advantage of enforcing its laws that are not enforceable in the official courts. Disobeying "an order against masquerading on a Sunday" is not a violation of any official government law applicable to Ajallị town. Therefore, an official court cannot legally convict or punish any person that disobeys such a law. It is only through the native, unofficial mechanisms of social control that a community can enforce this kind of law. The value of this law lies in its ability to assist in the sustenance and stabilization of the community's mores (Black, 1976; Dickson-Gilmore, 1992).

In Case Number 20 (Record of Proceedings, vol. 2, at p. 170, 1994), the incident leading to the case is that a masquerade, together with an accomplice,[17] assaulted the complainant. As in Case Number 4, the assault in Case Number 20 could find ground in criminal prosecution or civil claim in the official court. However, the complainant decides to have the case handled by the *Eze*-in-Council. The records actually refer to the second disputants as the "accused" (at p. 171). The accused persons are held responsible for the misconduct. The seriousness of the misconduct leads the council to ban the responsible persons from taking part in any masquerading activities in the town for two years. The council processes this case as a crime because of the general community interest in order maintenance.

The processing of Case Number 4 includes nine of the twelve themes of informal case processing. Case Number 20 complies with ten of those themes. However, each of the two cases fails to meet themes 5 (Punitiveness) and 9 (Record Management). Additionally, Case Number 4 does not meet the requirements of theme 12 (Peacemaking Emphasis). Both cases include theme 1 in their processes because the accused persons are tried before the *Eze*-in-Council. In Case Number 4, the council makes a clear reference to *omenala* Ajallị (Ajallị traditions, customs) [theme 1 (c)] when it states: "women are not to partake of the goat meat" collected as fines from the offenders[18] (at p. 61). As expected under theme 2 (Mediation), the proceedings in both cases are non-adversarial because there is no confrontation of the opponent. In fact, the accused persons are tried summarily. No witnesses are called. Themes 3 (Lawyer Involvement) and 4 (Litigiousness or Argumentativeness in a Legal Sense) are clearly identifiable in the cases because the accused are tried without lawyers. Contrary to theme 5 (Punitiveness), the proceedings emphasize placing blame. The processes in both cases stigmatize the accused persons (theme 6). Peers in such matters may no longer trust a person who has been convicted of breaking the laws and regulations on masquerading. The offender may therefore be denied certain sensitive offices in the community that relate to the secrets of masquerading (Cf. Becker, 1963). In Case Number 20, the *Eze*-in-Council bans the offenders from *otiti mmanwụ* and following *mmanwụ* (participation in masquerade displays) for two years (at p. 171).

The processes in Case Numbers 4 and 20 meet the predictions under themes 7 (Individualization), 8 (Proscriptiveness of Norms), 10 (Simplicity of Process), and 11 (Cost of Invoking Process) (see table 2.2). In addition, Case Number 20 meets the conditions of theme 12 (Peacemaking Emphasis). The punishment imposed on each offender in Case Number 4 depends on the seriousness of the offense (theme 7, Individualization). The laws and customs relied upon in both cases are uncodified (theme 8, Proscriptiveness of Norms). Neither case satisfies the "memory only (oral history)" record predicted under theme 9. However, both cases meet the "Simplicity of Process" expected under theme 10 because the proceedings in the cases are initiated orally. Also, consistently with theme 11 (Cost of Invoking Process), there is "no cost" to invoke the legal process in either case. Further, in Case Number 20, the disputants are encouraged to maintain peace and to cooperate with other community members (theme 12).

In Case Number 8 (Record of Proceedings, vol. 1, at p. 118, 1990), the second disputant has allegedly been "haunted and harassed" (at p. 125) by the members of his former *ụmụnna*, and that has led to fights between him and the first disputant. Part of the issue is a land dispute between the parties. One of the disputants takes the land case to the official court.[19] Subsequently, the first disputant brings the present case before the *Eze*-in-Council. The council concludes that the dispute before it deals with different issues from those involved in the case in the official court.[20] The present dispute is treated as a civil dispute.[21] As the council members view it, the responsibility of the council is that of "restoring peace among [the disputants]" (at p. 125). In recognition of this, the council decides as follows: "Both parties are hereby bound over from fighting or any behaviour calculated or likely to cause any breach of the peace. But their case in the [official] court is not the concern of the *Eze*-in-Council" (at p. 129).[22]

Case Number 8 meets eight of the twelve predicted themes of informal case processing (see table 2.2). The case is tried before the *Eze*-in-Council. Theme 12 (Peacemaking Emphasis) is clearly identifiable in the case. The record of proceedings (at p. 126) contains the following entry based on a resolution of the council: "The two families [are] accordingly to be informed to keep the peace among their members." The case is initiated by the *ịtụnye mmanya* procedure contrary to the expectations of theme 11 (table 2.1 and Appendix A). The record of proceedings in the case is complete and handwritten. This differs from the prediction under theme 9 (Record Management). Theme 6 (Stigmatization) is absent because neither of the disputants loses his dignity in the proceedings. However, both disputants lose their autonomy as a consequence of the council's interim injunction that prevents the parties from entering the disputed land. They are also directed to be of good behavior. The injunction and the binding over curtail the freedoms of movement, speech, and association of the disputants. Theme 2 (Mediation) is not identifiable in this case because the proceedings are adversarial.

The three cases examined in this subcategory (Case Numbers 4, 20, and 8) deal with assaults. The proceedings in Case Numbers 4 and 20 (criminal cases) are non-adversarial, while the proceedings in Case Number 8 (a civil case) are adversarial. The three cases are processed outside the official court system. The unofficial management makes it possible for the norms of the community to be applied, even where the official laws do not recognize the norms.

Dispute over an Act of Public Nuisance

The only case study in this subcategory is Case Number 6 (Record of Proceedings, vol. 1, at p. 80, 1989). This case involves tampering with public property. The Ajallị community treats Case Number 6 as a criminal case because the interest of the entire community is concerned. A "mass rally of Ajallịans" hears and determines this case. The mass rally is made up of all Ajallị community members that have attended a scheduled assembly. "The main object of the rally was on [*sic*] the gross indiscipline prevailing in the town" (at p. 80). This case is included in the record of proceedings of the *Eze*-in-Council because the case is later reported to the council. The report to the council is made as "a formality because most members of the Cabinet [council] were present at the rally" (at p. 80).

The offender in Case Number 6 climbs the ladder leading to the main water tank (reservoir) in the town. He lets out some water from the tank. The Central Executive Committee of the AWU deliberates on the matter but the offender fails to appear before the committee. He is subsequently brought before the mass rally of the townspeople, which holds him liable for his misconduct. For his punishment, "he [is] given a total of 24 strokes of the caine [*sic*] before the whole meeting as a disciplinary measure and also as a deterrent to others like him" (at p. 81). The process in the case satisfies ten of the twelve themes of informal case processing. The process does not satisfy themes 5 (Punitiveness) and 9 (Record Management). Contrary to the predictions under theme 5, the processing of the offender puts emphasis on placing blame and on guilt. He is given twenty-four strokes of the cane. The record of proceedings is in sketchy, handwritten files. This differs from an oral history record predicted under theme 9.

Although Case Number 6 is processed before a mass rally of Ajallịans, the mass rally, like the *Eze*-in-Council, is not created by, nor is it run by, any of the official governments. The process therefore meets the prediction under theme 1. The proceedings are non-adversarial as expected under theme 2. The satisfaction of themes 3 and 4 follows from the noninvolvement of any lawyer in the case processing. The prediction under theme 6 (Stigmatization) is met because the offender–who is given twenty-four strokes of the cane before the mass rally of the townspeople–has thereby become labeled and lost the respect of some of the community members. Case Number 6 is processed at the same rally where the complaint is made. Therefore, little or no time is lost in the process. The predictions under themes 7 (Individualization), 8 (Proscriptiveness of Norms), 10 (Simplicity of Process), 11 (Cost of Invoking Process), and 12 (Peacemaking Emphasis) for informal case processing are also clearly identifiable in Case Number 6 (see table 2.2).

The unofficial processing of Case Number 6 is intended to discipline and deter the offender and others like him (at p. 81). These objectives are to be achieved without incarcerating the offender. In an official process, he could have been incarcerated.

Disputes over False Accusations

The processes in the two cases in this subcategory (Case Numbers 9 and 17) are examined together. In Case Number 9 (Record of Proceedings, vol. 1, at p. 124, 1990), the first disputant complains to the *Eze*-in-Council that the second disputant "insulted and accused her of stealing a sheep" (at p. 124). The case does not continue through to conclusion before the council. The first disputant reports the matter to the *Ụmụ Ada* Ajallị (the association of all the daughters of Ajallị Town). The records are not clear on this, but it seems that the two disputing women belong to this association. While the case is pending before the *Eze*-in-Council, the *Ụmụ Ada* Ajallị sends a representative to the council with a message that the association has settled the dispute. The council cautions both disputants against any future occurrence of the dispute between them. The case is dismissed. The main issue in Case Number 17 (Record of Proceedings, vol. 2, at p. 56, 1992) is, according to the first disputant, that the second disputant has falsely accused the first disputant "of trying to seduce [the second disputant's] wife and causing a [*sic*] chaos in [the second disputant's] family" (at p. 56). The facts of this case sufficiently ground a civil action for defamation (slander) in the official court.

In each of Case Numbers 9 and 17, for a plaintiff to succeed in an official court action for defamation, there must be sufficient evidence that the second disputant has published the alleged defamatory statement to a third party. In Case Number 17, the second disputant has actually published the alleged defamatory statement to some third parties. He has reported to the first disputant's *ụmụnna* and church minister that the first disputant is trying to seduce the second disputant's wife and cause chaos in the second disputant's family. When asked about the publication, the second disputant claims that he has merely acted according to the *ichi* tradition (reporting a person's misconduct to another or others who have influence over the wrongdoer). However, according to the first disputant, "he was baffled when the matter was being rumoured in Ajallị [Town]" (at p. 64). If the second disputant is responsible for the rumor in the town and embarrassment to the first disputant, then the second disputant's claim of privileged communication could not stand even in an official court, except the second disputant successfully pleads the "truth" defense. Otherwise, making a defamatory statement available to the town's people goes beyond the *ichi* tradition privilege. There is no indication that the second disputant in Case Number 9 has published the alleged defamatory statement to a third party.

Insult or false allegation of a crime is a ground for legal action before the *Eze*-in-Council even if the official law would conclude that the complainant has not suffered any damage to reputation. The foci of the native Igbo justice system are to address grievances and conflicts before they grow into serious disputes and to maintain harmony and peaceful coexistence among the locals (Okereafọezeke, 1996; see also Todd, 1978; Pratt, 1995). While the proceedings in Case Number 17 are on, the first disputant also "appealed to [the second disputant] through the Cabinet to respect [the first disputant] at least for age reasons" (at p. 66). The *Eze*-in-Council handles Case Numbers 9 and 17 as civil disputes. The council, in its decision in Case Number 17, recognizes that the disputants have appeared before the council "for peace reasons." The record of proceedings reflects the council's decision as follows (at pp. 66-67): "Both [disputants] were cautioned to keep the peace. *Let bye gone be bye gone* from [*sic*] henceforth. Both parties were directed to keep off from each other's family."[23]

The process in Case Number 9 satisfies nine of the twelve themes in table 2.1. Case Number 17 meets eight of the themes. The themes that are missing in both cases are themes 6 (Stigmatization), 9 (Record Management), and 11 (Cost of Invoking Process). In addition, Case Number 17 does not satisfy theme 2 (Mediation). Therefore, the process in each case satisfies the predictions in themes 1, 3, 4, 5, 7, 8, 10, and 12 (see table 2.2). The major point of distinction between the processes in the two similar cases is theme 2 (Mediation). The prediction under this theme is that an informal case process would be non-adversarial. That is the situation in Case Number 9. But in Case Number 17, the proceedings are adversarial. It is not clear why this inconsistency exists, especially considering the fact that both cases are processed as civil cases by the *Eze*-in-Council.

The native, unofficial processing of Case Numbers 9 and 17 avoids the strict rules associated with the processing of defamation cases in an official court. Moreover, the unofficial processes are geared toward amicable settlement of the disputes between the parties.

Dispute over Stealing

In Case Number 10 (Record of Proceedings, vol. 1, at p. 131, 1990), the first disputant complains to the *Eze*-in-Council that the second disputant has cut and removed the first disputant's *achara* (bamboo) plant. The second disputant denies the allegation. He claims that in any case the first disputant has taken the matter before an official court where it is pending. The council concludes that the issue before it is different from that before the official court. The second disputant later admits that his son cut the *achara* plant. Cutting and removing the first disputant's plant could be grounds for a charge of stealing under the *Criminal Code Law of Anambra State*, which applies to Ajallị Town. A conviction under the *Criminal Code Law* for stealing attracts a term of imprisonment or, at a minimum, a substantial fine. However, since Case Number 10 is heard and determined by the *Eze*-in-Council, the council does not apply the official criminal laws. Rather, it applies the customary laws and traditions of the community. The records are not clear as to whether the case should be identified as criminal or civil. Thus, the author records its content as "None/Unclear" (see table 2.4). In its decision, the council holds as follows (at p. 149): "[The second disputant is] to appologise [*sic*] to [the first disputant] before the Cabinet for the destruction of [the first disputant's] *achara* plant." It is expected that an apology would lead to forgiveness for the second disputant. The process encourages the disputants to integrate with each other and the community (theme 12).

The process in Case Number 10 satisfies theme 12 (Peacemaking Emphasis) because the process includes the primary descriptor (Parties encouraged to integrate and cooperate with each other and with others in the community). However, the prediction under the same theme that a disputant in an informal case process would not stand against the system is not fulfilled in the case. The second disputant clearly stands against the system in two ways: first, when he claims that the council cannot hear the case because the case is already in the official court, and second, when, after submitting to the council's jurisdiction, he later rejects its decision. After the council has given its decision in the case, the second disputant, who has participated fully in the process, reacts adversely to the decision, and causes the following entry in the case record: "[The second disputant stated that] the *achara* matter was already in the [official] court and, therefore, [he] refused to accept the Cabinet decisions. Thereupon he walked away" (at p. 149).

In addition to meeting the prediction under theme 12, Case Number 10 meets the expectations for informal case processing under themes 1, 2, 3, 4, 5, 7, 8, and 10 (see table 2.2; Appendix A). The case does not meet the requirements under themes 6, 9, and 11. Theme 6 (Stigmatization) is not met because the loss of dignity predicted for an informal case process is absent. However, loss of autonomy by the disputants is clearly identifiable in the case. Before rendering a decision in the case, the council enjoins both disputants to stay away from the land at issue. This is a loss of autonomy under theme 6 (b). But this descriptor is not sufficient to satisfy theme 6. The "complete, handwritten files" maintained on the case are the reasons for the absence of theme 9 (Record Management). The case record deviates from the prediction of an "oral history"-based record for an informal case process. On "Cost of Invoking Process" (theme 11), it is not clear whether or not cost is incurred to invoke the process in this case.

Case Number 10 is processed unofficially by the *Eze*-in-Council, and as the case demonstrates, a party in such an unofficial process may reject a decision of the council. No such option exists in the official process.

Disputes over Insult and Disrespect for an Elderly Person, and Contempt of the Eze-in-Council

The processes in the two cases in this subcategory (Case Numbers 13 and 18) are considered together since the cases deal with similar issues. Also, the *Eze*-in-Council processes both cases as crimes. In Case Number 18 (Record of Proceedings, vol. 2, at p. 107, 1993), a member of the *Eze*-in-Council (cabinet member) is accused of having disrespected the *Eze*. It is alleged that on a previous occasion when the town's people gathered for a political event, the accused cabinet member said, in the presence of the townspeople, that the *Eze* was partisan. He allegedly called the *Eze* "a political chief" (at p. 107). All the members of the council regard the accused member's statement as an act of disrespect for, not only the *Eze* but also, the entire Ajallị Town. Their view of the seriousness of the member's statement leads the council to view the issue as a crime. The accused member admits that he made the statement. The council decides as follows (at p. 107):

> (i) The Cabinet [has] lost confidence in [the accused Cabinet member]. (ii) He should submit to the sect.[secretary] of[sic] the Cabinet the property of the body within 24hrs.[hours]. (iii) [His *ụmụnna* is] to be written to send a substitute to represent them in the *Eze*'s Cabinet. (iv) From today – 14/5/93 – [he is] no longer a member of the Cabinet of H. R. H. *Eze* C. O. Nwosu *Eze* VI of Ajallị.[24]

The newly divested cabinet member accepts the decision of his former colleagues but adds that he did not mean to disrespect or injure the *Eze*.

The distinction between Case Number 18 and Case Number 13 (Record of Proceedings, vol. 2, at p. 37, 1991) is that the act of disrespect in Case Number 18 is done outside the presence of the *Eze*-in-Council, whereas the act of disrespect in Case Number 13 happens in the council's presence. This distinction is similar to that between *contempt in the face of the court* and *contempt outside the court* in the official court proceedings. Case Number 13 is heard and determined by the *Eze*-in-Council. The conduct resulting in the case would not have been sufficient to ground a criminal or civil contempt case in an official court. However, the case is regarded as a criminal matter before the council. In Case Number 13, the accused person is summoned before the council to testify on an issue. At the end of his testimony, he leaves the hearing room. While he is still in the premises, a member of the council comes out from the room at the request of the council members to invite some other person into the room. The accused person threatens to "deal with [the member of the Council because the accused] had seen the role [the member] was playing [regarding the case]" (at p. 37). The member goes back into the room and reports the incident to the other council members. The council immediately sends someone to summon the accused back to the hearing room. The accused person refuses to deny or accept the member's allegation and leaves the premises.[25] He is held responsible. The offender, who up to this time has represented the town at *Ndịeni*[26] meetings, is punished as follows: "A letter should be written to *Ndịeni* meeting telling them that [the offender] from now would not represent Ajallị in the meeting" (at p. 38).[27]

The processing of Case Number 18 meets eight of the twelve themes of informal case management. Case Number 13 includes nine of the themes. Both cases meet themes 1, 3, 4, 6, 7, 8, 10, and 11 (see table 2.2; Appendix A). Also, Case Number 13 meets the requirements of theme 2. Both cases are tried by the *Eze*-in-Council (an unofficial tribunal as predicted under theme 1). The accused persons in both cases are tried without lawyers. This complies with themes 3 and 4. The punishment imposed on the offenders shows that the council blames the offenders for what they have done. This negates the prediction under theme 5 that an informal case management process would not emphasize blame. Therefore, the processes in both cases have failed to satisfy the expectations of theme 5. The stigmatization predicted under theme 6 is clearly identifiable in both cases. In Case Number 13, the offender is stripped of his position as the town's representative at *Ndịeni*. In Case Number 18, the offender, an *Eze*-in-Council member and office holder, is stripped of his office on the council and dismissed from the body. Both cases satisfy themes 7, 8, 10, and 11. On theme 11 (Cost of Invoking Process), as predicted, both cases are brought before the council at no cost. The council does not emphasize peacemaking in either Case Number 13 or Case Number 18. Therefore, neither case satisfies theme 12 (Peacemaking Emphasis).

Despite the similarities in the processes in Case Numbers 13 and 18, they differ on theme 2 (Mediation) ostensibly because the proceedings in Case Number 13 are non-adversarial, whereas that in Case Number 18 is adversarial. This difference may have been based on where each contemptuous act has occurred. The alleged contempt in Case Number 13 is done in the presence of the council, while the act of disrespect in Case Number 18 is done outside the council's presence.

Case Numbers 13 and 18 illustrate the ability of the unofficial processes to regulate behavior. Such regulation is necessary to maintain order in the community. As Case Numbers 13 and 18 show, the community rules and laws would be applied even if the official laws do not recognize them.

Dispute over Cost of Labor

In Ajallị Town, as in other Igbo communities, the *Eze*-in-Council hears and determines cases brought before it. However, this is by no means its only function regarding social control in the town. Sometimes, the council takes legislative steps to ease the economic burden on the community members, for example, by stipulating the amount of money a service provider may charge for his or her services. Admittedly, this is a form of price control. But every society, big or small, takes price control measures in one form or the other. This is still justifiable even in the so-called free economies. Price fixing or regulation of any kind is used to prevent the sellers of goods and services from "ripping off" their customers. In Ajallị Town, a breach of any of the town's rules on pricing is treated as a crime with the probability of a sanction.

In Case Number 21 (Record of Proceedings, vol. 3, at p. 13, 1994), the *Eze*-in-Council has determined that the rate of cutting palm fruits [five naira (N5:00) per head] is exorbitant. The council therefore summons the town's residents that provide the service. Some of the service providers are non-natives of the town. Two of the concerned persons fail to appear before the council. The council approves the sum of five naira as the charge for cutting *all the heads of palm fruits on a palm tree*, rather than five naira for cutting *one head of palm fruits*. The council goes on to decide that a certain service provider, a non-native of the town, should be asked to leave the town immediately. Another service provider, an indigene of the town, is suspended from his *ụmụnna* and suspended from climbing palm trees in the town.

The processing of Case Number 21 meets nine of the twelve themes of informal case management. The process includes themes 1, 2, 3, 4, 6, 7, 8, 10, and 11 (see table 2.2). Themes 5, 9, and 12 are not satisfied. The case is tried by the *Eze*-in-Council (theme 1), and no lawyer is involved in the proceedings (themes 3 and 4). As predicted under theme 2, the proceedings are non-adversarial and thus meet theme 2. However, contrary to expectation, the proceedings are not reconciliatory [see theme 2 (a)].

The proceedings in Case Number 21 are punitive. The following statement in the Record of Proceedings illustrates their punitive quality: "[A member of the council] emphasized that offenders/culprits of any laid down rule [such as the rule laid down in this case] must not go unpunished" (at p. 13). This emphasis detracts from the non-punitive proceedings predicted under theme 5 for informal case management. The stigmatization expected under theme 6 exists in the case. The decisions of the council to ask one of the alleged offenders to leave Ajallị Town, and to suspend the other from his *ụmụnna* and from climbing palm trees in the town amount to "denying or stripping disputant of a position" under theme 6. This case is concluded within one month of its commencement and after one adjournment. Thus, the disputants have not lost time in the process.

The process in Case Number 21 fails to satisfy theme 12 because the process does not emphasize peacemaking. The process shows only a slight indication of encouragement to the disputants to cooperate with others in the community. However, the process emphasizes that the interest of the entire community overrides that of an individual. The process in this case gives paramount consideration to *ọganiru obodo* Ajallị (the progress of Ajallị Town). The process does not meet the prediction under theme 9 (Record Management). The case record is complete and handwritten, rather than based on memory only as predicted for informal case management. The proceedings are initiated at no cost. This agrees with the prediction under theme 11.

Case Number 21 shows how the *Eze*-in-Council sometimes takes steps to protect the economic interests of Ajallị community members. By stipulating the cost of labor or service, the council tries to prevent the exploitation of the locals.

Dispute over Incestuous Act

Like many cultures, the Igbos regard incest as taboo. To the Igbos, an incestuous act is *arụ*, *alụ*, or *nsọ* (an abominable act; a crime that "pollutes the land"). The Igbos define incest as "sexual intercourse with a person one cannot marry" (Uchendu, 1966, at p. 42). This means sexual intercourse with a close blood relative. *Close blood relatives* include a son, daughter, brother, sister, half-brother, half-sister, nephew, niece, uncle, aunt, and first cousin. In Igbo, incest is a more serious crime than most other crimes. Incest also seems to be rare.[28] The Igbo look upon incest–like *ọchụ* (homicide)–as a crime that has the potential of affecting the future of the entire community. To avoid a negative effect on the community, the offender must be compelled to take responsibility for the evil deed and atone for it. In Case Number 24 (Record of Proceedings, vol. 3, at p. 66, 1994), the opinion of *ụmụ ada* Ajallị (the daughters of Ajallị Town) on the issue in the incest case are expressed as follows (at p. 66): "In their opinion, such a case should not be treated lightly since the whole town is bound to suffer the consequences. [The offender], they strongly recommended, should appease the gods in the proper way before he could be allowed to remain part of the community." Also, the Record of Proceedings shows that Case Number 24 is titled "[Offender's Name]'s *Abomination Case*"[29] (at p. 66). This highlights the special attention this case attracts among the community members. Incest is more than an ordinary crime; it is an abomination.

In Case Number 24, the accused person and the victim are father and daughter.[30] The father is accused of forcing the girl into sexual intercourse on three occasions. The events leading to these incidents are that the girl's mother, who is married to her father, has for some reason, left the matrimonial home to stay with the mother's sister. The incestuous acts are said to have taken place during the period when the girl's mother was away from their home. In addition to the acts of sexual intercourse, it is alleged that the accused person assaulted and battered the girl.

The alleged conducts amount to three counts of statutory rape under the official government *Criminal Code Law of Anambra State*, which applies to Ajallị Town. If convicted under the official laws, the father could be sentenced to years in prison on each of the counts. He could also be charged with assault and battery under the official laws. Convictions on these two additional counts would sentence him to more years in prison. However, the case is taken before the *Eze*-in-Council. The accused father denies the allegations. The council concludes that he is guilty. The case record contains the council's directives as follows (at p. 71): "1. [The accused person] was guilty of the offence and should appease the gods '*Ịkpụ Arụ*'. 2. A time limit was given [for] him to comply. 3. He should leave Ajallị [town] after the citizens are informed of this decision on Monday 12-12-94."[31]

The processing of Case Number 24 complies with eight of the twelve themes. The following four themes do not apply: themes 2 (Mediation), 5 (Punitiveness), 9 (Record Management), and 12 (Peacemaking Emphasis). The seriousness of the charge against the accused person explains the adversarial nature of the proceedings in this case. The adversarial proceedings are, however, contrary to theme 2. In an effort to determine whether or not the accused actually did the incestuous acts with which he is charged, the council allows him the opportunity to cross-examine the witnesses against him. It seems proper to allow the parties to cross-examine each other because the accused, if he were convicted, would be severely punished.

Theme 5 expects an informal case process to be non-punitive. This theme predicts that the process would not put emphasis on placing blame. The process in Case Number 24 puts emphasis on blaming the offender. Theme 5 also predicts that an informal case process would not emphasize guilt. Again, the process in the case emphasizes guilt. As already noted, the council pronounces the offender "guilty of the offence" (at p. 71). Also, the offender is stigmatized in various ways (theme 6). One of the consequences of conviction for the type of offense for which the offender is convicted is that the other community members would lose *ugwu* (respect) for the offender. The other consequence is that he would be regarded as a person who should not be looked up to, particularly by the younger members of the community. Moreover, the offender is stripped of a position or honor when the council decides that he should leave Ajallị Town. This is akin to a forced exile. There is no loss of time in the case. The council makes its decision on the same day that the case is brought before it. The case is instituted at no cost as predicted (theme 11). However, contrary to theme 12, the proceedings in the case do not emphasize peacemaking. The offensive nature of the alleged crimes explains the absence of peacemaking emphasis in the case processing. The council members understand that if the accused is guilty, he must be punished in the interest of the entire community. The record of proceedings in Case Number 24 is complete and handwritten, rather than based on memory only as predicted (theme 9).

In native Igbo, the blood relationship between the parties causes an incestuous act to be viewed as a more damaging act than simple sexual relationship. An incestuous act pollutes the land for all. Thus, the Igbo regard incest as a more serious crime than rape or sexual assault. The native, unofficial judicial process makes it possible for the accused in Case Number 24 to be tried for incest rather than for rape or sexual assault. The community members are thus able to show their aversion to the offender's crime.

Dispute over Ụmụnna Name

There are at least sixteen *ụmụnna*s (extended families) in Ajallị Town. Apart from the existing *ụmụnna*s, a new *ụmụnna* may be recognized from time to time.[32] Each of the sixteen or so *ụmụnna*s in the town is known by a different name. In Case Number 25 (Record of Proceedings, vol. 3, p. 59, 1994), two of the *ụmụnna*s are disputing over the name by which one of them is known. The second disputants are known by the same name as the *ọnụma* (village) that includes both the first and second disputing *ụmụnna*s. The first disputants claim that since the name of the second disputants is the same as that of the entire village, the second disputants are creating the false impression that they alone make up the entire village.

The dispute in Case Number 25 could legitimately be litigated in the official courts. However, this sort of case in an official court usually goes on for a long time. Moreover, a judgment by an official court would not necessarily put an end to the dispute between the *ụmụnna* groups. It is important to consider this since both *ụmụnna*s are part of the same town. They live together; they share many things; and they should cooperate with each other for the town's progress. Considering all these factors, if the dispute in Case Number 25 were dealt with in an official court, both the victorious party and the losing party would forfeit a lot of goodwill at the end – a pyrrhic victory for the *ụmụnna* that prevails.

The first disputants in Case Number 25 take the dispute before an *ad hoc*, mediation panel constituted to deal with the case. Twenty-three people: ten members of the *Eze*-in-Council, three representatives of the AWU, five representatives of the first disputants, and five representatives of the second disputants make up the panel. Before the panel begins deliberating on the dispute, *Eze* Ajallị, who chairs the panel, reminds all the panelists of "the sensitive nature" of the dispute (at p. 59). The dispute is treated as a civil case. The process in the case meets ten of the twelve themes of informal case processing. The absent themes are themes 6 (Stigmatization) and 9 (Record Management). Contrary to the prediction under theme 6, there is no stigmatization of any of the disputants in the case. No disputant loses dignity in the process. None of them loses either wealth or time. The panel reaches its decision at the same meeting where the case is begun. The complete and handwritten nature of the record of proceedings in the case detracts from the predicted "memory only (oral history)" record under theme 9. Therefore, the process in Case Number 25 does not meet theme 9.

Case Number 25, which is heard by an unofficial mediation panel, satisfies the prediction under theme 1 (Officialism). The proceedings in the case clearly reflect theme 2 (Mediation). In fact, the Record of Proceedings describes the meeting at which the dispute is discussed as the "meeting between the mediation panel and five representatives of [the disputing *ụmụnna*s]" (at p. 59). The proceedings are non-adversarial as predicted under theme 2. The final decision of the mediation panel further illustrates the mediatory nature of the proceedings. The panel decides that a more harmonious and lasting resolution of the dispute could be found among the members of the disputing *ụmụnna*s. Accordingly, the panel constitutes a committee of six persons (three individuals from each disputing *ụmụnna*) to settle the dispute. A member of the panel rationalizes this step as follows: "A lasting solution would only be found from within. Any decision handed over [*sic*] by the mediation panel would be an imposition" (at p. 61).[33]

The processing of Case Number 25 satisfies themes 3 and 4 because no lawyer is involved in the proceedings. On theme 5 (Punitiveness), the process in the case does not place any emphasis on blaming a guilty disputant. This is as predicted under the theme. The object of the proceedings is to find a lasting solution to the dispute. Consequently, there is no focus on proof. The process also complies with the flexible process predicted under theme 7 (Individualization). Further, the process accords with the unwritten character of traditions, customs, and laws expected under theme 8 (Proscriptiveness of Norms). In line with the simple procedure projected under theme 10 (Simplicity of Process), Case Number 25 is initiated orally. Also as expected, the case is brought before the mediation panel at no cost (theme 11). The process does not require either of the disputants to incur any cost for bringing the case. However, the second disputants have voluntarily given two gallons of palm wine and two Igbo kola nuts to the panel members. The gift could raise question regarding the panel's fairness to both parties: Does the panel favor the second disputants in the case? There is no evidence of unfairness by the panel. Moreover, the second disputants' gesture is not unusual among the Igbos in such situations. The gift, by itself, is not sufficient to question the panel's decision. Therefore, it is safe to assume that the panel has discharged its functions honestly and responsibly.

As anticipated under theme 12, the processing of Case Number 25 emphasizes peacemaking. One member of the mediation panel calls on the disputing *ụmụnna*s to be cautious "so as to bring about cooperate existence of both [*ụmụnna*s] in Ajallị" (at p. 59). The leaders of Ajallị community have tried to reconcile the disputing *ụmụnna*s to maintain harmony in the town. The leaders' steps toward reconciling the *ụmụnna*s do not involve the official processes.

Dispute over Ịkpa Asịrị (Peddling a False Rumor)

The last case in the "Informal" category involves rumor mongering in the community. Among the Igbos, elderly persons are highly respected, especially by the young. The need for the respect is probably more pronounced where an elderly person also holds an important position in the community. Any insult or disrespect to such a person is viewed as an insult or disrespect to the entire community. There is thus an involvement of the collective conscience of the community in any situation in which an elderly office holder is insulted or disrespected. The collective community conscience may be the reason for treating such cases as crimes. If an Igbo community reacts in this way to an insult or disrespect of one of its members, then there is no doubt that it will react even more strongly where the entire community is insulted or disrespected.

In Case Number 26 (Record of Proceedings, vol. 3, at p. 86, 1995), the accused young man is sent by an elderly member of the town to attend a gathering of the town's people. The young man is to collect some food items due to the elderly man. These food items, usually meat (called *ihe ndị oko ọha*), are specially reserved on such occasions for the community elders. At the gathering of the town's people, the young man allegedly insults the chairman of the occasion. The reason for the insult is not contained in the Record of Proceedings. The young man is immediately fined four gallons of palm wine for insulting the chairman. He later pays the equivalent amount of money for the wine. However, he goes on to tell "a blatant lie against Ajallị community that he, [his name], was fined N200 [200 naira] for daring to demand *ihe ndị oko ọha* for [the elderly man]" (at p. 87). He is penalized for peddling the false rumor (*ịkpa asịrị*).[34] His penalty for this second offense is more severe. He is ordered to pay "a big goat, 5 gallons of palm wine, and 8 Igbo kola nuts" (at p. 87). The elderly man, whom the accused person represented at the initial gathering, "petitioned" the *Eze*-in-Council to look into the case (at p. 86). The council upholds the fines with a minor change.

The process in Case Number 26 complies with eight of the twelve anticipated themes of informal case processing. However, the process does not meet themes 5 (Punitiveness), 9 (Record Management), 10 (Simplicity of Process), and 12 (Peacemaking Emphasis). The process clearly emphasizes the accused person's blame and guilt contrary to theme 5. The record of proceedings is complete and handwritten, which differs from the oral history-type record predicted under theme 9. A "petition" or "letter" initiates the process (at p. 86). The elderly member of the community whom the offender represents at the first gathering sends the petition or letter. This element of writing in the process negates the prediction under theme 10 that a case in an informal judicial process would be initiated orally. The case does not satisfy theme 12 because there is no clear indication that the council emphasizes peacemaking.

The proceedings in Case Number 26, which is heard by the *Eze*-in-Council (theme 1), are non-adversarial (theme 2) and without the involvement of lawyers (themes 3 and 4). The process stigmatizes the accused person as expected under theme 6. In its decision, the council "asked [the elderly man] to get another person to represent him in all future occasions" (at p. 87). This is a denial or stripping of the accused person of a position or honor under the theme. The resolution of the case is quick. The case is settled at the same meeting at which it is brought to the council's attention. Therefore, the parties do not lose time in the process. Also, the process complies with the individualization and bending of rules predicted under theme 7. Further, it complies with the uncodified brand of laws, customs, and traditions predicted under theme 8. The case is instituted at no cost to either party. This is as expected under theme 11. Case Number 26 shows how Ajallị community members would take unofficial steps to protect the image of the community against any person who presents it in bad light.

Summary of Contents and Processes Found in the Informal Category

The contents and processes in the twenty-two case studies found in the "Informal" category may be divided into three groups as follows:

1. The first group of cases is made up of those situations in which a disputant or group of disputants complains against another before an unofficial judicial tribunal. The tribunal summons the opposing disputant to appear before it and answer the allegations by the complainant. The tribunal handles most of

the cases in this group as civil cases. In the official courts, similar parties are known as "plaintiffs" and "defendants." Since the cases in this group are civil cases, the disputants are the parties to each of the cases. The community is not a party to such a case, except that the community has a strong interest in seeing to the settlement of every case whether it is civil or criminal. The contents of the cases found in the "Informal" category are land and land-related issues, destruction of property, breach of contract, *ụmụnna* name, and false accusations.

2. Another group of cases in the "Informal" category consists of those cases in which an individual, or group, reports to an unofficial tribunal that another has breached a tradition, custom, or law. Once a person lodges the report, he or she usually takes a back seat. He or she is not a party to the case. From then on, the dispute is between the alleged offender and the entire community. However, the complainant is usually required to testify at the proceedings. In few instances, the community may delegate a titleholder or respected community member to represent its interest at the tribunal. In most cases, however, the complainant and the other witnesses represent the community's interest by their testimony. But the community and the alleged offender are the parties to the case. All the cases in this group involve violations of Igbo traditions, customs, or laws. Some punishment is usually imposed for a violation. Thus, the society regards such a violation as a crime. Usually, the "accused" person is identified as such in the Record of Proceedings. The contents of the cases in this group are assault, battery, street fighting, disobedience of *iwu mmanwụ* (rules and regulations on masquerading), harassment, public nuisance, insult and disrespect, cost of labor, *ịkpa asịrị* (peddling a false rumor), and incest.

3. The last group of cases in the "Informal" category is made up of those cases in which the unofficial tribunal is a party. Cases of contempt or disrespect of the *Eze*-in-Council or its members in the face of the council fall into this group. The disputants in such a case are the disrespected member or the council, as the case may be, and the alleged offender. But the parties to the case are the disrespected member or the council, on behalf of the entire community, and the accused person. When, however, the contempt or disrespect occurs outside the council, the council asks the person reporting the alleged wrongdoing to show that it occurred.

SEMI-FORMAL CATEGORY

The "Semi-Formal" category is the third category on the informality-formality continuum (see table 2.3). The "Semi-Formal" category is made up of six subcategories. Each subcategory consists of cases dealing with similar subject matters. Seven of the forty-two case studies fall in the "Semi-Formal" category. The category includes all the cases that have five to seven of the predicted themes of informal case processing. The processes in five of the seven cases in this category meet seven of the twelve expected themes, while the remaining two cases contain six of the themes.

Nature and Kinds of Cases

Dispute Concerning Ostracism

Among the Igbos, ostracism may be used as a form of punishment to protest a disapproved or socially reprehensible conduct. Ostracism is an example of punishment by omission. The omissions by the persons meting out the punishment include refusal to exchange greetings and refusal to purchase goods from the ostracized person. Sometimes, the persons meting out the punishment make it expressly known to the ostracized person that he or she is no longer welcome as a full member of the group. Whatever the form of the ostracism, the ostracized is thereby socially handicapped.

The Igbos say: "*Ofu onye siere ọra, ọra erisia ya, mana ọra siere ofu onye, ọgaghị erisi ya.*" Literally, this translates as: "If one person cooks for the public, the public will eat it all, but if the public cooks for one person, he or she cannot eat it all." This expression represents the Igbo belief in the superior power of the aggregate group over the individual. Only rarely does an individual challenge the public and win, especially in a relatively homogenous, close nit community. Most Igbo communities are small, homogenous, and close nit (see Adeyemi, 1990, July; Anene, 1991). These small communities have "higher density of acquaintanceships" than larger and industrialized communities (Weisheit, et al., 1996, at p. 18).

Case Number 5 (Record of Proceedings, vol. 1, at p. 79, 1989) deals with ostracism. The processing of the case satisfies seven of the twelve themes of informal case processing predicted in table 2.1. The facts of the case are as follows. The first and second disputants belong to the same *ụmụnna*. The first disputant's case before the *Eze*-in-Council is that the second disputants (representing themselves and their *ụmụnna*) have ostracized him for ten years from their common *ụmụnna*. He wants the second disputants to explain the reason for his ostracism. He also wants them to accept him back fully into their *ụmụnna*. The second disputants state three main reasons why the first disputant is ostracized. First, when the first disputant's wife died, he shaved his own hair and took charge of the burial arrangements contrary to the customs. The second disputants consider this behavior taboo.[35] Second, on occasions when other persons died in their *ụmụnna*, the first disputant failed to take part in the burial ceremonies as is expected of every able-bodied, mature, member of the *ụmụnna*. Third, the first disputant has not paid his membership and other dues in the *ụmụnna* for years. In view of this, the second disputants have decided that in the best interest of their *ụmụnna*, the first disputant "should stand alone and outside [their *ụmụnna*]" (at p. 95).

Under the official government laws applicable to Ajallị town, ostracism *per se* is not actionable. Thus, an official court would not grant either of the reliefs that the first disputant seeks in Case Number 5. An official court could not invoke the principles of equity to order the second disputants to accept and treat the first disputant as one of their members. The reliefs that the first disputant asks for may only be granted through an out-of-court process, such as the *Eze*-in-Council represents. The council is not "set up by the Constitution or other law, nor is it established by the State" (theme 1, Officialism). Further on theme 1, the case is settled out-of-court. Also, the record of proceedings refers to *omenala* (tradition, custom) [theme 1 (c)]. The record further mentions that the person that previously tried to settle the dispute advised the first disputant "to swear on oathe[sic] to obey [his *ụmụnna*]" (at p. 95). This is clearly a reliance on the supernatural [theme 1 (d)]. There is no indication whatsoever that there are "specific locales of State authority" [theme 1 (e)], nor are "authority figures of State" [theme 1 (f)] involved in managing the case. None of the individuals holding positions in the process wears "uniforms/badges or other credentials" [theme 1 (g)].

The processing of Case Number 5 fails to meet the predicted mediation under theme 2. The expected non-adversarial procedure is not identifiable in the case. In fact, there are indications that each side to the dispute has cross-examined the opponent at the proceedings. However, the proceedings are somewhat reconciliatory. The first disputant himself describes his case against the second disputants as a "brotherly one" (at p. 94). By this statement, he shows that he recognizes his family relationship with the second disputants. No third party is involved in managing the case. Contrary to theme 2 (d), the process does not refer to order maintenance.

No lawyers are involved in the management of Case Number 5. Thus, themes 3 and 4 (Lawyer Involvement and Litigiousness or Argumentativeness in the Legal Sense, respectively) are absent in the record of proceedings. The record of proceedings in Case Number 5 shows that some emphasis is put on punitiveness, contrary to the prediction for an informal case processing (theme 5). Emphases on guilt [theme 5 (a)], placing blame [theme 5 (b)], and proof [theme 5 (c)] are at least somewhat identifiable in the record. The *Eze*-in-Council hears and deals with the dispute as a civil case. The council, in recognition of the sensitive nature of the dispute, decides (at p. 121):

> [The second disputants] were not at fault in any way, whereas [the first disputant] was liable all round. The [*ụmụnna*] should readmit [the first disputant] on condition that he brings 5 gallons of palm wine and 8 Igbo kola nuts with apologies for his wrongdoing. After his readmission then [the first disputant] should pay his debt en bloc or instalmentally.[36]

Theme 6 (Stigmatization) is not identifiable in the processing of Case Number 5. Contrary to the prediction, there is no loss of dignity by a disputant. Also, contrary to the anticipation of theme 6, there is a loss of time in the case processing. The case is brought before the *Eze*-in-Council in August 1989. It is settled in July 1990, after eight adjournments. Further, the case satisfies theme 7 (Individualization). Theme 7's prediction that persons holding positions in an informal process would bend rules and procedures to suit individual cases is clearly identifiable in the case. The council displays flexibility in the process by allowing the second disputants to put their case before the council even before they have complied with the conditions for *ịtụnye mmanya* (filing a suit).

The customary laws and traditions that the council applies to Case Number 5 are all uncodified. This accords with the prediction under theme 8 (Proscriptiveness of Norms). Under theme 9 (Record Management), it is predicted that the record of a case processed informally would be based on oral history (memory only). Contrary to this prediction, the record of the proceedings in Case Number 5 is handwritten and complete. Therefore, the case does not satisfy theme 9. However, the case partially satisfies theme 10 (Simplicity of Process). On the procedure for initiating a case, it is predicted under this theme that spoken words may suffice [theme 10 (a)]. The record of proceedings clearly shows that Case Number 5 is initiated orally, even though the first disputant later completes and signs Appendix B.

Contrary to the predicted "no cost" of invoking an informal judicial process (theme 11), each party presents eight Igbo kola nuts, two gallons of palm wine, and ten naira to the *Eze*-in-Council. Also, when the council's decision is read to the parties, the second disputants accept the decision. The first disputant rejects it. The rejection strongly suggests that he stands against the system contrary to the predicted "altruistic quality" of informal justice [theme 12 (c)]. But the fact that he has taken the case before the council in the first place indicates that he does not oppose the system. However, the processing of the case meets Theme 12 of informal case processing (Peacemaking Emphasis) because the council encourages the parties to integrate and cooperate between themselves and with others in the community. In addition, the record of proceedings contains some references to the community's interest in *udo* (peace). Further, there are clear indications that the second disputants have involved family relations, friends, and neighbors in efforts to resolve the dispute (theme 12).

Case Number 5 on ostracism could only have been processed unofficially. The official laws in Igbo do not afford an ostracized person a cause of action. The unofficial process is thus able to deal with a grievance based on ostracism, a grievance that could otherwise escalate.

Dispute over Breach of Business Financing Contract

Case Number 7 (Record of Proceedings, vol. 1, at p. 85, 1989) is the only case study found in this subcategory. This case illustrates, among other things, that people who live outside Ajallị Town may bring their case before the *Eze*-in-Council (based in the town) for settlement. The parties in this case reside in two different towns outside Ajallị (at p. 85). In the case, according to the first disputant, the second disputant has requested and received the first disputant's house lease and has used it as a collateral for a bank loan. The loan is to finance a cement business. The parties have agreed that the first disputant would take one-third of the profits from the business. The second disputant fails to meet his obligations under the contract. The bank is in the process of selling the first disputant's house because the second disputant has defaulted on the loan agreement. Although the agreement between the first and second disputants is oral, it is actionable in an official court. An official court would probably apply statutory and "common" laws rather than the Igbo customary law. The first disputant chooses to have the *Eze*-in-Council manage the dispute. He claims the sum of 125,000 naira, which is the amount of money owed him under the contract plus interest. The council treats it as a civil case.

The processing of Case Number 7 has seven of the twelve themes of informal case processing. Theme 1 (Officialism) is satisfied because the constitution or other law does not set up the *Eze*-in-Council nor is the council established by the state. In fact, this case satisfies all of theme 1's descriptors. The case does not satisfy theme 2 (Mediation). Contrary to theme 2, an adversarial procedure is at least somewhat identifiable in the process. The second disputant is cross-examined after he states his case before the council. The case also satisfies the other descriptors under theme 2.

No lawyer is involved in the management of Case Number 7. Thus, the process satisfies themes 3 and 4. However, the case fails to meet the requirements of theme 5 (Punitiveness). The Record of Proceedings shows that the trial emphasizes placing blame contrary to the prediction under theme 5. Moreover, the record clearly shows that the proceedings emphasize proof. Before deciding on the case, the council hears from both parties and examines some documents tendered before it. It decides as follows: "In view of the whole evidence before the Cabinet, it is the *unanimous* opinion of the *Eze*-in-Council that [the first disputant] has got a genuine case. [The second disputant] should pay to [the first disputant] his claim of N125,000.00 (One hundred and twenty-five thousand Naira)" (at p. 121).[37]

There is no indication that either of the parties in Case Number 7 is stigmatized. Neither party has lost dignity in the process. There is clearly a loss of time in the process. The case, commenced in October 1989, is decided in June 1990, after six adjournments. The case clearly shows individualization in that persons involved in the process have bent rules and procedures to suit the case as predicted under theme 7. Persons holding positions in the process could, and have, exercised discretion. The customary laws and traditions applied by the council are uncodified (theme 8).

The type of record management (theme 9) employed for preserving the proceedings in Case Number 7 is complete and handwritten contrary to the memory-only (oral history) type record predicted for an informal case processing. Case Number 7 is initiated orally. The parties later pay a small amount of money and make minor gifts to the council. The money and gifts comply with the requirements for *ịtụnye mmanya* (filing suit). In the proceedings, the council clearly shows its emphasis on peacemaking. The council encourages the disputants to integrate and cooperate with each other and with others in the community. The Record of Proceedings shows that the council "thanked [the first disputant] for bringing the matter to the Cabinet as a peaceful move for settlement. Both persons were enjoined to exercise some patience and to rethink the issues involved more soberly" (at p. 92).

Case Number 7 illustrates that the *Eze*-in-Council, an unofficial judicial tribunal, is capable of resolving cases, including those involving large sums of money. The amount of money involved in this case is substantial in the circumstances of the case.

Disputes over Land Ownership and Trespass to Land

The issues in the two cases in this subcategory (Case Numbers 11 and 27) are somewhat similar. However, the cases are considered separately to adequately describe the peculiarities of the processes in each case. In Case Number 11 (Record of Proceedings, vol. 1, at p. 157, 1991), the first and second disputants own adjacent pieces of land. The first disputant claims before the *Eze*-in-Council that the second disputant has trespassed on the first disputant's land. The council treats the case as a civil dispute. Six of the twelve predicted themes of informal case processing are identifiable in the case.

The fact that the *Eze*-in-Council is neither created by, nor under the influence of, the official government means that the process in Case Number 11 satisfies theme 1 (Officialism). However, the case does not satisfy theme 2 (Mediation) because each party is cross-examined after he states his case (adversarial quality). The process satisfies themes 3 and 4 because it does not involve lawyers. There is some indication of punitiveness in the process contrary to theme 5. Furthermore, it is predicted under theme 5 that an informal case process would not focus on proof. The process in Case Number 11 shows some focus on proof. The Record of Proceedings supports this conclusion. The record states as follows (at p. 119): "Evidence before the *Eze*-in-Council indicates that the whole piece of land under dispute appears to belong to [the first disputant]."[38]

Case Number 11 fails to satisfy the prediction under theme 6 (Stigmatization) that a disputant would lose some dignity in the process. Also, the case shows a loss of time by the disputants contrary to theme 6. The case, which is instituted in March 1991, is finally settled in August 1993, after twelve adjournments. The *Eze*-in-Council has employed an individualized process to suit the case as predicted under theme 7. The council members have bent rules and procedures to accommodate the needs of the case by visiting and inspecting the disputed lands (at p. 115). In line with theme 8, the traditions, customs, and laws applied to the case are all unwritten.

Case Number 11 does not satisfy theme 9 (Record Management) because the record of the case is complete and handwritten. It is not based on memory only as predicted. The case is initiated in a simple way consistently with theme 10 (Simplicity of Process). Note, however, that although the first disputant is able to initiate the case by spoken words, he later completes and signs Appendix B before the council entertains the case. Contrary to the prediction under theme 11, there is some cost in invoking the process for this case. Both parties comply with the requirements of *ịtụnye mmanya* (filing a suit). Peacemaking emphasis (theme 12) is lacking in this case. The record of proceedings shows only minor indications that the disputants are encouraged to integrate and cooperate with others in the community as expected. However, both parties show altruistic qualities by accepting the council's decision (at p. 127).

In Case Number 27 (Record of Proceedings, vol. 3, at p. 88, 1995),[39] the first disputant claims before the *Eze*-in-Council that the second disputant has threatened to destroy the first disputant's crops and plants on an identified piece of land if the first disputant farms on the land. According to the first disputant, the second disputant, together with the second disputant's relatives, has divided up the disputed land among themselves. The first disputant wants the council to return the land to him because it belongs to him. The bases of the suit are the second disputant's threat to destroy anything that the first disputant may plant on the land as well as the action of the second disputant and his relatives in dividing the disputed land. Therefore, the first disputant could sue in the official court all those that have taken possession of his land unlawfully. Instead, he sues the second disputant before the *Eze*-in-Council. The council handles the case as a civil dispute.

Seven of the twelve predicted themes of informal case processing are present in Case Number 27. The case is initiated by the *ịtụnye mmanya* procedure, that is, the parties present minor gifts and the sum of fifty naira[40] to the council. The gifts and money contradict the "no cost" predicted under "Cost of Invoking Process" (theme 11). This case satisfies theme 1 (Officialism) and all its descriptors. However, theme 2 (Mediation) is absent in the process. Each of the parties presents his case and is cross-examined by the other party. The process fully satisfies themes 3 and 4. There is an absence of lawyers in the case management. The process contains theme 5, which predicts that there would be no emphasis on placing blame in informal case processing. Theme 6 (Stigmatization) is absent in the case. The theme predicts that a disputant in an informal justice process would lose dignity. That is not so in Case Number 27.

Theme 7 (Individualization) is clearly identifiable in Case Number 27. The *Eze*-in-Council's action in allowing a third party, who is neither a disputant nor a witness in the case, to address the council meets the predicted flexible procedure under theme 7. The council allows the third party to address them because the members believe that his statements would assist them in coming to a just decision in the case. The Record of Proceedings presents this act of individualization as follows (at p. 91): "[The third party] stated that he was not present as a witness to any of the disputants. But he was allowed to have his say in the matter. In that capacity, he asked the following questions to [*sic*] [the first disputant]."

Consistently with theme 8 (Proscriptiveness of Norms), none of the traditions or customs applied to Case Number 27 is codified. The case record is complete and handwritten contrary to the predicted record based on memory only (theme 9). Theme 10 (Simplicity of Process) is identifiable in the case. But the simple process applies only to the initiation of the case. As argued earlier, the author, having considered the circumstances of the unofficial and official proceedings, is of the view that the simple case initiation procedure sufficiently supports a finding that the judicial process at issue satisfies the expectations of theme 10. In partial satisfaction of theme 12 (Peacemaking Emphasis), there is only a slight indication that the disputants are encouraged to integrate and cooperate with others in the community. The case contains some references to the community's interest in peace. However, both disputants accept the *Eze*-in-Council's jurisdiction as predicted.

Ownership of Economic Trees

The issue of the ownership of economic trees is treated as a separate subcategory because under the Igbo customary law, what is affixed to land is not considered part of the land. Therefore, under this legal system, a person who owns a piece of land may not be the owner of the economic trees that grow on it. The dispute in Case Number 15 (Record of Proceedings, vol. 2, at p. 52, 1992) is over the ownership of some palm trees from which the second disputant harvests some fruits. The first disputant reports the matter to the official police. According to the first disputant, the police say that they are unable to do anything because the second disputant claims that the palm trees belong to him. The first disputant then withdraws the case from the official system and files a suit before the *Eze*-in-Council. The council deals with the case as a civil dispute.

Case Number 15 contains seven of the twelve themes of informal case processing predicted in table 2.1. The suit is commenced by means of *ịtụnye mmanya*, which involves some cost, rather than the "no cost" predicted under theme 11. The process in the case satisfies theme 1 (Officialism). The case is heard and determined by the *Eze*-in-Council, which is an unofficial body. There is no mediation (theme 2) in the case processing. Contrary to the non-adversarial procedure predicted under theme 2, each disputant is cross-examined after he presents his case. However, the council takes some steps to maintain order between the disputants. While the case is pending before the council, it is reported that the second disputant has harvested and sold some of the disputed palm fruits. The council orders him to deposit the proceeds with the council. The council's decision concerning the money is as follows (at p. 55): "Whoever wins will claim the amount involved. The two parties [are] banned from cutting the oil palm fruits to keep the peace within the period before the final settlement of the case." Contrary to the prediction under theme 5, the process in Case Number 15 puts some emphasis on placing blame. Moreover, the word *wins* in the quoted portion of the council's judgment strongly suggests that the council is focused on proof contrary to the prediction. The Record of Proceedings (at p. 170) also includes a statement to the effect that the second disputant has entered and cleared the part of the land involved in the dispute "contrary to the Cabinet's injunction to the two parties to desist from entering the area of the land involved in the dispute until *the determination of the real owner*."[41]

Case Number 15 meets the expectation of non-involvement of lawyers in informal case processing (themes 3 and 4). However, contrary to theme 6, stigmatization is not identifiable in the process. Theme 6 also predicts that there would be no loss of autonomy by disputant. But there is a loss of autonomy resulting from the council's interim injunction against the disputants. The council enjoins them against entering or removing anything from the land involved in the dispute. To minimize losses of wealth by the parties, the council appoints a third person to cut and sell the fruits from the disputed palm trees. The third party is to deposit the money realized from this with the council (at pp. 67 and 73). This is a prudent step taken by the council because the case processing lasts from March 1992 to July 1995 [Contrast the no loss of time predicted under theme 6 (d)]. In July 1995, the first disputant unilaterally takes the case to the official High Court. Consequently, the *Eze*-in-Council adjourns the case "indefinitely" (at p. 84).[42]

The *Eze*-in-Council, in appointing a third person to cut, sell, and deposit the money from the palm fruits, seeks to accommodate the peculiar needs of the case (theme 7, Individualization). The non-proscriptive nature of the customs and traditions applied to the case accords with the prediction under theme 8. Theme 9 is not satisfied because the record of the case is complete and handwritten, rather than the predicted oral history-type record. The process in the case meets the prediction under theme 10 to the extent that the case is initiated by spoken words. Peacemaking emphasis (theme 12) is clearly identifiable in the process. The disputants are encouraged to integrate and cooperate with others in the community. However, the first disputant's decision to take the case from the unofficial *Eze*-in-Council to the official High Court contradicts the altruistic qualities predicted under theme 12.

Defamation of Character – Slander

Case Number 23 (Record of Proceedings, vol. 3, at p. 44, 1994) falls in this subcategory. In the case, the first disputant is an official government worker involved in the transfer of schoolteachers. He claims that the second disputant has falsely accused him of transferring some teachers who prefer not to be transferred. The first disputant denies any involvement in the transfers. Based on his allegations, the first disputant may institute a legal action for defamation in an official court because the allegation by the second disputant may have lowered the first disputant's reputation in the eyes of the locals. A legal action in an official court would be based on the official law of torts applicable to Ajallị Town. However, Case Number 23 is taken to the *Eze*-in-Council for settlement. The council treats it as a civil case.

The process in Case Number 23 meets seven of the twelve predicted themes of informal case processing. The case satisfies theme 1 (Officialism) because the *Eze*-in-Council is independent of official creation and controls. Theme 2 (Mediation) is absent in the case processing. The non-adversarial procedure predicted under theme 2 is not identifiable in the case. The proceedings include cross-examination. The case is handled without the involvement of any lawyer. Therefore, themes 3 and 4 are fully satisfied. The case meets theme 5 (Punitiveness), which predicts that there would be no emphasis on placing blame. Under theme 6 (Stigmatization), it is predicted that a disputant in an informal judicial process would lose dignity. However, no loss of dignity is identifiable in this case. Thus, the case does not meet the requirements of theme 6.

Case Number 23 satisfies the individualization predicted under theme 7 in that persons holding positions in the process bend rules and procedures to suit the case. Also, the process fully meets theme 8 because, as predicted, the customary laws and traditions that the council applies to this case are uncodified. The predicted oral history-type record under theme 9 (Record Management) is absent in the case. Instead, the proceedings are recorded in complete, handwritten files. Theme 10 (Simplicity of Process) is clearly identifiable in the case based on the author's earlier conclusion that an invocation of a judicial process by spoken words would be sufficient for the process to be regarded as informal. The first disputant would later complete and sign Appendix B. The case is brought by the *ịtụnye mmanya* procedure. Thus, both disputants make minor gifts and pay small amounts of money to the *Eze*-in-Council. The procedure differs from the "no cost" predicted under theme 11 (Cost of Invoking Process). The case does not meet the prediction under theme 12 (Peacemaking Emphasis). There is no indication that the disputants are encouraged to integrate and cooperate with others in the community.

Dispute over Destruction of Property

Case Number 31 (Suit No. CCA/12/87) in this subcategory is handled both in and out of court before it is finally settled. First, there is an unsuccessful attempt to resolve the case at the *ụmụnna* level. The case is then taken to the *obodo* Ajallị level, but it is not resolved there either. The aggrieved party subsequently institutes a civil suit in the Customary Court (an official court). The plaintiff claims before the Customary Court that the defendant has forcefully entered the plaintiff's land and damaged the plaintiff's cocoyams and cassava plants. The plaintiff asks the court to award him the sum of 1,000 naira as damages for the destroyed property. He also wants 500 naira as damages for trespass and an injunction restraining the defendant and his agents from further entry into the land. The defendant denies responsibility for any of the plaintiff's claims. The case proceeds through trial from February 1988 to January 1989.[43] Before the court reaches a judgment in the case, the plaintiff files a notice discontinuing the suit because the case has been settled out of court. The record of the proceedings relating to this case is part of the court's archives.[44]

Case Number 31 defies precise categorization because of the multiplicity of judicial bodies involved in its management. However, the case provides a very good illustration of the continuous nature of Igbo justice from the lowest unofficial level through the highest official level. Despite the difficulties of classification, the process in Case Number 31 is determined to possess six of the twelve predicted themes of informal case processing. The process meets the requirements of theme 1 (Officialism). Although the case is tried in the Customary Court, it is *finally* settled in an out-of-court arrangement. Therefore, the case is resolved unofficially as predicted for an informal case management process. Moreover, theme 1 asks whether there is any indication in the report showing that the dispute is settled in *ụnọ ikpe* or court. The Case Report clearly states that the dispute is settled in an out-of-court arrangement. According to the report: "The plaintiff filed notice of discontinuation of the suit as a result of mutual understanding between the two parties who also agreed to close ranks without seeking for costs" (at p. 21).

Theme 2 (Mediation) is not identifiable in Case Number 31. The non-adversarial procedure envisaged by the theme is absent in the case processing. Each witness in the case, including the plaintiff and defendant, is cross-examined by the opposing side. This case satisfies themes 3 and 4, which predict the non-involvement of lawyers in informal case processing. Both in and out of court, no lawyer plays a part in the resolution of the case. Theme 5 (Punitiveness) is only somewhat identifiable in the case. There is some indication that the case processing in the Customary Court puts emphasis on placing blame contrary to the prediction under theme 5. The case is therefore classified as not meeting the requirements of theme 5.

Theme 6 (Stigmatization) is clearly identifiable in Case Number 31. It is predicted under this theme that an informal case process would cause a disputant to lose some dignity and that this would be "clearly identifiable" in the proceedings. Loss of dignity is indisputable in the case. The parties have lost the respect of some of the other community members. At the proceedings, a witness for the plaintiff expresses his frustration over the case and his impression of the disputants as follows (at pp. 9 and 11 of the Case Report):

> I am ashamed that this family matter which would have easily been resolved within the rank and file of the family is brought before this court. The elder and the younger failed to do their duties. In fact I am confused and find it very difficult to come and expose members of the same family in court. The plaintiff and the defendant are of the same family and we are also of the same family with them. I am very ashamed that such a brotherly matter is dragged to this court.

The process in Case Number 31 does not satisfy theme 7 (Individualization). The prediction under the theme that "persons holding positions in the process bend rules and procedures to suit individual cases" is not clearly identifiable as expected. However, there is some indication of flexibility in the process. For example, the Customary Court allows many second-hand statements into evidence in the proceedings. In the higher courts, such statements would not be allowed in because they are not based on the perceptions of the witness but on what the witness has been told by another person.[45] Case Number 31 satisfies theme 8 because none of the rules of customary law applied to the case is codified. The oral history-type of record predicted under theme 9 (Record Management) is not identifiable. The record of the case is in the form of complete, typed files.

Case Number 31 does not possess the simplicity of process predicted under theme 10. The expectation that spoken words would suffice as a means of initiating a case is not realized. The case is initiated by following the usual formalized steps for filing a suit in an official court. The steps include informing the court in writing about the prospective plaintiff's claim. There is no room for initiating a case in the Customary Court by spoken words. The cost of invoking the process in the case is relatively high. Although the parties have not hired lawyers to assist them in the case, they still have to pay the court fees before the court entertains the action. Additionally, on one occasion the defendant fails to attend a scheduled court session due to his wife's illness. The court orders him to pay 20 naira (N20.00) as costs to the plaintiff, even though the defendant has written to the court explaining why he could not attend the court session. There is peacemaking emphasis (theme 12) in the case. The disputants are encouraged to integrate and cooperate with each other and with others in the community.

Summary of Contents and Processes Found in the Semi-Formal Category

The seven case studies that fall in the "Semi-Formal" category are between private individuals and groups. An individual or group institutes each case against another individual or group. Such cases are processed as civil cases. Accordingly, all the cases in the "Semi-Formal" category are civil cases. The issues in the cases in this category are ostracism, breach of contract, land and land-related issues, defamation, and destruction of property.

The fourth category in the informality-formality continuum is the "Formal" category, which is made up of four subcategories that deal with similar subject matters.

FORMAL CATEGORY

The "Formal" category contains the case studies that possess one to four of the predicted themes of informal case processing. Of the forty-two cases, twelve fall in the "Formal" category (see table 2.3). One of the twelve cases has four of the themes, five cases have three, four have two, and two cases contain one theme each.

Nature and Kinds of Cases

Disputes over Land Ownership, Possession, Trespass, and Economic Trees

Nine of the twelve case studies in the "Formal" category deal with the issues in this subcategory. For a better appreciation of the procedures followed in the cases, each case is considered distinctly. In Case Number 29 (officially listed as Case No. 42/57), the plaintiff brings a civil suit in the Customary Court, Ajallị, against six defendants claiming a declaration of title to a piece of land, and money damages for trespass on the land and the harvesting of economic trees on the land. The defendants deny the plaintiff's claims. The case therefore proceeds through trial. The management of Case Number 29 contains three of the twelve projected themes of informal case processing. The process does not meet theme 1 (Officialism), which expects that the tribunal in informal case processing would be independent of the state. The Customary Court is a creation of the official government. Also, the Customary Court judges and other court officials involved in managing the case are officers of the state contrary to theme 1. The expectation under theme 2 (Mediation) that the procedure in informal case processing would be non-adversarial is not realized in the case. The Case Report contains clear statements that cross-examination of the witnesses in the case is a part of the proceedings. The record reflects this when it states that the case is adjourned to a future date: "Defendant to complete her statement [on the adjourned date]. Then she can be examined" (at p. 12 of the Case Report). In the circumstances, it is reasonable to read the word "examined" as "cross-examined." Cross-examination is a key ingredient of the adversary process.

No lawyer plays a part in the management of Case Number 29. The absence of lawyers in the process satisfies themes 3 and 4 (Lawyer Involvement and Litigiousness or Argumentativeness in a Legal Sense, respectively). However, the case does not satisfy theme 5 (Punitiveness). Contrary to the primary focus of theme 5, the process places emphasis on blame. While discussing the circumstances that have led to the case before it, the court places the blame squarely on the first defendant's shoulders when it states (at p. 17 of the Case Report): "The No. 1 defendant has actually recked [*sic*] up an old trouble." Further on theme 5, a focus on proof is also clearly identifiable in the case contrary to the prediction. In reaching its decision on the case, the court relies on a sketch of the disputed land that a mediator has prepared (at p. 17 of the Case Report). The sketch helps to convince the court that the disputed land belongs to the plaintiff rather than the defendants.

Contrary to expectation, stigmatization (theme 6) is not identifiable in Case Number 29. Theme 7 (Individualization) is only somewhat identifiable in the case. Theme 7 predicts that persons holding positions in the process would bend rules and regulations to suit individual cases. The only indication of this in Case Number 29 is that during the trial the judges ask some questions of the witnesses. This is not unusual as it happens even in the most formal of judicial proceedings.[46] What Theme 7 expects is some step or activity on the part of the judicial position holders to accommodate the peculiar needs of the individual case. There is no such step or activity in Case Number 29. Therefore, the case does not meet theme 7. The case satisfies the expectation of theme 8 (Proscriptiveness of Norms) that the rules and laws applied to the case would be uncodified. None of the customary laws applied to the case is codified.

The record of the proceedings in Case Number 29 is complete and typed contrary to the oral history-type record predicted under theme 9 (Record Management). Under theme 10 (Simplicity of Process), it is expected that a case may be initiated and conducted orally in an informal judicial process. This, however, is not the situation in this case. The case is properly filed in written form with the Customary Court before the court entertains it. Even the initiation of the proceedings has to be done in writing. The cost of invoking the process in the case is high contrary to the "no cost" predicted under theme 11. The parties to the case have paid court fees to invoke the court processes. The fees include the filing fees and the payment for developing a survey plan to assist the court in the proceedings. Further, the disputants have paid extra money for the court's visit to the *locus in quo* (visit to the place in dispute) for the purpose of inspecting the disputed land so as to allow the Customary Court judges the opportunity to see the property for themselves rather than rely exclusively on witness testimonies. All the required payments in the case have to be made before the case proceeds to final judgment.

The main focus of theme 12 (Peacemaking Emphasis) is that disputants would be clearly encouraged to integrate and cooperate with others in the community. This is, at best, somewhat identifiable in Case Number 29. The court, while awarding the title to the disputed land to the plaintiff, states that the defendants "must live and use the area according to the sketch made by [the maker's name] after the [previous case on the same land]" (at p. 17 of the Case Report). The court's statement reads more like an *order* than the *encouragement* envisaged by theme 12. Thus, the process in Case Number 29 does not satisfy the peacemaking emphasis expected under theme 12.

Case Number 34 (Suit No. 28C/61) is also a Customary Court case. In the case, ten joint plaintiffs bring a civil action against the defendant. They ask the court to hold that a certain piece of land belongs to them and that the defendant has trespassed on the land. The processing of the case includes three of the twelve themes of informal case processing. The Customary Court is an agency of the official government. Therefore, Case Number 34 does not comply with the prediction under theme 1 (Officialism). All the position holders in the court, including the president, judges, and registrar or clerk of the court, are employees and officers of the official government. This is contrary to the expectations of theme 1. Theme 2 (Mediation) predicts a non-adversarial procedure in case processing. The primary indicator of this form of case processing is an absence of cross-examination in proceedings. This expectation does not materialize in Case Number 34. Persons who have testified during the proceedings are cross-examined by the rival party. Indeed, the case report includes a subheading that reads (at p. 2): "Cross Examination Open." Therefore, theme 2 is not identifiable in Case Number 34. However, the case meets the conditions of themes 3 and 4. These two themes expect that no lawyer would be involved in informal case processing. No lawyer is involved in managing the case.

Theme 5 (Punitiveness) predicts that there would be no emphasis on placing blame. Such emphasis is somewhat identifiable in Case Number 34. Moreover, there is a clear focus on proof contrary to the theme's expectation. In reaching a judgment for the plaintiffs, the court cites the irregularities in the defendant's case. In essence, such irregularities have interfered with the believability of the defendant's case. In short, the defendant has not proved his case. There is absence of stigmatization (theme 6) in the process. The predicted loss of dignity by a disputant is not identifiable in the case. Therefore, the case does not meet the expectations of theme 6. Similarly, individualization (theme 7) is only somewhat identifiable. This theme expects persons holding positions in an informal judicial process to bend rules and procedures to suit individual cases. The only indication of this in Case Number 34 is the fact that the court asks questions of the witnesses. As already explained, there is nothing unusual about this. The case, however, meets the expectations of theme 8 (Proscriptiveness of Norms). The customary laws and traditions applied by the Customary Court are uncodified.

The form of the record on Case Number 34 is complete and typed. Under theme 9 (Record Management), it is predicted that the record of the proceedings in informal case processing would be based on memory only. That is not the situation in this case. The simplicity of process envisaged by theme 10 is not identifiable in the case. The expectation that spoken words would suffice to initiate a case does not materialize. The case is initiated in writing by filling out forms, signing them, and filing them with the court. The cost of invoking the judicial process (theme 11) in the case is a large amount of money. Over and above the fees paid to file the suit, each of the disputants pays for an inspection of the disputed land as well as for a survey of the land. Thus, the prediction of no cost under theme 11 is unrealized in this case. There is no peacemaking emphasis (theme 12) in the case. At no point in the trial does the court encourage the disputants to integrate and cooperate with others in the community as expected by this theme. Additionally, the fact that the plaintiffs take the case to an official court rather than have it settled outside the official system contradicts the absence of self-help predicted under theme 12 (d). Theme 12 (d) expects that a disputant would involve family relations, friends, volunteers, and neighbors in efforts to resolve a dispute rather than take it to an official government agency. This expectation does not materialize in Case Number 34.

Case Number 35 (*Ezeokafor v. Otaluka*, Suit No. FSC 214/63) begins in a state High Court, an official court. The plaintiff brings a civil action against the defendant to recover possession of the plaintiff's family land, a declaration of title to the land, damages for the defendant's trespass on the land, and perpetual injunction against the defendant. The land at issue has been rented to the defendant under a kola tenancy (an Igbo customary law land lease procedure). The defendant subsequently makes another agreement whereby he purports to buy the same land from another person. Because of the later agreement, the plaintiff sues the defendant unsuccessfully in the High Court. The plaintiff appeals to the Supreme Court.[47]

Three of the twelve predicted themes of informal case processing are present in Case Number 35. However, the case does not meet theme 1 (Officialism), since both the High Court and the Supreme Court that process the case are official government institutions contrary to the prediction under theme 1. On the Supreme Court procedure and theme 2 (Mediation), the process in Case Number 35 is non-adversarial as predicted. During the proceedings, the parties are not subjected to cross-examination by the opposing side. However, the absence of cross-examination is a part of most proceedings in the Supreme Court. Being basically an appellate tribunal, the Court reaches a decision on an appeal before it based on the record of proceedings in the lower court. The Supreme Court very rarely invites persons to testify before it. Therefore, the absence of an adversarial procedure before the Supreme Court should not be interpreted in the same way that a similar situation before the *Eze*-in-Council, for instance, is interpreted.

Case Number 35 does not meet the expectations of either theme 3 (Lawyer Involvement) or theme 4 (Litigiousness or Argumentativeness in a Legal Sense). Lawyers are involved in the case management. Indeed, there is lawyer involvement prior to the institution of the action in the High Court. Before the court action, the plaintiff's attorney, acting on the plaintiff's behalf, writes to the defendant (then "tenant") asking the tenant to give up possession of the land (at p. 235 of the Case Report). The court action follows when the tenant refuses to comply. Theme 5 (Punitiveness) expects that an informal case process would not put emphasis on placing blame. There is clearly an emphasis on placing blame in Case Number 35. The Supreme Court, in rejecting the defendant's defense, puts the blame for the situation on him when it states (at p. 237 of the Case Report): "The plaintiff succeeds, and the defendant must accept the consequences of being defeated in the court dispute which he provoked."

Theme 6 (Stigmatization) predicts that a loss of dignity in informal case processing would be clearly identifiable. That is not so in Case Number 35. None of the three predicted indicators of loss of dignity is identifiable in the case. There is no indication that a disputant loses respect in the process, there is no indication that a disputant should no longer be looked up to, and neither of the disputants is denied or stripped of a position or honor. Individualization (theme 7) is clearly identifiable in the processing of Case Number 35. In processing the case, the Court exhibits flexibility by granting a relief not specifically sought in the plaintiff's suit. This is an act of bending the rules and procedures to suit the case. The Court grants the relief after explaining that "no useful purpose can be served by another suit for forfeiture" (at p. 237 of the Case Report). This form of flexibility in a judicial process is consistent with the prediction under theme 7. The process in Case Number 35 meets the non-codification of the laws predicted under theme 8 (Proscriptiveness of Norms). The laws and rules applied to the case are unwritten.

The record on Case Number 35 is complete and typed. Under theme 9 (Record Management), it is expected that the record in an informal process would be based on memory only. Therefore, this case does not satisfy theme 9. The case does not support the expectation that spoken words would suffice to initiate a case (theme 10, Simplicity of Process). The case is initiated in writing. Also, the case does not satisfy theme 11 (Cost of Invoking Process). The process is invoked by means of a "large amount of money" contrary to the predicted "no cost." Over and above the court fees paid by the parties, they have paid for their attorneys' services. Lawyers who appear in the Supreme Court are usually the more experienced ones. These lawyers are more expensive to retain than the average lawyer. Also, there is no peacemaking emphasis in the case processing. The court does not advise the parties to co-exist peacefully as predicted under theme 12.

Another case that deals with land and land-related issues in this "Formal" category is Case Number 36 (*Nzekwu and Others v. Nzekwu and Others*, 1989 2 NWLR 373). This is an appellate case, which begins at the High Court level. It is appealed through the Court of Appeal to the Supreme Court. The first plaintiff is the widow of the first defendant's late uncle. After the uncle's death, the first defendant becomes the eldest male member of their *ụmụnna*. He sells a piece of land occupied by the first plaintiff. He claims that, as the eldest male member of their *ụmụnna*, an Onitsha (an Igbo community) custom entitles him to alienate the property as an absolute owner. The first plaintiff brings a civil action in the High Court for recovery of possession of the land. She succeeds in the High Court. The defendants appeal unsuccessfully to the Court of Appeal. They appeal further to the Supreme Court.

The processing of Case Number 36 before the Supreme Court satisfies two of the twelve themes of informal case processing. The case does not satisfy theme 1 (Officialism) because, contrary to the theme's expectation, the Supreme Court is a state agency. It operates with the authority of the state. The non-adversarial nature of the proceedings in the Supreme Court means that theme 2 (Mediation) is identifiable in the case. However, the point made earlier concerning the general absence of cross-examination in appeals in the Supreme Court also applies here. Lawyers are involved in Case Number 36 even before the dispute is taken to court. Lawyer involvement continues through the proceedings in the Supreme Court. Therefore, themes 3 and 4 are absent in the case. The case clearly shows an emphasis on placing blame. The court puts the blame for the problems leading to the case on the defendant who unilaterally disposes of the family property as if it were his personal property. Therefore, the case does not satisfy theme 5 (Punitiveness).

Case Number 36 does not meet the requirements of theme 6 (Stigmatization). Neither disputant has lost dignity in the process. However, both disputants have lost some wealth in the process because of the court order that some of the rents collected on the disputed property be paid into the court pending the determination of the case. In the meantime, the disputants lose the use of the rents contrary to theme 6 (c). This is particularly relevant since the case lasts from 1972 through 1989 in the High Court and the Supreme Court. In the Supreme Court alone, it lasts from 1985 through 1989. This contradicts theme 6 (d). Theme 7 (Individualization) is clearly identifiable in the case because persons holding positions in the process, especially the justices of the Supreme Court, exercise discretion and bend the rules and procedures to suit the case. Thus, the Supreme Court upholds the trial court's conclusion that the Onitsha custom, which entitles the first defendant to alienate the *ụmụnna* property as an absolute owner, is an unacceptable custom. The Court states (at p. 396 of the Case Report): "Any Onitsha custom which postulates that [the eldest male member of an *ụmụnna*] has the right to alienate property of a deceased in the lifetime of his widow is a barbarous and uncivilized custom which should be regarded as repugnant to equity and good conscience and therefore unacceptable."[48] This statement is a classic example of the ways in which the official government agencies, particularly the courts, shape Nigeria's customs, traditions, and native laws. The official government laws empower the official courts to refuse the enforcement of any customary law, which is adjudged repugnant to natural justice, equity, or good conscience, or contrary to any official law.[49] This official mandate is a very important justice policy in Nigeria. It has negatively affected the development of the traditions, customs, and native laws of the Igbo and the other nations of Nigeria.

Contrary to the uncodified rules predicted under theme 8, the court proceedings in Case Number 36 rely on the provisions of the official *Evidence Act*.[50] The memory only-type of record management expected under theme 9 is absent in the case. Also, from the beginning, the procedure for initiating and conducting the case involves writing. There is no opportunity for the use of spoken words to initiate or conduct the case. Thus, the case does not satisfy theme 10. Further, the large amount of money expended by the disputants in the invocation of the judicial process runs counter to the prediction under theme 11. Finally, the peacemaking emphasis envisaged under theme 12 is not observable in this case. At no point does the Supreme Court emphasize to the parties the community's interest in peace. The Court does not encourage them to integrate with others for peace.

Case Number 38 (*Ome and 14 Others v. Ugeze*, Suit No. AB/CC/3A/92, Decided in May 1993) is a civil case. It is first tried in the Customary Court. The case is later appealed to the High Court. In the Customary Court, the plaintiffs have asked for a declaration of title to a piece of land. They base their claim on a customary right of occupancy.[51] The plaintiffs also ask the court for an injunction against the defendants and their agents from further trespassing on the land. The plaintiffs succeed in the trial court. The defendants appeal to the High Court. The appeal is dismissed. The processing of Case Number 38 in the High Court contains only one (theme 7, Individualization) of the twelve predicted themes of informal case processing. The case record shows that the High Court exercises discretion in its efforts to do justice between the disputants. The court's decision relies on "substantial justice" based on the unique circumstances of the case. In justifying its act of individualization, the court states (at p. 5 of the Case Report): "This court is enjoined to do substantial justice between the parties. See *S. 20 of the Customary Court Edict*."[52]

In Case Number 39 *(Nwomeji and Others v. Nwegbe*, Suit No. AB/27CCA/88, Decided in July 1993), the second disputants allegedly enter the first disputants' land and plant yams and cassava in the land. The issue is taken before the traditional ruler of the disputants' Igbo town (not Ajallị). The traditional ruler is unable to settle the dispute. The first disputants take the case to the Customary Court, and thus the first disputants become the plaintiffs. The Customary Court gives judgment for the plaintiffs. The court relies, at least in part, on the statement of a person who is neither called as a witness in the case nor cross-examined in the process. The defendants' appeal to the High Court is allowed. The High Court sets aside the Customary Court judgment and remits the case to the Customary Court for rehearing before different judges (at p. 13 of the Case Report). The traditional ruler, the Customary Court, and the High Court all treat Case Number 39 as a civil case.

Like Case Number 38, Case Number 39 contains only one of the twelve themes of informal justice. Only theme 7 (Individualization) is present in the processing of the case. The case report does not show how flexibly the traditional ruler handles the case. But the report shows that both the Customary Court and the High Court act with noticeable flexibility during the proceedings. The High Court exercises its discretion and, after considering the circumstances of the case, holds that the Customary Court should not have relied on the statement of a non-witness. However, in bending the rules and procedures to suit Case Number 39, the High Court pays heed to the injunction that "an appellate court should not interfere with the trial court's findings of fact or decision unless the same was perverse, unreasonable or unsound or a substantial principle of law or procedure had been violated or there had been a miscarriage of justice" (at p. 7 of the Case Report). This injunction is particularly relevant when the appellate court hears an appeal against the judgment of a Customary Court, which is enjoined by the *Customary Court Edict*[53] to exercise discretion and do "substantial justice."

Case Numbers 41 and 42 are Supreme Court cases. The civil disputes in both cases are based on disagreements over land. Case Number 41 is about redemption of a piece of land that is pledged under the Igbo customary law. Case Number 41 (*Ezeanya and Others v. Okeke and Others*, 1995 4 SCNJ 60) is an appellate case that starts in the High Court. It is appealed through the Court of Appeal to the Supreme Court. In the suit before the High Court, the plaintiffs contend that they, as the surviving family members of their deceased relative, should be allowed to redeem a piece of land that the deceased has pledged to the defendants under the Igbo customary law. The defendants agree that the land once belonged to the deceased. However, they contend that the land has become irredeemable because, under the native laws and customs that apply to their (Igbo) town, "the traditional slaughtering of a goat or goats in respect of such land transaction [as performed in the transaction at issue], confirms the irredeemability of the land so given or surrendered" (at p. 70 of the Case Report). The High Court dismisses the case. The plaintiffs appeal to the Court of Appeal. The Court of Appeal, on its own, raises the official justice policy question as to whether or not the customary law pleaded by the defendants is repugnant to natural justice, equity, and good conscience, or contrary to an official law. Without allowing the parties to address the question, the Court of Appeal decides that the customary law relied upon by the defendants is repugnant to natural justice, equity, and good conscience and would therefore not be enforced. The defendants appeal to the Supreme Court. The Supreme Court restores the judgment of the High Court. However, the point made earlier should be borne in mind here: Under the Igbo customary law, the general law is that a pledged land is perpetually redeemable (*Ekpendu v. Erika*, 1959 4 FSC 79; *Nzekwu and Others v. Nzekwu and Others*, 1989 2 NWLR 373; *Ome and 14 Others v. Ugeze*, Suit No. AB/CC/3A/92, Decided in May 1993). It is up to the party contending otherwise to produce evidence of a different intention.

The processing of Case Number 41 before the Supreme Court complies with two of the twelve anticipated themes of informal case processing. The themes found in the process are themes 2 and 7. Theme 2 (Mediation) anticipates a non-adversarial procedure in an informal process. This is the situation in Case Number 41. However, as has been pointed out, the non-adversarial nature of proceedings in the Supreme Court is an essential element of the Court's role as an appellate tribunal. The presence of theme 7 (Individualization) in the case processing is more significant. The Supreme Court exercises its discretionary powers and finds that the Court of Appeal's decision on the official justice policy question without reference to the parties has prejudiced the defendants. Based on this finding, the Supreme Court concludes that the circumstances of the case warrant the restoration of the judgment of the High Court.

In Case Number 42 [*Iroegbu (For himself and as representing the Chiefs and people of Avonkwu Ibeku) v. Okwordu and Nwubani (For themselves and as representing the Chiefs and people of Eruete Ibeku)*, 1995 4 SCNJ 7], each of two Igbo communities claims the ownership and possession of the disputed piece of land. The case is first litigated in the High Court where the defendants lose. They appeal to the Court of Appeal. The Court of Appeal affirms the High Court's decision. The defendants further appeal to the Supreme Court. The Supreme Court affirms the judgments of both the High Court and the Court of Appeal, which have awarded the disputed land to the plaintiffs.

The Supreme Court processing of Case Number 42 includes two of the twelve themes of informal case processing: themes 2 and 7. The non-adversarial nature of the process accords with theme 2 (Mediation). Usually, no witness is called in proceedings before the Supreme Court. The fact that none of the other descriptors under theme 2 is identifiable in this case further testifies to the need to attach little importance to the non-adversarial nature of the process in the case. Also identifiable in Case Number 42 is theme 7 (Individualization). Once again, the Supreme Court exercises its discretion and adopts the findings of the High Court and the Court of Appeal. The two lower courts have found that the plaintiffs' account of the traditional history leading to their ownership of the land under Igbo customary law is more believable than the defendants' account.

The last case in this first subcategory (on land and land-related disputes) of the "Formal" category concerns a dispute over an economic tree that stands on the plaintiff's land. It is allegedly cut and sold by the defendant. Case Number 33 (Suit No. CCA/5/90, Decided in February 1990) particularly illustrates the relationships among the various levels for case processing in Igbo. The case involves more case management levels than most other cases. When the disagreements between the disputants break over the tree, both parties decide that each of them should invite a person (a local) who knows about the disputed tree to assist thc parties in resolving the dispute. On the agreed date, the disputants and the invited locals meet at the agreed place. According to the first disputant (who later becomes the plaintiff), the two locals support the first disputant's claim. However, the second disputant (later, defendant) does not accept the outcome of the meeting. He invites other community members to settle the dispute between him and the first disputant. The community members conclude that either disputant should swear to *Iyi* (a shrine) to buttress his claim of ownership of the disputed tree. Before the swearing ceremony is carried out, the second disputant resumes work on the disputed tree. At this juncture, the first disputant (plaintiff) institutes a civil action in the Customary Court against the second disputant (defendant).

In the Customary Court, the plaintiff claims 1,800 naira, allegedly the value of the economic tree, which the defendant has cut and sold. The proceedings in the Customary Court include four of the twelve themes of informal case processing. The themes found are themes 3, 4, 7, and 8. None of the remaining themes is identifiable in the case. Case Number 33 satisfies themes 3 and 4 because, as predicted, the case is processed out of court and in court without the assistance of lawyers. Theme 7 on Individualization of the process is clearly identifiable in the case. The Customary Court takes two steps, which it considers appropriate for a determination of the issue in the case. First, the court goes and inspects the tree in dispute. Second, during the inspection of the tree, the "court also interrogated [a young lady] who herself never appeared for once before the court" (at p. 18 of the Case Report). The court's actions are necessitated by the need to gather relevant information, which it would otherwise not have to decide the case. In particular, the interrogation of the stranger constitutes a bending of the rules and procedures to suit the individual case. The court dismisses the case on the ground that the plaintiff has not proved his case. This focus on proof contradicts theme 5 of informal justice.

The case studies in the first subcategory (Disputes over land ownership, possession, trespass, and economic trees) of the "Formal" category illustrate that the unofficial judicial processes, as well as the official processes, among the Igbos are capable of effectively managing such cases. The unofficial processes provide several advantages over their official counterparts, including the facts that the official processes are more time consuming and more expensive than the unofficial processes.

Dispute over Adultery

Case Number 30 (Suit No. CCA/7/87, Decided in June 1987) is the only case study in this subcategory. In the case, like in many others in this book, an out-of-court settlement is apparently attempted without success. The plaintiff, who hails from an Igbo town other than Ajallị, alleges that his wife is having an affair with the defendant. According to the plaintiff, he has complained about his wife's "immoral behaviours" to his brother-in-law (at p. 5 of the Case Report). However, the brother-in-law denies this claim before the Customary Court. In any case, the alleged effort to involve a third party in managing the dispute [see theme 2 (c)] does not result in settlement. The plaintiff then takes his complaint to the Customary Court in the form of a civil suit. In the suit, the plaintiff claims the sum of 1,900 naira from the defendant for the defendant's adultery with the plaintiff's wife. The plaintiff also asks the court to restrain the defendant from further "meddlings with [the plaintiff's] wife" (at p. 3 of the Case Report). The plaintiff tells the court that he and his friends have once caught the defendant and the plaintiff's wife in the plaintiff's house. They severely beat the defendant.

In the Customary Court proceedings in Case Number 30, three of the twelve themes of informal case processing are identifiable. These are themes 3, 4, and 8. Themes 3 and 4 are clearly identifiable because, as expected for an informal process, the case is processed without the involvement of any lawyer. The procedure in the case satisfies theme 8. The customary laws and traditions applied to the case are uncodified. However, although the Igbo customary law is uncodified, the judges understand the relevant customary rules and traditions. Thus, the Customary Court observes that adultery contravenes the Igbo customary law. The court states (at p. 7 of the Case Report): "The act is untidy and against our custom and tradition. It could cause serious provocation which may lead to disaster."

In concluding the proceedings in Case Number 30, the Customary Court decides that the plaintiff has not "proved" that the defendant has committed adultery with the plaintiff's wife (at p. 29 of the Case Report). This is clearly a focus on proof contrary to the prediction for informal case processing [Theme 5 (c)]. Before dismissing the plaintiff's case, the court advises that the plaintiff should have done more to have the case resolved out of court. The court also warns against aggrieved persons taking the law into their own hands as the plaintiff has done in beating the defendant. According to the Case Report (at pp. 28-29):

> The Court observed with regret that the plaintiff failed to apply any of *our traditional methods of dealing with a house wife found or suspected [of] flirting*, but rather adopted a ruthless, delicate stringent measure which nearly led him to [commit] murder. This is dangerous as [it] is irresponsible and tantamounts to one taking the law into his hands. The Court seriously warned against its repetition.[54]

The Customary Court's use of the word *flirting* in the circumstances of the case is rather misleading. To flirt is to tease, play, or entice. For a husband to invoke the native Igbo means of dealing with an unfaithful wife, the wife would have done more than *flirt*. Even in Case Number 30, the plaintiff alleges that the defendant has committed *adultery* with the plaintiff's wife; that is, there is an allegation of sexual intercourse, which is much more than *flirting*.

The *traditional methods of dealing with a housewife found or suspected [of unfaithfulness]* to which the Customary Court in Case Number 30 makes reference include the following: (1) reporting the wife to the *onye aka ebe* (middle man) in the marriage negotiations; (2) reporting her to her parents and *ụmụnna*; (3) reporting her to *ụmụ ada* (the daughters of the town). Each of these persons or groups could bring such pressure on the unfaithful wife that she would change her ways. Failing the above options, the aggrieved husband may (4) simply end the marriage by sending the unfaithful wife back to her maiden home. The *traditional methods of dealing with a housewife found or suspected [of unfaithfulness]* are unofficial methods of case management. The Customary Court's statement acknowledges the ability of the unofficial processes to resolve the dispute in Case Number 30.

Contempt of Court

In Case Number 32 (Charge No. CCA/53C/89, Decided in October 1989), two persons are charged with contempt of the order of the Customary Court. The court has previously issued an order restraining all parties to a pending case from plucking pears from a certain pear tree. The two accused persons have allegedly plucked and sold the pears contrary to the order. They are charged under *sections 39 and 59 of the Anambra State Edict No. 6 of 1984*. Among other things, the law mandates the Customary Court to punish for contempt outside the court. The Case Report lists the court as the prosecutor.

Thus, the court in Case Number 32 plays two roles at the same time: prosecutor and judge.[55] However, the double roles are not sufficient to satisfy the requirements of theme 10 (Simplicity of Process) because the primary descriptor under the theme, which is that spoken words may be sufficient to initiate a case, is not identifiable in the case.

Themes 3 and 4 are the only themes of informal case processing found in Case Number 32. In line with themes 3 and 4, the accused persons are prosecuted without lawyers. Also, the court clearly shows the focus of the proceedings on proof (theme 5) when it states (at pp. 8-9):

> In the absence of [corroboration], and in the absence of either yam or pear, tendered before the Court as Exhibits, [the] Court has no doubt that the complainant merely based his complaint on hearsay. With lapses such as these, [the] Court is left without any doubt that *the complainant has not proved his case beyond all reasonable doubts*. In the light of these circumstances [the] court has found both 1st and 2nd accused not guilty on both counts and therefore are *discharged and acquitted*.[56]

In Case Number 32 the accused persons are prosecuted under a written law in the Customary Court, which is an official court. Under the official laws of Nigeria, an accused person cannot be prosecuted or convicted of a crime in any official court unless the crime is defined in writing and the penalty therefor similarly spelled out [*Section 36 (12), 1999 Constitution*]. This rule does not apply to criminal cases processed unofficially, for example, by the *Eze*-in-Council.

Dispute over the Validity of Marriage, Inheritance, and Succession to Village Headship

The only case in this subcategory is a Supreme Court case. Case Number 40 (*Okonkwo v. Okagbue and 2 Others*, 1994, 12 SCNJ 89), a civil matter, is first instituted in the High Court where the plaintiff loses. He appeals unsuccessfully to the Court of Appeal. He appeals further to the Supreme Court. In the case, the plaintiff brings a civil suit in the High Court against three women: two of them are his aunts (his late father's sisters), and the third woman is someone whom the first two defendants have married for the plaintiff's deceased father after he died. The plaintiff asks the court (for himself and on behalf of his four brothers) to declare the marriage of the third defendant void. Further, he asks the court to declare that the six children borne by the third defendant are not the children of his late father and as such cannot inherit his late father's property or title. The first two defendants claim that "under Onitsha [an Igbo town] native law and custom, a sister is entitled to marry a wife for and in the name of her brother, be he dead or alive even if the brother has surviving male issue" (at p. 90 of the Case Report). The High Court accepts this native law and custom and dismisses the plaintiff's case. The plaintiff appeals to the Court of Appeal, which affirms the High Court decision. On further appeal to the Supreme Court, the Court decides that the native law and custom pleaded by the defendants and upheld by both the High Court and the Court of Appeal is "repugnant to natural justice, equity and good conscience"[57] (at p. 105 of the Case Report). Therefore, the marriage is void.[58]

There is some indication in the Case Report that some unsuccessful efforts are made to settle Case Number 40 out of court. However, the process in the Supreme Court contains three of the twelve themes expected in an informal case processing. The following themes are found: Mediation, Stigmatization, and Individualization (themes 2, 6, and 7, respectively). Theme 2 is present in the process because, as predicted, the procedure before the Supreme Court is non-adversarial. There is no confrontation of the witnesses for the opposing side. However, as noted, this is a standard appellate procedure in Nigeria. Therefore, it does not necessarily mean informality.

The "loss of dignity" predicted under theme 6 is clearly identifiable in the Supreme Court's judgment. The Court decides that the third defendant is not the wife of the deceased because the first and second defendants could not marry a wife for their dead brother. This amounts to "denying or stripping [the third defendant] of a position or honor" under theme 6 (a).[59] Also, the process includes theme 7 because the Supreme Court uses its discretion to accommodate the unique native law and custom issues raised by this case. Case Number 40 shows the importance of reasonably re-evaluating the customs and traditions that apply in the Igbo communities. The reasonable evaluation done by the Supreme Court in this case leads to the conclusion that the custom of marrying a wife for a dead man is unsustainable in the contemporary Igbo society.

Summary of Contents and Processes Found in the Formal Category

One of the twelve cases in the "Formal" category is a criminal case. The rest are civil cases. In the criminal case (contempt of court), the dispute is between the public, which is represented by the official Customary Court, and the accused. The court serves as both the prosecutor and the judge. The alleged contempt of court is reported to the court. The court prosecutes the accused persons. In the civil cases, the disputes are between private persons. In each of the civil cases, the court–Customary Court, High Court, Court of Appeal, or the Supreme Court, as the case may be–serves only as judge. The cases are initiated and conducted by private persons. The issues in the civil cases in the "Formal" category are land and land-related issues, issues of adultery, the validity of marriage, inheritance, and succession to village headship.

Each of the twelve cases in the "Formal" category is processed in an official court. However, the cases also contain various elements of the different levels available for case management in the relevant Igbo community. For each of the cases, the native means of case management is explored before the commencement of the action in the official court system.

VERY FORMAL CATEGORY

This category contains one of the forty-two case studies: Case Number 37. A case in the "Very Formal" category is managed in such a way that its process does not satisfy any of the twelve predicted themes of informal case processing. The "Very Formal" category is the opposite of the "Very Informal" category.

Nature and Kind of Case

Preliminary Objection to the Competence of an Appeal from a Customary Court

Case Number 37 (Suit No. AB/CC/8A/91, Decided in October 1992) is a civil case. The issue before the High Court is whether or not the procedure followed in filing an appeal in the High Court against a Customary Court judgment accords with the prescribed practice. The respondent in the appeal claims that because the appellant's attorney–rather than the appellant himself as mentioned by the *Customary Court Rules*–has signed the Notice of Appeal, the appeal is incompetent. He asks the High Court to dismiss the appeal for that reason. The court rejects the argument, ruling that the appellant or his attorney may sign the Notice of Appeal.

The issue in Case Number 37 is very technical. Therefore, as expected, the processing of the case is very technical. This accounts for the absence of all the twelve themes predicted for informal case processing. What actually puts the case in this extremely formal category is the fact that the issue before the High Court is not the merits or demerits of the Customary Court's decision. Rather, the issue before the High Court relates to the usually complex appeals process. Thus, it is important to bear in mind in interpreting the process in this case that the High Court has not gone into the merits of the parties' cases. Case processing in Nigeria's official courts is highly structured. As Case Number 37 shows, the process is even more structured in appeals. The rules regulating appeals in the official courts do not apply in unofficial processes.

OTHER CONTENTS FOUND IN THE RECORD OF PROCEEDINGS

The forty-two case studies surveyed in this book are those completely processed before the data collection. In addition to the completed cases, there are other incomplete cases. The incompletes do not contain sufficient information to answer the process issues in this book. However, they are helpful in answering the content issues because the records reflect the subject matters involved in these yet-to-be-completed cases. However, not all the uncompleted cases in the Record of Proceedings are discussed here. The cases discussed are those that add new dimensions to the nature and kinds of cases processed under the native Igbo justice system. Thus, the contents of the uncompleted cases are included as further illustrations of the issues anticipated and managed by the Igbo justice system. There are five such cases in the records. These yet-to-be-completed cases are assigned numbers 43A, 44A, 45A, 46A, and 47A to distinguish them from the completed cases. The content of Case Number 47A has been discussed (see the introduction to chapter 3). The contents of Case Numbers 43A through 46A are examined next.

There are three issues in Case Number 43A (Record of Proceedings, vol. 1, at p. 133, 1990). First, the second disputant claims that the first disputant has made the following statement to the second disputant: "*Onye lọrọ gị gburu nwanyị na afọ ime*" (may be translated as: "In your previous life, you killed a pregnant woman") (at p. 133). Second, the first disputant claims that the second disputant has said that the first disputant is not the father of the first disputant's son, that someone else impregnated the first disputant's wife before she became married to the first disputant. Third, the first disputant further claims that the second disputant has told some people that the first disputant has taken part in preparing some traditional medicine to kill the second disputant and his family members.

Each of the allegations in Case Number 43A is a serious charge in the disputants' community, and among all Igbos for that matter. The second and third allegations in particular may be actionable in the official courts. If the second allegation attributed to the second disputant does not reflect the truth, the first disputant could bring civil proceedings on the ground that the statement has lowered his standing in the community and defamed him.[60] However, thc first disputant's wife could successfully sue for defamation. The first disputant may also succeed in an official court action for defamation on account of the second disputant's third allegation. The first allegation may not be civilly or criminally actionable under the official laws applicable to Ajallị Town. The three allegations are, however, taken before the *Eze*-in-Council for settlement.

Case Number 44A (Record of Proceedings, vol. 2, at p. 12, 1991) deals with an allegation that an Ajallị Town member contravened the rules and regulations governing masquerading in the town during *ikeji* (an Igbo annual festival). He is alleged to have invited some masquerades to his home on a certain day contrary to the directives of the town's rulers, which directives stated that the masquerades should only assemble at the town's main square. The accused person is arraigned before the *Eze*-in-Council to be tried for contravening *iwu mmanwụ* (the rules and regulations on masquerading). The rules and regulations are not enforceable in the official courts.

In Case Number 45A (Record of Proceedings, vol. 2, at p. 90, 1993), an elderly male member of an *ụmụnna* group reports two other members of the same *ụmụnna* to the *Eze*-in-Council on the ground that "his family members were not giving him his due respect" (at p. 90). He pleads with the council to invite the two *ụmụnna* relatives and advise them to accord the elder his due respect. At this time, the two relatives of the elderly man reside in other parts of Nigeria. The council therefore advises the elderly man to inform the secretary to the council whenever the relatives visit home so that "necessary letters of invitation" to a meeting could be issued to them (at p. 90).

Case Number 46A (Record of Proceedings, vol. 2, at p. 134, 1993) is based on a land dispute. However, unlike other land cases in the Record of Proceedings, two *ụmụnna* representatives bring this case. They (the first disputants) bring the case for themselves and on behalf of all the *ụmụnna* members. The case is against an individual, non-member of the *ụmụnna.* The first disputants bring the case before the *Eze*-in-Council claiming that the second disputant has trespassed and wrongfully entered their *ụmụnna* land.

SUMMARY

The range of the grievances, conflicts, and disputes processed either unofficially or officially in Nigeria's Igbo is wide. Theoretically, judicial processes in cases could fall in the five categories created in the informality-formality continuum (Very Informal, Informal, Semi-Formal, Formal, and Very Formal – see table 2.3). However, of the forty-two cases studied for their relative informality, none falls in the "Very Informal" category. Each of the other four categories contains a number of cases. Overall, the processing of the cases is less informal than anticipated. The maintenance of written records is a prominent feature of formality found in all the cases. Reliance on evidence and proof constitute the other major features of a formal judicial process found in the cases managed in the official courts as well as those managed in the unofficial tribunals.

NOTES

1. "Subcategories" are the groups into which the cases in each of the five categories in table 2.3 have been sorted. Subcategories are created according to the subject matters of the cases. The "Informal" category is made up of eleven subcategories. The first subcategory is "Dispute over Contract to Perform Services and Sell Product." The "Very Informal" category contains no subcategory. The "Semi-Formal" category consists of six subcategories. The "Formal" category is made up of four subcategories. Finally, the "Very Formal" category consists of one subcategory.

2. These crimes are defined and punishable under the *Criminal Code Law of Anambra State*, which applies in Ajallị Town (the place where the contract is entered into).

3. This act of the second disputant in sending someone to represent him at the hearing of the dispute angers the council members. They regard it as a contemptuous behavior – a "gross disrespect and slight of the Council" (at p. 31 of the Record of Proceedings, vol. 1). He is expected to be personally present at the hearing. The council fines him for this misbehavior.

4. In further reaction to the second disputant's failure to appear before the council, the council members also mention his failure to honor the agreement between him and the first disputant. This, however, does not qualify as an "emphasis on placing

blame," especially since the mention is made after the second disputant has admitted the claim against him.

5. The prospective buyer is also the head of a primary school in the area. However, there is no indication that this has influenced the council's handling of the case. The council would probably handle it in the same way, no matter who was involved.

6. In the example of Ajallị Town, the minor gifts and small amount of money constitute *ịtụnye mmanya* (filing a suit) according to the town's customs. The *ịtụnye mmanya* procedure is explained fully in chapter 5 of this book.

7. An economic tree is a tree that reaps monetary value as in the instance of a kola nut tree, a palm tree, or a breadfruit tree.

8. Italics added.

9. In 1984, General Muhammadu Buhari's military regime established this program, which according to the regime, was designed to curb all aspects of "indiscipline" in the lives of Nigerians. The program was administered at the federal, state, and local levels in the country. All the administrators were officials of the Federal Military Government. The succeeding military junta of General Ibrahim Babangida continued this program (from 1985) until the program was allowed to die.

10. Cf. the "retreatist" in Merton's (1957) Anomie Theory.

11. Contrast the position of the English law of real property that adheres to the Latin maxim: *quicquid plantatur solo, solo cedit* ("whatever is attached to land is a part of the land").

12. Italics added.

13. The record on Case Number 28 is obtained from the AWU, which managed the case even though the record shows that the case was first reported to *Eze* Ajallị. According to the first disputant, when the dispute began he reported the matter to the *Eze*. However, when the *Eze* "did not act, he [the first disputant] took the matter to the A.W.U. Central Executive" (at p. 1). It should be mentioned here that this case illustrates the fluid nature of out-of-court case processing. In the official court structure, a litigant must first take his or her case to an inferior court before appealing to a higher tribunal. In an out-of-court case management process, there are no strict rules requiring a disputant to take a dispute to one avenue rather than another. That is why an Igbo litigant in the official courts must first go to the High Court before he or she can proceed on appeal to the Court of Appeal. In an out-of-court setting, the disputants may have their dispute managed by whomever or wherever they want, however lowly or highly placed.

14. Italics added.

15. *Iwu mmanwụ* is made up of the customary rules, regulations, and laws that guide masquerade displays in an Igbo community. The rulers and elders of the community take a breach of any of these unwritten laws seriously. Such breach is an example of a "crime" in the native Igbo justice system. A series of punishments, ranging from fines to the destruction of the offender's home and other property, may be imposed.

16. The annual yam festival (*otute*) is celebrated to herald the beginning of the new harvesting season and to thank God for the yields from the farmlands.

17. As a reminder, a masquerade "accomplice" is a person, usually young or adult male, who is initiated into the secrets, rules, and regulations of masquerading and who accompanies the masquerade during an outing. The masquerade and the accomplice visit private homes, business premises, and public centers in the community entertaining people, sometimes for minor gifts. The accomplice's responsibilities include announcing the approach of the masquerade so that the uninitiated males and females may avoid the masquerade. The accomplice carries out this responsibility with the aid of his metal

gong. A person with a complaint concerning a masquerade must proceed against the masquerade's human partner since the Igbo regard masquerades as the spirits of the dead and so beyond human reach.

18. As stated earlier, this is one of the laws on masquerading among the Igbos. Apart from very few elderly and highly respected women, such as title-holders, masquerading is exclusively for initiated males. Thus, no female may eat any food associated with masquerades.

19. The Record of Proceedings does not disclose who initiated the lawsuit pending in the official court.

20. The council's ruling resulted from a *preliminary objection* raised by the second disputant to the council's competence to hear the present case considering the lawsuit pending in the official court.

21. Note that this is the main difference between Case Number 8 and Case Numbers 4 and 20.

22. Italics added.

23. Italics added. The italicized expression is a colloquial way of asking the disputants to forgive each other for their wrongdoings.

24. Italics added.

25. Although the Record of Proceedings does not support the following point, the researcher's knowledge and understanding of the culture and tradition of the relevant Igbo community lead to the following conclusion. The accused person refuses to deny the (true) statement because to do so would be to lie. He would be lying to the *Eze* and his council members as well as to the ancestors, customs, and traditions of Ajallị Town, which the *Eze*-in-Council represents. This is particularly significant considering the location of the meeting venue (*Ogbiti Otti*). The venue, which is the residence and office of *Eze* Ajallị, is the town's symbol of authority.

26. Italics added. *Ndịeni* is a loose association of about seven towns and communities adjacent to one another, including Ajallị Town. The association is similar to a confederation. The constituent towns and communities cooperate on cultural, social, economic, and political issues.

27. Italics added.

28. Based on the author's knowledge of the study setting, incest is a rare crime there. However, it is possible that, as in many cultures, most of the incestuous acts are never reported.

29. Italics added for emphasis.

30. The girl's age is not stated. However, she was a primary school student at the time of the alleged crimes. Therefore, she was probably less than twelve years old.

31. Italics added.

32. Any group that wishes their new *ụmụnna* to be recognized by the town must follow a certain procedure that includes presenting some gifts to the townspeople and convincing the town that the new *ụmụnna* is capable of fulfilling the responsibilities associated with such recognition. In particular, a new *ụmụnna* must demonstrate that it is capable of meeting its financial obligations toward the town's endeavors.

33. Apparently, the mediation panel is not reconciliatory enough, hence the constitution of the committee of six.

34. It is not clear who has decided what this second penalty should be. However, the townspeople at a later gathering probably decided it.

35. Under the customs and traditions of Ajallị and other parts of Igbo, a bereaved person should leave the responsibilities for such ceremonial activities to the members of the *ụmụnna* and *ọnụma*.

36. Italics added.

37. Italics added. Does the use of the word *unanimous* in the council's decision mean that the council may reach a majority decision? That is conceivable. But there is nothing in the Record of Proceedings to support this opinion.

38. Italics added.

39. Although this case had not been completed at the time that the Record of Proceedings was obtained, the case was included here for two reasons. First, at the time of collecting this part of the data for this book, the case was one of the most recent case studies. Thus, it adds to the contemporary understanding of the judicial processes being examined. Second, the record shows that the case has gone on sufficiently long for a reasonable understanding of the process used in it.

40. By the date this case is brought before the council, the amount of money required for *ịtụnye mmanya* has become fifty naira.

41. Italics added.

42. Even though this may be speculative, it seems that the first disputant took the case to the official court because he had not received the quick settlement that he expected in the out-of-court, unofficial process. Before he decided to go to the official court, his case had been adjourned for more than fifteen times in the time period between March 1992 and July 1995.

43. This time period is long enough to be a "loss of time by disputant in the process" contrary to the prediction under theme 6 (Stigmatization).

44. The archives, obtained from the court, differ from the *Eze*-in-Council's Record of Proceedings.

45. The legal jargon for this rule of evidence in official court proceedings is the "hearsay rule."

46. In this connection, the Supreme Court of Nigeria has rightly drawn a distinction between a judge asking questions of a witness to clarify relevant points and assisting a party at the expense of the other party. The Court maintains that a judge should not do the latter. In *Nzekwu and Others v. Nzekwu and Others* (1989) 2 NWLR 373 at 379, the Court states: "A judge should regard himself as an impartial arbiter and has no right to prop up the weak case of one party or to assist that party to make out a case different from that which has been set up by the litigant." See also *Ochomma v. Unosi* (1965) NMLR 321. This Supreme Court injunction applies to all official judges and magistrates, including those applying the Igbo customary law.

47. Case Number 35 predates the creation of the Court of Appeal as an intermediate appeals court between the High Court and the Supreme Court.

48. Italics added.

49. See the discussions of this policy in chapters 7 and 8 of this book.

50. The *Evidence Act* comprises the guiding rules and regulations of judicial proceedings in Nigeria's official courts. However, the provisions of the Act do not apply to proceedings in the Customary Courts. But the Act is applied in appellate proceedings on a customary law issue in the High Court, the Court of Appeal, or the Supreme Court.

51. A "customary right of occupancy" is a right of land possession assigned by the official government. This right is contained in the *Land Use Act, 1978*, which governs land ownership, possession, use, and disposition. What used to be known as the "right of *ownership* of land" prior to the Act, is now called the "right of *possession* of land."

52. Italics added. The *Customary Court Edict* is an official law of Anambra State. Other states have equivalent laws.

53. Or the equivalent law.

54. Italics added.

55. In Nigeria, it is usual for a court, including the Customary Court, to be the judge and also act as some kind of a prosecutor in the consideration of an alleged contempt committed in the face of the court (in the court). When, however, the alleged contempt occurs out of the court's face (outside the court), the prosecution may be left to the state's attorneys, although the court may, as has happened in Case Number 32, consider an allegation of contempt outside the court without formally referring the allegation to the state's attorneys.

56. Italics added for emphasis. In Nigeria, if an accused person is *discharged* from official criminal court proceedings, he or she may be tried later for the same or similar offense. If, however, the accused is *acquitted* or *discharged and acquitted*, he or she may not be tried again for the same or similar offense.

57. Chapters 7 and 8 include discussions of the effects of this official Nigerian justice policy on the development of Nigeria's native justice systems.

58. In the case, the Supreme Court also makes the points that since the purported husband in the marriage arrangement was dead before the alleged marriage, the consummation of the marriage became impossible from the very beginning. Therefore, what has taken place between the first and second defendants and the third defendant is, at best, a marriage between two women and a woman. The Court restates its decision in an earlier case (*Meribe v. Egwu*, 1976 3 SC 23) that such an association between persons of the same sex is "repugnant to natural justice, equity and good conscience" and therefore void.

59. Having noted that the "loss of dignity" *expected* under theme 6 exists in Case Number 40, it should also be observed that the "loss of time" *not expected* under the theme also exists in the case. It took more than fifteen years for this case to be processed from the High Court through the Supreme Court. It lasted for about one year in the Supreme Court.

60. The husband may also succeed if he claims that his wife has thus been defamed and that he has incurred some loss as a result of her pain and suffering.

Part II

Aspects of Justice in Contemporary Traditional Igbo

4

Law-making Techniques in Contemporary Traditional Igbo and the Growth of Nigeria's Native Justice Systems

INTRODUCTION

Law-making techniques and practices have predictably changed in traditional Igbo. The changes that have taken place are in line with the changes in the lifestyles, mores, and overall circumstances of the Igbos. Prior to the British colonization of Nigeria, writing was not a part of Igbo law making. Laws were typically "customary laws" based on the generally understood and accepted conduct norms. The natives relied on their individual and collective memories to ascertain the controlling legal authority on an issue. Because of the high integrity and honesty level among community members, the absence of written documents as objective statements of the laws was not a major handicap to ascertaining and applying laws. The relatively homogenous, pre-colonial Igbo population (Anene, 1991; see also Adeyemi, 1990, July), which was based on great respect for community authority figures, facilitated the general acceptance of the unwritten, customary laws.

In contemporary Nigeria, with the immense social, economic, political, religious, and other changes that have occurred in the society, it is necessary to change some of the techniques used to make laws in traditional Igbo. As in many other world populations, written laws are indispensable in Igbo. Writing is an important element in the development of a system of laws. Writing helps greatly to minimize ambiguity and confusion and to ensure clarity and certainty in the legal provisions. A written law should be preferred to an unwritten law. In the particular area of criminal law and procedure, basic fairness dictates that if a person is to be held criminally responsible and punished for a crime, the crime should first be expressly defined in such a way that the average person in society understands the restrictions of the society. With the proper language and adequate publicity, writing could be the most effective way of defining society's expectations. This chapter examines the process of law making in contemporary traditional Igbo and investigates related ways in which the body of the Igbo native laws and customs could be strengthened, diversified, publicized, and grown to increase the capacity of the native Igbo justice system for social control in Nigeria.

The following questions have guided the research leading to this chapter: What is the procedure for making laws in contemporary traditional Igbo? Does the procedure distinguish between criminal and civil laws? Are contemporary traditional Igbo laws written or unwritten? How, if at all, could writing enhance the growth of the native Igbo justice system? What other policy issues does the data highlight regarding law making in contemporary traditional Igbo and how to expand the capacity of the native Igbo justice system for social control in Nigeria?

CONTEMPORARY PATTERNS OF LAW MAKING AMONG THE IGBOS

The Igbo customary law has long recognized the need to have different kinds of rules and regulations governing different species of grievances, conflicts, and disputes. Thus, this system of laws distinguishes among "(a) purely social obligations (such as the duty to honour invitations), (b) duties imposed by custom only (for example, a father's duty to provide his male children with their first wives in order of seniority), and (c) legal duties which can be enforced against the will of the party on whom such a duty lies" (Obi, 1963, at p. 27). The distinctions exist in the making, application, and enforcement of Igbo traditions, customs, and laws.

In contemporary traditional Igbo, there are numerous enforceable traditions, customs, and laws that regulate interpersonal (civil) relations among the members of each community. The traditions, customs, and laws include the rules and regulations governing the acts and omissions that the English law calls torts. Also in this category are those rules and regulations governing such things as contracts; land ownership, use, and transfer; marriages; matrimonial relations; deaths and burials; inheritance (of property); succession (to title, office, etc.); and laws passed from time to time by the local leaders in each community to address the needs of the community. Other customary laws deal with crimes, including assault, battery, street fighting, insulting an elderly person or an authority figure, breaking any of the governing rules and regulations on festivals and public displays (*iwu mmanwụ* inclusive), *ọchụ* (homicide), and other *arụ* or *alụ* (crime that pollutes the land, such as incest or the desecration of a place of worship, such as a shrine).

In pre-colonial Igbo, laws were uncodified. The law-making process involved an assembly of all the community members or, in some circumstances, a selected group that looked into the issue to be addressed. The people assembled would discuss how best to deal with the issue before them. At the end of the discussions, a few leading members of the community would confer with one another and come up with the final proposal of the law. All the community members (or a majority) would approve the proposal before it became law (Uchendu, 1966). The law was unwritten.

The data show that the outlined law-making procedure is still largely followed in Igbo. The changes to the process include the presence of writing. Law making in contemporary traditional Igbo now includes writing in some instances, even though the written laws are still uncoordinated. When the members of an Igbo community gather as they did before the coming of the British, there is often a person designated as a secretary. The secretary records the major points raised and made at the gathering in a "minutes book." The proceedings are usually conducted in the Igbo language or a mix of Igbo and the English language. However, it is fashionable to appoint as secretary a person who speaks and writes the English language, albeit only smatteringly. Even if the secretary is only half-literate in the English language, the community members usually expect the proceedings to be recorded in that language. As unfortunate as this attitude is, it is not surprising, since so many Igbos seem unable to distinguish between knowledge or intelligence and the language medium through which an idea is communicated. No language–however widely it appears to be spoken–is a repository of knowledge or intelligence. Insistence on the use of the English language to record Igbo proceedings sometimes results in inaccuracies in the records because the English language does not fully capture the meanings of Igbo words and phrases. Moreover, the secretary may simply use wrong words in translating statements from Igbo to English (Okereafọezeke and Austin, 1996; Okereafọezeke, 1998b).

When the issue being considered for a law is not complex or when the community leaders need to act immediately, they go ahead and make the law (Case Number 21, Record of Proceedings, vol. 3, 1994, at p. 20). Some issues are complex, and lengthy deliberations and consultations are necessary in enacting laws for them. For such issues, it is necessary to come up with laws that not only address the issues at stake but are also acceptable to the community members. Thus, the community leaders make sure that they involve all the necessary parties in the law-making process. The parties are given time and opportunity to make their contributions to the process by suggesting what they believe the proposed law should contain. If necessary, the community leaders will meet with the necessary parties to iron out some differences before the new law is enacted (Record of Proceedings, vol. 3, 1995, at pp. 79 and 81). The issues involved in Appendices C and D ("Marriage in Ajallị – Regulations" and "Death and Burial Ceremonies in Ajallị – Regulations," respectively) are complex. Therefore, consultations preceded the two laws.

Appendices C and D illustrate the Ajallị community's attempts to codify the Igbo traditions, customs, and laws as they apply to Ajallị. As an example, Appendix D sets out in detail the procedure for marriage in the town. The legislation is made up of ten sections and sixteen sub-sections. Section 3 (a) provides that "[Bridal price] should not exceed Two thousand Naira, N1,500 for the father and N500:00 for the mother irrespective of status. For non-indigenes, bridal price is limitless or negotiable." Section 9 criminalizes a breach of the legislation thus: "Anybody who contravenes the marriage regulations or part thereof is liable to a penalty of N1,000:00 (One Thousand Naira)." Under section 10, the marriage celebrant is required to inform named community leaders to witness the ceremonies. The leaders are obliged to report a breach of the legislation to the *Eze*-in-Council, which takes steps to enforce the penalty.

When a law is enacted, it is published to all the community members. The importance of publishing the new law is twofold: to get the maximum compliance with the law and to make it impossible for any member of the community to plead ignorance of the law as a defense. In the example of Ajallị Town, where a new law is made at the town level, it may be published at a meeting of the townspeople (Record of Proceedings, vol. 3, 1995, at p. 79). Appendices C and D are published in this way. In some circumstances, a new law may be published through the town's various *ụmụnna*s. The *Eze*-in-Council sends a message to each head of the sixteen *ụmụnna*s advising the head to inform the *ụmụnna* members about the new law. This is the most frequently used means of publication. Alternatively, announcing it through the town criers may publish a new law.

To publish a law through the town criers, each town crier is assigned to a part of the town. He is to use his *ogene* (metal gong) to attract the community members' attention and then announce the law at intervals. This method of publication is frequently used when the law is of an *ad hoc* nature. An example of an *ad hoc* law is where all adult male members of the town are directed to assemble at the town hall the following morning. Any adult male who fails to attend will be fined the sum of twenty naira.[1] If the law is made at the *ọnụma* or *ụmụnna* level, it is similarly published.

The recognized organs of the Igbo communities make some of the laws just described. There are other laws that are passed on from one generation to another as unenacted rules of behavior (customs and traditions). For example, quite apart from the official, governmental laws, the unenacted custom against homicide is well understood among the Igbos. Also well understood is the unwritten customary law that prohibits incestuous acts. In traditional Igbo, *arụ*, *alụ*, or *nsọ*, which are the most serious crimes – crimes that pollute the land, for example, incest and *ọchụ* (homicide) – remain uncodified. Further, there are numerous uncodified rules and regulations that govern social interactions among the members of each Igbo community. Respect, especially for the elderly and one's ancestors, and the social duty to participate in community engagements are examples. The rules and regulations that apply to these interactions in contemporary Igbo are still borrowed from the past.

PROBLEMS LIMITING THE GROWTH OF THE IGBO TRADITIONS, CUSTOMS, AND LAWS

Lack of Codification of the Igbo Customary Law

The data reveal a lack of effort by the official governments to codify the rules of the Igbo customary law. Most of the traditions, customs, and laws applied to the cases studied for this book are uncodified. The Igbo customary law remains fluid and often uncertain. A person who intends to rely on a principle of the customary law has to establish it by evidence. The fluid and uncertain nature of the law discourages adherence to the common trends that exist in the law. Emphasis is placed on those elements that localize, rather than generalize, this system of laws.

Insufficient Publication of Decided Cases

The data reflect that the only customary law cases published in Nigeria are those decided by the Supreme Court and the Court of Appeal. Cases decided by the Customary Court are not published. Only a fraction of the cases decided by the High Court is published. The cases decided unofficially at the *ezi na ụnọ*, the *ụmụnna*, the *ọnụma*, and the *obodo* levels (see figure 5.1) are never published (Okereafọezeke, 1996; also Okereafọezeke, 2000a). Igbo unofficial courts are not courts of record. That is, they are not required to reduce their judgments and the reasons therefor to writing. However, the data show consistent efforts by the various unofficial courts and tribunals to maintain written records of the proceedings before them. That explains the availability of archives for this research even at the most local level. Despite being available, all the unofficial and most of the official records of proceedings are never published.

SUGGESTIONS FOR THE DEVELOPMENT AND GROWTH OF IGBO JUSTICE AND LAW

Based on the data, the author offers the following suggestions on codification, teaching and research curricula, as well as publication for the development and growth of Igbo law and justice.

Codification

A major way to encourage the growth of the Igbo customary laws and traditions is to codify them. The state and local governments can help make this possible. Codification is already happening unofficially (without official government involvement) in parts of Igbo. In the course of this research, the author has discovered several documents containing written laws enacted by the Ajallị community. These laws are unofficial, non-governmental (see Appendices C and D). However, unlike the Appendices D and E, meaningful codification of the Igbo traditions, customs, and laws should be done in the Igbo language, which is the native language of the population. Translated copies of the codified laws may be provided for persons who speak other languages, including the English language. The Igbo customary law codification should begin at the community levels. If the codification were begun at the community levels as suggested here, the procedure would clearly establish any differences that may exist among the communities. Based on the local enactments, the local and state governments, through policy makers who understand the Igbo customary laws and traditions, would be able to synthesize these local enactments into generally acceptable, comprehensive codes.

Teaching and Research Curricula

Nigerian teachers and researchers at lower and higher institutions of learning should create teaching and research curricula emphasizing how to improve the native systems of justice and law. At present, native justice and law systems are barely addressed, particularly in teaching curricula. Even where a curriculum touches on native justice, it is limited to the immediate ethnic location of the particular institution of learning. Thus, a university professor at an institution in Enugu state limits his discussion of native justice to the Igbo system. He makes no effort to examine the native systems of the other ethnic nations in the country. The author recognizes that increasing funding for research in this regard would help a great deal in broadening appreciation for other native systems. There are numerous field opportunities for research on the native justice systems in Nigeria. What is lacking is the funding for such research activities. Both government and private funds are necessary to support these activities.

Publication of Judicial Decisions

The various federal and state ministries of justice, as well as private groups and individuals, should collaborate and publish judicial decisions by official and unofficial tribunals on the Igbo customary law. Publication would help to develop the case law on Igbo native laws and customs. In particular, it would assist the unofficial and official judges to determine how an issue facing them might have been handled in a previous case. The need for such coordination among case management bodies is based on the recognition of the important role of the doctrine of precedent to the development of any set of laws. Moreover, publication of judicial decisions would reduce the need to expend time in each case ascertaining the relevant customary law or tradition by evidence. That would also help educate the general public on the laws and customs that regulate their lives. At present, the data shows that publication is limited to the judgments of the Supreme Court, the Court of Appeal, and some judgments of the High Courts. Without seeking to formalize the largely informal native justice systems, the local, state, and federal governments should encourage private persons and groups in efforts to publish all the judicial decisions on the native laws and customs. This is essential to building a worthy justice and legal system with which the Nigerian peoples can identify.

The exact financial cost of codifying the Igbo (or other Nigerians') customary laws and publishing the judicial decisions is not known, but such an endeavor would be expensive. However, the cost to the official governments would be reduced if private individuals, groups, and educational and research institutions are involved in the activities. The services of the more than eighty universities and colleges, as well as the thirty-seven ministries of justice in Nigeria could be used to accomplish this, thereby reducing the cost to the official governments. For too long, justice commissioners and ministers (at both the state and federal levels) have limited themselves and their organizations to copying and redating foreign-made laws, especially those from Britain. It is time these custodians of justice among Nigerians spearheaded efforts toward making the country's justice systems and processes fundamentally relevant to Nigerians and their native institutions.

SUMMARY

This chapter has described and explained the contemporary features of unofficial (non-governmental) law-making processes, strategies, and practices in Igbo. The data show that the law-making techniques in present-day, traditional Igbo differ in some respects from the pre-colonial procedures. Prior to the British colonization of Nigeria, Igbo traditions, customs, and native laws were unwritten. The data reveal that writing is now a fairly common feature of traditional, unofficial law making among the Igbos. Different kinds of written evidence of made laws are found at the different levels of the community studied. Several examples are found of local, community efforts to legislate in writing the traditions, customs, and laws governing conduct in the community. Examples of such written laws are "Marriage in Ajallị – Regulations" and "Death and Burial Ceremonies in Ajallị – Regulations" (Appendices C and D, respectively). However, the data also show that both unofficial and official judicial decisions on the Igbo native laws and customs are rarely published. Thus, developments in this law are seldom publicized and shared, leading to a limitation on the opportunities for this law to grow and establish a meaningful body of case law. Further, justice and law research and teaching curricula in Nigeria pay little or no attention to the development of the country's native laws and customs. Well-coordinated written legislation, in combination with increased publication of the legislation and case law and a diversification and strengthening of justice and law research and teaching curricula, with more attention to customary law, would lead to the growth and strengthening of Nigeria's native justice systems.

NOTE

1. The term *law* is used to describe this directive because even though the order is "temporary" rather than "permanent," it bears the necessary characteristics of a law: It is a directive from a political authority to a subject to carry out a duty, failing which the subject will be sanctioned in the stated manner.

5

Methods and Procedures for the Application of Igbo Traditions, Customs, and Laws

INTRODUCTION

This chapter examines justice processing in Igbo. The data sources are archives, interviews, and field observations. Based on a content analysis of the relevant, available archives collected from official, governmental, as well as unofficial, non-governmental organs in Nigeria, cases are used to illustrate the mixed Igbo and English views of justice, justice processing mechanisms, and the hierarchy of unofficial and official justice-processing tribunals. Other data are based on face-to-face interviews and the author's field observations in Nigeria. The Igbo and English perspectives of justice often conflict with, and oppose, each other. As a solution to the finding of a diverse and uncoordinated justice system, the author recommends a synthesized justice-processing mechanism. However, the new system must clearly and strongly recognize the native justice institutions and practices as the bases for the new justice system.

This chapter also studies the contemporary role of native means of case management in Igbo. Two sets of research questions addressing "content" and "process" issues guide this chapter:

Research Question 1 (Content) – What are the kinds of civil and criminal grievances, conflicts, and disputes (cases) processed through the traditional, unofficial Igbo case management system, rather than through the English-style, official, government system?

Research Question 2 (Process) – What are the avenues for case management among the Igbos? What are the hierarchical levels, if any, in case management among the Igbos? What is the nature of the relationships among the identified avenues? How do the data reflect on the ability of the native Igbo justice system to regulate behavior among the Igbos in contrast to the English-style justice system?

The official case management methods are universal throughout the Igbo. The unofficial methods are also found throughout Igbo land. However, there are some differences among the communities regarding the unofficial processes. Thus, for an understanding of the unofficial justice processes, the author relies on an Igbo town, Ajallị. This serves as a sample community to explain the workings of the Igbo unofficial justice processes. In using Ajallị as a sample Igbo community, the author does not mean that all Igbo communities are structured in the same way. Ajallị Town is used in this study because the author, an Ajallị native, has maintained the necessary contacts to gain the needed data from the community.

The data show that writing is frequently used to record judicial proceedings. The finding of written records and opinions at all justice-processing levels among the Igbos is particularly significant considering that writing, as a method of recording judicial proceedings among the Igbos, derives mainly from the British colonialists. Overall, the data show that both the unofficial and official courts insist on recording their proceedings in the English language even though some of the human recorders are not fluent in that language (Okereafọezeke, 1996). However, the author is confident that the proceedings studied in this book have been recorded reasonably accurately and consistently. Inquiry about the processed cases among the members of the communities where the cases occurred has checked the accuracy and consistency of the unofficial records. There is no way of checking the accuracy of the official courts' records, however. Instead, the author relies on the fact that the official courts usually make use of expert or competent recorders.

RESEARCH QUESTION 1 (CONTENT)

The data reveal a wide range of issues among the parties to the cases studied. There are criminal (felony and misdemeanor) as well as civil (at law and equity) issues. The crimes covered by the cases include assault, battery, street fighting, disobedience of *iwu mmanwụ* (the rules and regulations on masquerading),[1] public nuisance, contempt of community institutions and officers, incest, and contempt of the (official) court. Incest and *ọchụ* (homicide) are two of the most serious crimes in native Igbo. Hence, both crimes are categorized as *arụ*, *alụ*, or *nsọ* (crimes that are serious enough to "pollute the land"). An offender must follow specially laid out procedures to cleanse him or herself, as well as cleanse the community of *arụ*. The data show that the unofficial, local courts exercise jurisdiction over incest.

Some of the civil cases deal with land and land-related disputes, such as ownership of economic trees and destruction of property, which the English-style law identifies as torts. Even in situations where land is held in the name of the community, the unofficial and official courts recognize private property rights in so far as the community has given the complainant possession of the property. Some other cases deal with other kinds of torts, such as defamation, false accusations, insult and disrespect of an elderly person, and ostracism. The other issues in the cases are those concerning inheritance, succession to village headship, and various forms of contract, including business-financing contract, contract to perform services and sell product, and validity of marriage.

The great majority of the issues may be processed either unofficially or officially based on the same set of facts. Only a few of the issues, such as ostracism and disrespect for unofficial, community institutions and personnel, may be processed only unofficially through non-governmental case management tribunals. The official laws do not consider issues such as ostracism *per se* actionable. Case Number 5 (Record of Proceedings, vol. 1, at p. 79, 1989) illustrates the efficacy of the native, unofficial processes to anticipate, recognize, and manage important issues that the official, English-style justice system does not address. Briefly, the facts of the case are that the disputants belong to the same *ụmụnna*. The first disputant alleges before the *Eze*-in-Council that the second disputants, who represent themselves and their *ụmụnna*, have ostracized him for ten years from their common *ụmụnna*. He wants the second disputants to explain the reason for his ostracism. He also wants them to accept him back fully into their *ụmụnna*. The second disputants state three main reasons why the first disputant is ostracized. First, when the first disputant's wife died, he shaved his own hair and took charge of the burial arrangements contrary to the customs, which require him to leave the arrangements to his *ụmụnna*, *ọnụma*, etc. The second disputants consider his behavior taboo. Second, on occasions when other persons died in their *ụmụnna*, the first disputant has failed to take part in the burial ceremonies as is expected of every able-bodied, mature, member of the *ụmụnna*. Third, the first disputant has not paid his membership and other dues to the *ụmụnna* for years. In view of all these, the second disputants have decided that in the best interest of their *ụmụnna*, the first disputant "should stand alone and outside [their *ụmụnna*]"[2] (at p. 95).

Under the official government laws applicable to Ajallị Town (the *locus* of this case), ostracism *per se* is not actionable. Thus, an official court cannot grant either of the reliefs that the first disputant seeks in this case. An official court cannot invoke even the principles of equity to order the second disputants to accept and treat the first disputant as one of their members. Such an order would be extremely difficult, if not impossible, to enforce, and equity does not act in vain. Thus, an official court, not wanting to act in vain, is very unlikely to grant either of the reliefs. The reliefs can be granted only through an out-of-court process, such as the *Eze*-in-Council represents in Ajallị Town. Case Number 5 illustrates that the issues with which the Igbo native laws and customs deal are broader than those anticipated and managed under the official, English-style justice system. Thus, the native Igbo justice system anticipates and manages a wider range of issues, some of which are not actionable under the English-style justice system.

RESEARCH QUESTION 2 (PROCESS)

The data reveal nine avenues for case management among the Igbos. Figure 5.1 illustrates these avenues and their hierarchical relationships. The data show that Igbo justice is both pluralistic and hierarchical. Justice in Igbo is based on two systems: the native system that has survived British colonization of Nigeria and the imposed English system. The native laws and customs are officially subjected to the imposed English and English-style laws (*Proclamation No. 6 of 1900* and the equivalent laws in different parts of Nigeria). Note that the British colonialists received the English laws and justice system and subjected Nigeria's native justice and law to their English counterparts without consulting Nigerians.

Among the Igbos, the social organizational make-up of justice begins at the *ezi na ụnọ*, or family level. This is the lowest, recognizable, institutional (or quasi-institutional) body. Beyond the *ezi na ụnọ* are the *ụmụnna*, or extended family; the *ọnụma*, or village; the *obodo*, or town; Customary Court; Customary Court of Appeal in some areas; Magistrate Court; High Court; Court of Appeal; and the Supreme Court of Nigeria. The first four avenues or levels (the *ezi na ụnọ*, the *ụmụnna*, the *ọnụma*, and the *obodo*) are non-governmental, unofficial avenues. The remaining five avenues (Customary Court, Magistrate Court, High Court, Court of Appeal, and the Supreme Court) are governmental, official bodies. The Supreme Court is Nigeria's highest official court.

Igbo Case Management Avenues in Figure 5.1

The Igbo customary law recognizes three main categories of persons: natural persons, corporate persons, and supernatural persons. A natural person is an adult human being. Such a person is a full legal personality. Irrespective of his or her mental state, the person may invoke the legal processes to enforce rights. However, a natural person who is mentally deficient is more likely to have his or her rights enforced by the relatives. Also, a mentally deficient person may not be legally responsible. Even a child can enforce his or her rights, especially property rights. Corporate persons are associations of persons and groups, which the Igbo customary laws and traditions recognize as property-owning groups. Examples of such corporations are the *ụmụnna* and the *ọnụma*. The corporate persons can sue and defend legal actions in the enforcement of their collective proprietary or nonproprietary rights. Supernatural persons are the conceptual entities, which the Igbos regard as controllers of human affairs. An example is a shrine located in a forest. Typically, the forest is known by the name of that shrine, which would own the forest. The shrine may alienate its rights to the property. One of the ways in which it does so is by gift. Since the shrine cannot physically alienate the property by itself, it acts through its *alter ego*, who is the chief priest of the shrine. Any of the three categories of persons may invoke the judicial processes under the Igbo justice system.

Figure 5.1
Case Management Avenues among the Igbos

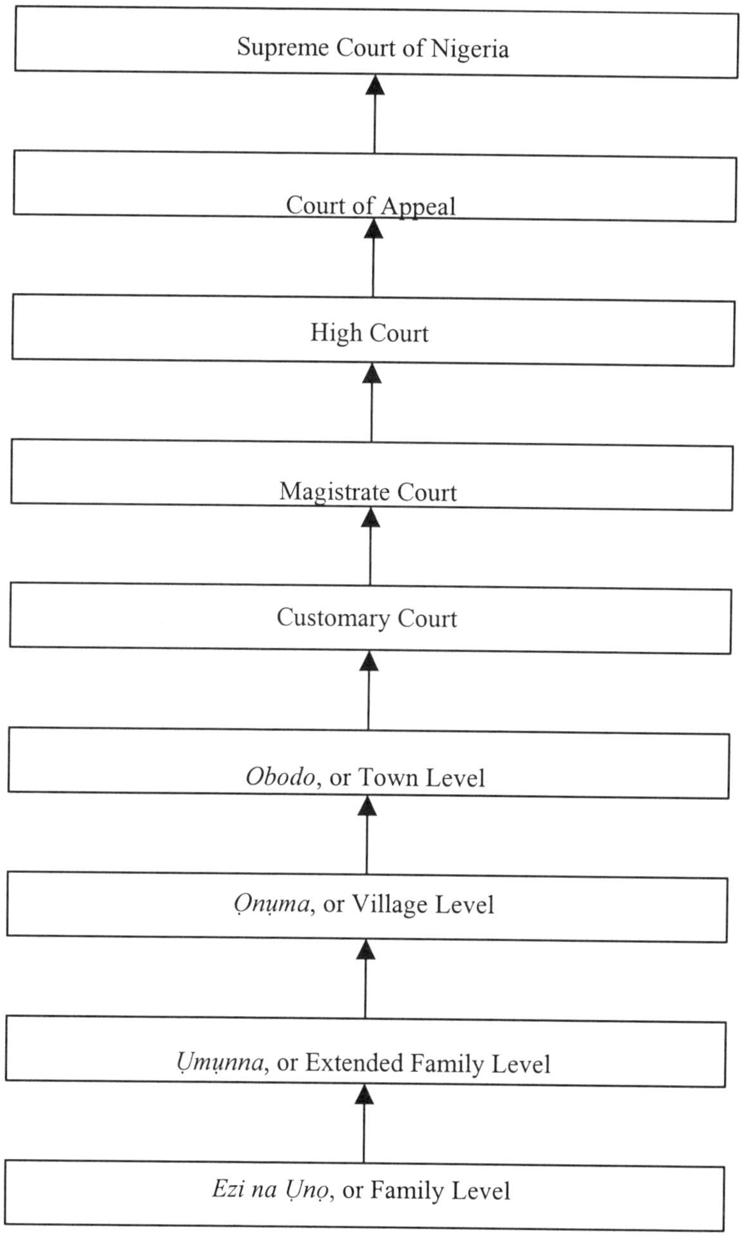

The native Igbo judicial procedures reflect recognition of the distinctions between purely social obligations, which are not enforceable, and legal obligations, which are enforceable. The justice system has established procedures for the settlement of disputes over property and other rights. The procedures for the application of the relevant Igbo customary laws and traditions to cases vary somewhat from one kind of case to another. Thus, the procedure for managing a land dispute differs in some respects from that for dealing with a case of stealing. The procedures also differentiate among grievances, conflicts, and disputes. In Case Number 45A (Record of Proceedings, vol. 2, at p. 90, 1993, on disrespect of an elder), the first disputant brings his complaints to the *Eze*-in-Council *by following the procedure outlined for filing a suit*. The council members decide to return the money he has paid as part of the procedure "since he [is] not suing the persons concerned" (at p. 90). He is *merely reporting* them to the council.

The following are the various steps, methods, and procedures followed to manage cases in Igbo. The case management processes examined here extend from the lowest unofficial avenue (*ezi na ụnọ*) to the highest official avenue (the Supreme Court). The data show that the methods and procedures used in processing a case depend, first and foremost, on where the case is processed (the avenue). Second, certain characteristics of the methods and procedures, particularly the level of proof, depend on whether the case is civil or criminal. Third, among civil cases, there are some distinctions between the proof of a property-oriented civil case and a nonproperty-oriented civil case. Among criminal cases, there are some distinctions between the proof of a crime affecting public security and a crime affecting public morality.

A case is capable of moving through the nine avenues illustrated in figure 5.1. The avenues apply whether a case is civil or criminal. The data examine the last six avenues (*obodo* level, Customary Court, Magistrate Court, High Court, Court of Appeal, and Supreme Court) in greater detail than the preceding three avenues. The first four avenues are unofficial avenues, while the remaining five are official. The data suggest that any case in Igbo may be resolved in an official court or out of the official courts. The choice is that of the parties to each case. A person who resides in a different town may take his or her case back to the hometown for resolution. Such is the situation in Case Number 7 (Record of Proceedings, vol. 1, at p. 85, 1989, on dispute over breach of business financing contract), where both disputants live outside Ajallị Town. The following are the processes in the nine avenues in figure 5.1.

Ezi Na Ụnọ, or Family Level

The *ezi na ụnọ* in Igbo is more inclusive than the Western "family." Thus, the *ezi na ụnọ* includes the husband, the wife or wives, their children, the wives of the married male children, and house helps. Sometimes, the *ezi na ụnọ* refers to all the persons residing in a household. In this social group, civil and criminal grievances, conflicts, and disputes sometimes arise. When that happens, and the parties are unable to settle it between themselves, they are expected to report the matter to the head of the *ezi na ụnọ*. The head, usually male, invites the disputants to tell him their sides of the issue. The *ezi na ụnọ* is not a creation of the official government. Thus, official laws do not regulate its proceedings.

The primary aim of the judicial proceedings at the *ezi na ụnọ* level is to find an amicable settlement of the issue. The proceedings are non-confrontational. The head of the *ezi na ụnọ* calls on the parties to make compromises to accommodate each other. In most cases, they recognize the need for cohesion among the *ezi na ụnọ* members. This encourages the parties to compromise. Efforts to settle an issue at the *ezi na ụnọ* level may apply even where the parties come from different *ezi na ụnọ*s. In the latter situation, both *ezi na ụnọ*s may cooperate to settle the issue. Also, a member of a different *ezi na ụnọ*, who is not involved in an issue, may be invited to help resolve it, as happens in Case Number 31 (Suit No. CCA/12/87, on trespass and destruction of property). In the case, two members of other *ezi na ụnọ*s try unsuccessfully to help resolve the dispute. Whether the parties come from the same *ezi na ụnọ* or different *ezi na ụnọ*s, an issue may not be successfully managed at the *ezi na ụnọ* level, in which case it may be taken to the next level (the *ụmụnna*). However, a party may bypass the *ezi na ụnọ* level and take his or her case to the *ụmụnna* level. The more serious a case is, the more likely that the *ezi na ụnọ* will be bypassed. Also, where a case is criminal in nature, it is likely to go beyond the *ezi na ụnọ* level.

Ụmụnna, or Extended Family Level

A person who wants a civil case to be settled at this level must bring the case to the attention of the *ụmụnna* members by means of *ịtụnye mmanya* (filing a suit). The requirements for *ịtụnye mmanya* vary somewhat from one *ụmụnna* to another. But the basic requirements are that the person bringing the suit must make small gifts to the *ụmụnna*. The gifts are usually one or two gallons of palm wine and some Igbo kola nuts (Case Number 16, Record of Proceedings, vol. 2, at p. 55, 1992, particularly at p. 60). Some *ụmụnna*s require the person sued to respond to the suit by bringing similar items. If the conduct at issue is a crime, the complainant is not required to present any gifts to the *ụmụnna*.[3] The complainant simply brings the crime to the attention of the *ụmụnna* leaders. Once this is done, the *ụmụnna* takes over from there and acts as prosecutor in the case. In Case Number 24 (Record of Proceedings, vol. 3, at p. 66, 1994, a case of incest), the alleged crime is reported to the leaders of the victim's *ụmụnna*. The leaders prosecute the accused person at both the *ụmụnna* and *obodo* levels.

The judicial proceedings at the *ụmụnna* level are independent of official controls. The proceedings are usually part of the regular (monthly) meetings of the *ụmụnna* members. Like the proceedings at the *ezi na ụnọ* level, the proceedings at the *ụmụnna* level are geared toward amicable settlement. However, depending on the subject matter of a case, the proceedings may be confrontational. To illustrate, the natures of the proceedings on each of the following subject matters differ. First, where the issue is a civil assault, or stealing (a crime), the proceedings focus more on reconciling the disputants. Where possible, the proceedings in the case of stealing concentrate on returning the stolen property. There is not much confrontation between the disputants. Cross-examination may not be necessary at the proceedings. Second, where the issue is land ownership, the proceedings are aimed at determining the true owner of the disputed property (Case Number 3, Record of Proceedings, vol. 1, at p. 43, 1988). Thus, on a land issue, and in all cases on property, the level of proof tends to be higher than that on other issues. At the proceedings in a property-related case, the *ụmụnna* members (through their leaders) invite the disputants to state their cases. The opponent is given the opportunity for cross-examination. The *ụmụnna* gives opportunities to persons other than the disputants or the accused person, who are present at the proceedings, to address the *ụmụnna* on the issues or to ask relevant questions. The *ụmụnna*'s decision and some aspects of the proceedings are usually included in the "minutes book," used to record the *ụmụnna* proceedings. A disputant or accused person, who is not satisfied with the decision of the *ụmụnna* or who wishes to bypass this avenue, may take the case to the *ọnụma*, or village level.

Ọnụma, or Village Level

The *ọnụma* is a collection of *ụmụnna*s. Each of the four *ọnụma*s that make up Ajallị Town consists of about four *ụmụnna*s. There is no standing leadership at the *ọnụma* level. The different *ụmụnna*s cooperate as necessary to deal with the issues that affect their common interest. However, in each *ọnụma*, or village, there are some persons who are popular among the locals and are highly respected. Such people tend to be the village leaders. A party may take a case to such a person or persons. Alternatively, a party may invite the entire village to intervene and settle an issue as in Case Number 33 (Suit No. CCA/5/90, Decided in February 1990, in which the defendant allegedly cut and sold the plaintiff's economic tree). A disputant invokes the jurisdiction of the *ọnụma* level by presenting, at least, Igbo kola nuts to the villagers (Case Number 33, at p. 2 of the Case Report). Inviting the entire village to hear and determine a case is common where the issue is a crime. As obtains at the *ụmụnna* level, a person who wishes to report a crime to the village leaders does not need to present them with any gifts. Once the report is made to the village leaders, they take over the case on behalf of all the villagers.

The proceedings at the *ọnụma* level are similar to the ones at the *ụmụnna* level. The important distinction is that more people participate as witnesses, observers, judges, and other court personnel in the proceedings at the *ọnụma* level. Even persons who are not directly involved in a pending case may address the villagers or ask questions of the parties. A party who disagrees with the decision of the villagers may take the case further to the *obodo*, or town, level. As an alternative, the case may be taken to the town level without first going through any of the preceding three levels (*ezi na ụnọ*, *ụmụnna*, or *ọnụma*).

Obodo, or Town Level

The most prominent avenue for case management at the Ajallị Town level is the *Eze*-in-Council. The council meets regularly once every month. But, whenever necessary, it meets *ad hoc* on an emergency basis. A person who wishes the council to settle a civil dispute must initiate the proceedings by means of *ịtụnye mmanya* (filing a suit). The *ịtụnye mmanya* procedure at the town level requires each disputant to present specific gifts[4] to the council members. In July 1987, the council deliberated on the conditions for *ịtụnye mmanya* and decided as follows (Record of Proceedings, vol. 1, at p. 22, 1987):

> *Ịtụnye mmanya* cases according to Ajalli custom. It was decided (i) it [is] the responsibility of *Eze*'s Cabinet to hear such cases; (ii) both parties each should present [10 Naira], 2 gallons of palm wine and 4 kola nuts (*Ọjị* Igbo); (iii) the party that loses, loses the money [10 Naira] and the other party that succeeds regains his [10 Naira]; the money thus gained from the loss of one of the parties goes to the Cabinet treasury to run its affairs.[5]

In February 1993, the requirements for *ịtụnye mmanya* were slightly amended by increasing the amount of money to be paid by each disputant from ten naira to twenty naira (Record of Proceedings, vol. 2, at p. 92, 1993). The amount of money has further been increased to fifty naira (Case Number 27, Record of Proceedings, vol. 3, at p. 88, 1995). The inflationary trend in Nigeria has apparently necessitated yet another increase of the amount of money to 100 naira. Thus, in line with the inflationary trend in Nigeria, the amount of money required for *ịtụnye mmanya* is frequently reviewed, mostly upward. The council's stipulations and the amendments thereto are examples of some modern-day attempts, however localized, to codify some of the Igbo customary laws and traditions. The council's stipulations of the items required to invoke the judicial processes means that a prospective party before the council must meet these procedural requirements. Additional examples of local attempts at codification are attached as Appendices C and D.

In addition to presenting the items to the *Eze*-in-Council, the first disputant has to complete and sign the form attached hereto as Appendix B. When the first disputant has completed the form, the council sends a message to the prospective second disputant to respond to the *ịtụnye mmanya*. The message to the prospective second disputant is sent mostly by word of mouth through a council member, as is the procedure in Case Numbers 3, 10, and 14. In Case Number 14, the *Eze* Ajallị, who heads the council, acts as the messenger. Sometimes, the council may write to the prospective second disputant asking him or her to respond to the *ịtụnye mmanya* as illustrated by Case Number 16. Responding to the *ịtụnye mmanya* entails presenting to the council items similar to those presented by the first disputant. Whether it is the first or second disputant that is presenting the items, the council members insist that he or she presents "good palm wine" (Case Number 23, Record of Proceedings, vol. 3, at p. 44, 1994, particularly at p. 52). If the palm wine is not "good," the council will reject it and direct the party in default to replace it at the next meeting (Record of Proceedings, vol. 2, at p. 99).

The complainant simply reporting an alleged crime to any of the council members or a community leader initiates a criminal case before the *Eze*-in-Council. The complainant does not incur any financial or material cost in this process. The complainant may also be the victim. Once the report is made, the case becomes the community's concern. The community leaders see to it that the alleged offender is brought to trial. The complainant and others with relevant information may be called upon to testify at the proceedings. In Case Number 20 (1994), a masquerade and its accomplice have allegedly assaulted the complainant, who reports the matter to the town's leaders. He later testifies at the proceedings before the *Eze*-in-Council.

The proceedings in a civil case are usually more prolonged than those in a criminal case. In civil proceedings, the *Eze*-in-Council makes sure that the disputant who gets their judgment is the one who should have it. Such disputes often involve proprietary rights. In Case Number 19 (1993), the issue is the rightful owner of a disputed piece of land. The council hears evidence from the disputants. It also reads the reports prepared by a previous arbitration panel. The council then reaches a decision based on the evidence and the reports. The proceedings in all the property-oriented case studies are adversarial. Each disputant has the opportunity to present his or her case personally and through witnesses. Neither the disputants nor the witnesses are sworn. However, it is unlikely that a person would knowingly lie to the council. That would amount to lying to the ancestors and the entire community. A person who lies in such circumstances is believed to risk serious repercussions from the supernatural forces. In Case Number 13 (1991), the accused person refused to talk rather than lie to the council.

After presenting a case, a disputant may be cross-examined by the opposing party. The council members also ask some questions of the disputants to clarify the issues. In a land or land-related dispute, the council members often go to the location of the property and inspect it, as in Case Numbers 2 (1988), 3 (1988), 14 (1991), and 19 (1993). However, the council will only carry out a land inspection if each disputant presents certain additional items to the council. In Case Number 19 (Record of Proceedings, vol. 2, at p. 127, 1993, particularly at p. 131), the council spells out the requirements for property inspection as follows: "(a) *aka na ụtakụ* ['decent meal'], (b) N50.00 [Fifty Naira] land inspection fee, (c) kola nuts, (d) palm wine." The council expects the disputing parties to present the items before the inspection is carried out. But, sometimes, the council makes exceptions and carries out the inspection before the items are presented. When the council visits a property location, it may make a sketch of the inspected property. In Case Number 14 (Record of Proceedings, vol. 2, at p. 19, 1991), where the issues are the ownership of an economic tree and the destruction of property, the council visits the property involved in the dispute and prepares a detailed sketch, which it uses in deciding the case.

Where the issue in a case involves a less serious crime, for example, assault, the proceedings are less time consuming. In many instances, there is a witness to the crime. In Case Number 4, for example, seven young men, who commit various acts of assault, battery, and street fighting, and disobey *iwu mmanwụ* (masquerading rules), are processed together. The trial is summary because there are witnesses to the crimes. The trial is non-adversarial and non-confrontational. However, when there is no witness to the alleged crime, the proceedings are adversarial. Also, the more serious a crime, the more adversarial and confrontational the proceedings will become. The proceedings in Case Number 24 are adversarial and confrontational because the issue (incest) is one of the most serious crimes among the Igbos.

In both civil and criminal proceedings, persons present at the proceedings, such as the *Eze*-in-Council members, witnesses, and observers, may ask questions of the parties. When the council members have heard all the evidence offered in a case before them, they might deliberate on the case in the absence of the parties (*ịchị izu*). In Case Number 15 (1992, a land case), the council, after hearing from the disputants, asks them to leave the hearing room for the council members to deliberate on the issues before giving a decision. In particular, the council deliberates on a case away from the parties if the issue is highly sensitive. Examples of highly sensitive issues are found in Case Number 14, where someone seems to question the council's impartiality, and Case Number 24, where the accused person is alleged to have had an incestuous relationship with his young daughter.

The *Eze*-in-Council's judgment, as well as other aspects of the proceedings in a case, is reduced to writing. Typically, the council renders its decision in a criminal case at the same meeting where the accused is tried. In a complex civil case, it may take six months (six monthly meetings) for the council to render its decision.[6] A party to a case on which the council renders a decision may obtain a copy of the judgment with the payment of twenty naira to the council and paying the cost of typing the judgment. In Case Number 7 (Record of Proceedings, vol. 1, at p. 85, 1989), the issue is the breach of a business-financing contract. The first disputant claims the sum of 125,000 naira from the second disputant. After giving its decision for the first disputant, the council allows him to obtain a copy of the judgment (at p. 130).

In Ajallị, the *obodo*, or Town, level is the last avenue for non-governmental, unofficial case management. A disputant who rejects a decision at the *obodo* level may take the case to the next level (Customary Court), which is an official avenue. From the level of the Customary Court to the Supreme Court, the courts entertain only civil and criminal cases recognized by the official laws. Under the official laws of Nigeria, a person cannot be prosecuted or convicted of any crime in an official court unless the law creating the crime is written, and the elements of the crime and the punishment therefor are outlined in writing (*Section 36 (12), 1999 Constitution*). Thus, the customary law crimes that can be enforced in the official courts are only those that are also recognized by, and defined in, the official laws.

Further Discussion of Case Management Avenues in Figure 5.1

The following are the official and unofficial tiers of administration for the Igbo (from the most to the least powerful): Government of Nigeria, State Government, Local Government, *Obodo* (Town), *Ọnụma* (Village), *Ụmụnna* (Extended Family or Kindred), *Ezi na Ụnọ* (Family). The *ezi na ụnọ*, *ụmụnna*, *ọnụma*, and *obodo* are unofficial administrative levels, while the remaining three are official. Regarding case management, a case may be managed at the *ezi na ụnọ* level by the head or other key member of the *ezi na ụnọ*. Beyond the *ezi na ụnọ*, the *ụmụnna* is a prominent case management level in Igbo. In Ajallị, a chairman leads the *ụmụnna*. The *ụmụnna* chairman is elected for two years. All the taxable adult male members of the *ụmụnna* present at a scheduled general meeting elect him. After two possible tenures of two years each, he may not be elected to the same position. He may serve in another capacity.

As stated, in Ajallị there is some variation between *ụmụnna*s on the requirements for initiating and conducting a case before the *ụmụnna* and other judicial levels. However, the requirements and procedures are very similar. Including the most recent amendments, the *ịtụnye mmanya* (filing a suit) requirements and procedures in the town are as follows. The first disputant presents two gallons of palm wine and four Igbo kola nuts and deposits 100 naira cash with the *ụmụnna*. Note that the previous amount (50 naira, Case Number 27, Record of Proceedings, vol. 3, at p. 88, 1995) has been increased. The second disputant deposits 100 naira as well. The parties are invited for hearing on a day, time, and place certain. The plaintiff and defendant present their cases in turn. A party may invite witnesses to testify on his or her behalf. Each party or witness is questioned by the other side and by the *ụmụnna* members present. After the testimonies, questions, and the parties conclude their cases, there is the *ịchị izu* (the *ụmụnna* meets in a closed-door session minus the disputants; the parties are excluded from the hearing room). Every *ụmụnna* member present is allowed to express a view on the case, taking into account the parties' cases. The parties are invited back into the hearing room. The *ụmụnna* chairman summarizes the members' views and delivers the verdict. The verdict may be a fine or advice to the guilty party to apologize and beg for forgiveness, or the parties are advised to overlook the issues and interact with each other peacefully. Penalty may be imposed on the party determined to be at fault who, additionally, loses the N100:00 deposit. The other party is refunded his N100:00 deposit. An unsatisfied party may "appeal" to the *ọnụma*, or village council, and from there to the *obodo*. Before or instead of involving the *ụmụnna* in the management of a case, a disputant may select a group of persons conversant with the issue(s) to help settle the case even if they do not belong to the same *ụmụnna* as the parties. Even after the *ụmụnna* delivers its verdict, a dissatisfied party may select a group he or she likes to help resolve the case without involving the *ọnụma* or the *obodo*.

The *ọnụma*, or village council, comprises selected members of all the *ụmụnna*s that make up each village. The hearing and adjudication take the same form, and the requirements are the same as those at the *ụmụnna* level. Unsatisfied party may appeal to the *obodo*. In appealing to the *obodo*, different organs are involved depending on the issue at stake. If the issue involves a tradition or custom, an appeal goes to the *Eze*-in-Council. If the issue is on any other matter, an appeal goes to the Ajallị Wefare Union (AWU). If the issue is both political and traditional, an appeal goes to a joint *Eze*-in-Council and AWU.

The requirements for lodging an appeal with the *Eze*-in-Council, AWU, or a joint session of the two bodies are as follows. For an appeal to the *Eze*-in-Council, the appellant is required to present two gallons of palm wine and four Igbo kola nuts to the council. For an appeal to the AWU or to the joint *Eze*-in-Council and AWU, there is no charge. The appellant may, however, voluntarily give something to the AWU. In each appeal, the appellant needs to submit to the body to which the appeal is lodged a write-up of the case appealed. There is no definite form of the expected write-up. However, its basic contents are the identification of the issue(s) involved in the case, the verdict appealed, and a statement of how the verdict was reached. The procedures for the hearing and determination of an appeal (presentation of case-in-chief, questioning of witnesses, and reaching a verdict inclusive) are similar to those followed at the *ụmụnna* level. In what may be regarded as a continuation of the judicial process, a dissatisfied party may *appeal* further to the Customary Court, which is an official judicial tribunal.

Both civil and criminal cases may be managed outside the official court process if the parties agree. In a pending case, two medical doctors (male, about forty-five years old, and female, about thirty-three years old, members of one village) were killed by a motor vehicle in circumstances that support official homicide charges against the driver. The victims' relatives state that they do not want the police and the official justice processes to be involved in the management of the case. Instead, the relatives demand the sum of 100,000 naira compensation as settlement for each victim. The offender's relatives offer to pay 70,000 naira for each victim. The negotiations continue. The victims' relatives are reluctant to involve the official police and other official case management agencies in the matter because the relatives believe that they would spend much money, time, and other resources in prosecuting the offender, and yet they (the victims' relatives) would not gain anything. If the offender were imprisoned, the victims' relatives would not gain anything. If he were fined, the fine would be paid to the official court, not to the victims' relatives.

At each of the unofficial levels of case management, where a fine is imposed, the focus is not so much on the sum of the fine as it is on peace making. Such fine is a way of encouraging the party at fault to comply next time for the peaceful coexistence of the community members. A small amount of money may suffice for the purpose of encouraging the guilty or responsible party to comply. Thus, fine is imposed on a guilty or responsible party according to his or her ability to pay. A fine is not imposed on a party if the fine will be too much for him or her to pay or too burdensome to bear. This judicial attitude is consistent with the essence of native Igbo case management, which is to build and maintain peace among the community members. The objective is not to punish; it is not to repay an aggrieved party monetarily. The objective is peace making.

A disputant has the option to cut off the four preceding unofficial levels for case management (*ezi na ụnọ*, *ụmụnna*, *ọnụma*, and *obodo*) and take a case directly to an official court. The official court may be the Customary Court, the Magistrate Court, or the High Court, depending on the issue.[7] The processes in the official courts are examined next.

Customary Court

A disputant who disagrees with a decision of an *ọnụma* tribunal, for example, and moves a case from the *ọnụma* level to the *obodo* level may be said to have appealed the decision. But a disputant who takes a case beyond the decision at the *obodo* level to the Customary Court, Magistrate Court, or High Court has not appealed the town's decision in the official justice sense. The tribunal at the *obodo* level is not *formally* recognized as a part of the official judicial hierarchy in Nigeria. However, where a case is moved from the *obodo* level to the Customary Court, for example, there is some unofficial, *informal* continuity in the judicial process. Customary Court judges have no formal legal education.[8] However, they are presumed to have a very sound understanding of the customary laws and traditions that apply to their areas of jurisdiction. The judges are elderly community members. Until recently, they were almost exclusively the traditional rulers of their communities. Now, the state appoints nontraditional rulers as Customary Court judges. It seems reasonable to expect that when Customary Court judges preside over a case in which a traditional ruler or a respected community member has given a judgment at the *obodo* level, the judges are likely to give serious consideration to the previous decision even though they are not required to do so. This is very likely in view of the fact that the area of jurisdiction of each Customary Court is relatively small. Therefore, the judges of each Customary Court may have personal knowledge of the traditional rulers and other key members of the constituent communities in the court's geographic jurisdiction.

The *Anambra State Customary Courts Law, 1984* establishes the present Customary Court system in the state. The Law stipulates the court's geographic jurisdiction. The Ajallị Customary Court used to be the Ajallị Native Court during the British colonial rule of Nigeria. The Ajallị Native Court's geographic jurisdiction extended to as far away as Inyi, Achị, Ọrọ, and Ụmụnze in the present Anambra State. The court's jurisdiction was probably the largest in colonial Igbo. Its contemporary geographic jurisdiction covers all the towns in Orumba North Local Government Area of Anambra State, namely: Ajallị, Amaetiti, Amaọkpala, Awa, Nanka, Ndịkeliọnwu, Ndịokoro, Ndịowuu, Ndịọkpalaeke, Ndịọkpalaeze, Ndịukwuenu, Oko, Okpeze, Ọgbụ, Ọmọghọ, and Ufuma. By law, a Customary Court may try a case from outside its jurisdiction if the case is transferred from that other jurisdiction. Transfer may be applied for even during the course of the trial.

The proceedings in the Customary Court are by far more flexible than those in the other official courts. For example, the rules of evidence, which apply to the other official courts, do not govern proceedings in the Customary Court. Instead, the Customary Court is enjoined to do substantial justice in the cases brought before it. However, when a case is filed in the Customary Court, the court must first decide whether to enter summary judgment or invite the party bringing the case to call evidence to prove the case (see examples, *Rules 23-25 of the Customary Court Rules of Anambra State*). Thus, a party to a case before the Customary Court has to meet a standard of proof necessary to present the evidence in support of his or her case as well as establish a customary law or tradition on which the case is based. There are two alternative ways to establish an Igbo customary law or tradition before a court. The first way is to lead evidence to prove the tradition, custom, or native law. The second (alternative) way is for the official court to accept, by judicial notice, the tradition, custom, or native law as proved if, for example, it has been held by the Supreme Court to have the force of law [see *Section 73 (1) of the Evidence Act*; *Nzekwu and Others v. Nzekwu and Others*, 1989 (Case Number 36); *Ezeanya and Others v. Okeke and Others*, 1995 (Case Number 41)].

In proceedings before the Customary Court, the court gives the parties reasonable opportunities to present their cases personally and through witnesses. In a criminal case, the evidence of a minor is inadmissible. In Case Number 32 (Charge No. CCA/53C/89, October 1989, case of contempt of the Customary Court), the prosecutor seeks to prove the contempt charge with the evidence of a minor. The court rejects the evidence. The opposing side in a case may cross-examine the other party. The records refer to the questions asked in this context as "cross-examination" (Case Number 33, Suit No. CCA/5/90, Decided in February 1990, case of dispute over an economic tree allegedly cut and sold by the defendant). The judges almost always ask questions of the parties and their witnesses in efforts to better appreciate the issues in a case. In Case Number 31 (1988, a case of trespass and destruction of property on land), the subheading to the court's questions reads "Crossexamination by the Court" (at p. 18 of the Case Report). The same procedure is followed whether a case is civil or criminal, for examples, Case Number 30, 1987, civil case; Case Number 33, 1990, civil case; and Case Number 32, 1989, criminal case.

The parties to a case before the Customary Court usually conduct their case by themselves, that is, without the assistance of attorneys. Although the amended *Constitution of Nigeria, 1979, Section 33 (6)*, as well as the *Constitution of Nigeria, 1999*, allows every person accused of a crime in Nigeria to legal representation, it is impractical to have an attorney appear and argue legal issues before Customary Court judges who are not lawyers. Thus, a lawyer may not conduct a case before the Customary Court except if he or she is a party to the case, in which instance the lawyer conducts the case strictly as *party* not *attorney*. A Customary Court judge interviewed for this book informed the author that there is a case pending before his court to which a lawyer is a party. The lawyer is free to conduct his case personally.

In the year 2000, the Anambra State legislature passed legislation requiring the inclusion of at least one lawyer as a judge of each Customary Court jurisdiction in the state. Non-lawyers, especially, opposed the legislation. The opposition to it is predicated on the belief that the legislation would, by means of the proposed Customary Court lawyer-members, transfer English native laws and customs to Igbo. Many lawyers lobbied hard for the legislation because of their exclusion from lucrative law practice at the Customary Court level where most land cases are tried. The interviewed Customary Court judge opines that lawyers should not be involved at the first stage of official trials (Customary Court Level) to ensure that cases are decided according to the Igbo traditions, customs, and native laws. He expresses the view that to do otherwise would be to legislate against custom. He warns: "If you legislate against a custom, you fail" (Obu, interview, July 2000).

A Customary Court judge in Anambra State is appointed for a three-year period. The State Judicial Service Committee (SJSC) chaired by the state chief judge makes the appointment. A judge may be reappointed for a second and final term. Originally, Customary Court judges were traditional rulers. But the SJSC no longer appoints traditional rulers to the Customary Courts. A Customary Court may, however, *suo motu* invite a traditional ruler to testify in a case before the court. As a full court, the Customary Court is made up of three judges, including the president. Any two of the three is a quorum. If, at any time, the president's office is vacant, the two judges may hear and determine cases pending the appointment of a president.

The Customary Court applies the traditions, customs, and native laws of the relevant communities but not necessarily in accordance with the official laws. The court sometimes applies the laws of the applicable local government and the laws of the relevant state. Further, the court applies laws such as those unofficially made and sometimes written by a community within the court's jurisdiction if the unofficial laws are established by evidence as the traditions, customs, or native laws of the relevant community. Thus, the court will apply the provisions of Appendices C and D if they are established as parts of the Ajallị traditions, customs, and laws.

The Customary Court handles both civil and "quasi-criminal" cases (Obu, interview, July 2000). Quasi-crimes include contempt of the court for which it has powers to punish and violations of local government by-laws. Some of the civil issues that the court hears and determines concern land, some others deal with administration of estates situated in rural areas for persons who die intestate. Regarding land cases, the Supreme Court expresses two apparently contradictory positions. The Court has indicated that all legal actions over lands in rural areas should start in the Customary Court. According to the Supreme Court, it is unreasonable for a High Court judge, for instance, who is far removed from the property at issue to place restrictive injunction on the property when the judge is not close enough to the property to ascertain all the facts. However, the Supreme Court later expressed a different position as follows: Since the High Court is a court of unlimited jurisdiction, a case over land in a High Court jurisdiction may be tried before the High Court instead of the Customary Court. A clearer guidance is necessary.

In Anambra State, the Customary Court does not handle a case in which the claim is worth more than 2,000 naira. However, the court allows the parties to determine the value of a disputed property. In one case, a party claims that land covering the equivalent of Ụmụabịama and Ụmụeve (two of Ajallị's four villages) is worth ten naira and the court accepts jurisdiction even though the judges are familiar with the land and can ascertain its correct monetary value if they wish to do so. Thus, for the purposes of determining jurisdiction, the Customary Court would accept whatever value the parties place on a disputed property.

The Customary Court is an official tribunal. Official laws regulate its proceedings. However, these laws do not apply strictly to the court (Case Number 38, in which the appellate court warns against expecting the rules to apply strictly to the Customary Court). The language of proceedings in the court is Igbo or English, depending on each party's preference. If either party does not speak or understand the English language, Igbo is used, in which case the proceedings are translated into English for recording. As much as possible, all proceedings are recorded in the English language. The court's proceedings (including its decision) are recorded in writing. Decisions are reached on the basis of the evidence and witnesses that the parties present. A decision may be unanimous or by a majority of the judges. The Customary Court adheres to the repugnancy test in that the judges try to ensure that their judgments follow the spirit of some of the official laws without formally citing those official laws. For example, if a custom threatens a party's fundamental human right, the court will not apply the custom. The Nigeria Police Force (NPF) enforces the court's judgments in criminal cases as well as orders stemming from civil proceedings in the same way that the NPF enforces the judgments of the country's other official courts. The losing party in a civil case has up to thirty days to appeal a verdict. After the thirty days, he or she must obtain leave to appeal. Such party may also apply for stay of execution of judgment. The Customary Court or a higher court may allow such application for stay. A party who is not satisfied with the decision of the court may take the case to the Magistrate Court or the High Court, as the case may be, since the Customary Court of Appeal has not been constituted in Anambra State.

Magistrate Court

The official Magistrate Court tries minor crimes and limited amount civil claims. It is also a court of initial appearance for serious crimes, such as murder. Thus, an accused person may be arraigned before the Magistrate Court even if the alleged crime is so serious that the court has no jurisdiction to try the case. In the circumstance, the court's responsibility is to take the accused person's plea and decide whether or not to grant bail. Because of its limited jurisdiction, the Magistrate Court does not try serious crimes such as murder and armed robbery. As noted, the court may however hold a preliminary hearing pending trial in the High Court.

The High Court hears appeals from the Customary Court and the Magistrate Court. In Anambra State, a Notice of Appeal from the Customary Court to the High Court must be filed within thirty days. There are procedural differences between the High Court's exercises of its original and appellate jurisdictions. Thus, the court's procedures are presented in two parts: High Court as a trial court, and High Court as an appellate court.

High Court as a Trial Court

In its original and appellate jurisdictions in cases based on the Igbo customary law, the High Court is enjoined to do substantial justice between the parties [*Section 20 of the Customary Court Edict, 1984 (CCE)*]. In Case Number 38 (*Ome and 14 Others v. Ugeze*, Suit No. AB/CC/3A/92, Decided in May 1993), the appeal before the High Court is on a land ownership case previously tried in the Customary Court. The High Court refers to *section 20 of the CCE* and holds that the High Court's duty is "to do substantial justice between the parties" (at p. 5 of the Case Report). This means that, like the Customary Court, the High Court should be flexible in cases based on customary laws and traditions. To achieve this, the court should exercise discretion in the circumstances of each case. However, the proceedings in such cases before the High Court are more formalized than the proceedings before the Customary Court. A party to a customary law case before the High Court is expected to comply with the High Court rules, which govern proceedings in the court. Also, lawyers are almost always involved in customary law proceedings in the High Court.[9] The involvement of lawyers in these proceedings usually makes the proceedings more confrontational and more adversarial.

As in the proceedings before the Customary Court, a party wishing to establish a customary law or tradition in the High Court has to provide evidence to prove it. An exception is made when the Supreme Court has decided that the particular customary law or tradition has the force of law (*Nzekwu and Others v. Nzekwu and Others*, 1989 2 NWLR 373). Partics to a case before the High Court present their cases personally or through their attorneys. The court affords the adverse party a reasonable opportunity to cross-examine the opponent. The court issues written judgment, which the judge usually reads to the parties. A party may obtain a copy of the judgment on the payment of a reasonable fee. A party who disagrees with a High Court judgment may appeal to the Court of Appeal.

High Court as an Appellate Court, the Court of Appeal, and the Supreme Court

The High Court as an appellate court, the Court of Appeal, and the Supreme Court are examined together in this section because their duties regarding cases based on the Igbo customary laws and traditions are identical. None of the three courts tries an appealed case afresh. Instead, each court evaluates the trial done in the lower court. If a case is tried in the Customary Court and later appealed to the High Court, the Court of Appeal, or the Supreme Court, the appellate court focuses on ensuring that the Customary Court has acted fairly.

The appellate court is enjoined to focus more on the substance of a trial in the Customary Court than on its form. Thus, the appellate court will not reverse a Customary Court decision simply because the Customary Court has not followed the official rules of evidence and procedure [*Ezeanya and Others v. Okeke and Others*, 1995 (Case Number 41)]. Such a decision may be reversed only if there has been a substantial miscarriage of justice. According to the Supreme Court:

> The courts hearing appeals from Customary or Area Courts or District Courts, whatever the designation of these courts presided over by laymen, should be wary to apply the strict technicalities of procedure or *Evidence Act* in reviewing those appeals if such application will destroy the substance and merits of the matters heard in those inferior courts (*Afonja v. Aiyelagbe*, FSC 317/61; see also *Osu v. Igiri*, 1988).[10]

In Case Number 38 (*Ome and 14 Others v. Ugeze*, Suit No. AB/CC/3A/92, Decided in May 1993), the High Court hearing an appeal from a Customary Court decision applies the Supreme Court's injunction when the High Court holds as follows (at p. 4 of the Case Report):

> To expect that a customary court composed entirely of laymen presiding over a dispute instituted by the natives not knowledgeable in the art of drafting claims should in the circumstances as the instant matter concern itself with the subtle matter as it were as the legal distinction between suing the defendants jointly as against suing them jointly and

severally and because of that to urge on this court as an appellate Court to rely on the failure to appreciate the distinction and the effects thereof to disturb the judgment of the trial court otherwise correct is to misconceive the purpose or aim which the setting up of such [customary] courts was intended to serve.

Thus, in determining appeals in customary law cases, the High Court, the Court of Appeal, and the Supreme Court will not interfere with the lower court's decision unless the lower court has made a substantial error (Case Numbers 38 and 41).

Unofficial, Non-Governmental Case Management Avenues

The data show that the position holders in the administration of justice at the first four levels of case management (see figure 5.1) are mostly community leaders. An aggrieved person is at liberty to complain to any of the four lower, unofficial case management avenues. There are no strict rules requiring that a particular level must manage a case before it could be appealed to another. However, the opportunities for appeals exist. Thus, a decision of the *ezi na ụnọ* may be appealed to the *ụmụnna*. It may be appealed further to the *ọnụma*, to the *obodo*, and beyond. In the Ajallị Town example, the community recognizes a multiplicity of avenues for case management. However, the *Eze*-in-Council and the AWU are the unofficial, non-governmental courts of last resort.

Official, Governmental Case Management Avenues

Beyond the *obodo* level, case management is in the hands of the official governments and their agencies (Customary Court, Magistrate Court, High Court, Court of Appeal, and Supreme Court).[11] The official Nigerian justice system is made up of two jurisdictional entities: the federation and the states. At the federal level, the justice system is based on the Nigerian constitution, other statutes (including military decrees, edicts), case law, and elements of the English common law. The laws are enforced in cases involving the government of Nigeria. A case between the federal government and an individual or group is brought initially at the Federal High Court. An appeal from the Federal High Court is taken to the Court of Appeal. A further appeal goes to the Supreme Court. However, a suit involving an important constitutional question or a case between governments may be instituted directly at the Supreme Court. Therefore, except for those few cases in which the Supreme Court may serve as a court of original jurisdiction, it is an appellate court.

The Magistrate Court or the High Court of a state officially manages cases that arise in the state on the basis of a statute or the common law. Whether it is managed in the Magistrate Court or the state High Court depends on the value of the civil claim or the seriousness of the criminal charge. The Magistrate Court hears and determines matters that involve relatively small claims and less serious criminal charges. The High Court has much wider jurisdiction than the Magistrate Court. The High Court is, in fact, known as a court of general jurisdiction. Thus, it is empowered to hear and determine any case brought before it, except where the issue involved has been specifically reserved for a specialized court or tribunal. A case tried in the Magistrate Court may be appealed to the state High Court. A further appeal may be taken to the Court of Appeal. Finally, a dissatisfied party may appeal to the Supreme Court. If a case is tried in the High Court, it may go on appeal through the Court of Appeal to the Supreme Court. Although the Court of Appeal and the Supreme Court are federal courts, whenever either court hears and determines a case based on the laws of a state, the court must apply the laws of the relevant state, rather than federal laws.

Although the official laws do not set up unofficial courts, these courts are not prohibited. Thus, if the parties to a case wish to do so, they may manage their case unofficially. However, if the case is of interest to the official government, such as when a serious crime is involved, the government is likely to insist on official management of the case. Such insistence would prevent an unofficial court from hearing and determining the case. No official rules are found in the data on the issue of appeals from unofficial Igbo courts to the official courts. Thus, a case taken from an unofficial tribunal to an official court is tried *de novo*. However, the data show that when an official court action is brought on a case previously managed unofficially, the official court may rely partly on evidence of the earlier effort to deal with the case. This is more common in the Customary Court.

A Supreme Court decision in a state or federal case is the final determination in the case. Although the Supreme Court has been Nigeria's highest official court since October 1, 1963, in practical terms, the Court does not question a decision of any of the country's special military tribunals [see examples, *Okeke v. A-G Anambra State*, 1992 1 NWLR (Part 214) 60, at p. 85, per Uwaifo, JCA; *Abacha and Others v. Fawehinmi*, Appeal No. SC, 45/1997, S.C.N, Judgment on April 28, 2000]. The enabling decrees and edicts specify that a decision of such a tribunal cannot be questioned in any court. The tribunals have been common in post-independence Nigeria, the last batch holding sway through May 29, 1999. In many instances, only the ruling military council could review, approve, or disapprove of the tribunal's verdict. Thus, figure 5.2 realistically represents the hierarchical structure of Nigeria's official courts and tribunals before May 29, 1999. In post-military rule Nigeria, the Supreme Court is the ultimate official court.

RECOMMENDED CHANGES TO JUSTICE PROCESSING IN IGBO

Based on the issues and problems revealed by the data, the following changes to the Igbo justice system are recommended.

Figure 5.2
Hierarchical Structure of the Official Courts and Tribunals in Nigeria – Federal and State Jurisdictions

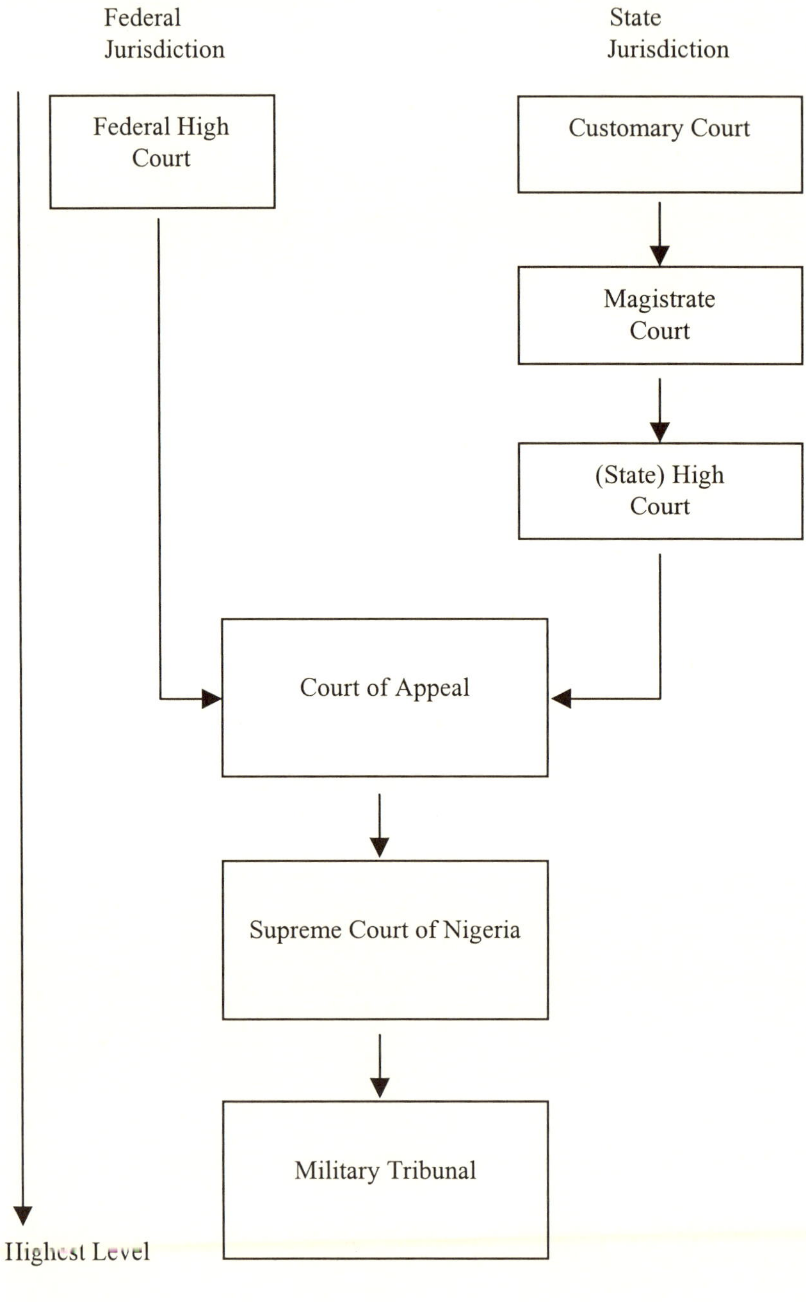

Recommendation 1

Officers of all the case management avenues (see figure 5.1) should accord more recognition to the Igbo customary laws and traditions. The data show that the Igbos widely follow the native methods of case management. What is required is for the official governments and their agencies to recognize this fact. The lopsided official regard in favor of the foreign, English-style justice system further complicates the situation. The data show that the English-style justice system enjoys the primary place in the eyes of the official government despite the fact that the native justice systems manage more cases than the English-style justice system. Moreover, the data show that the native methods are effective and efficient approaches to justice for the locals. The official governments should also encourage these native, traditional methods to increase their effectiveness and efficiency levels. In recognition of the dynamic nature of the Igbo society, outdated Igbo customs and traditions should be revised to conform to the Igbo contemporary ways of life. However, the official courts should not be too eager to discard a custom or tradition without proper evaluation. In *Ezeanya and Others v. Okeke and Others*, 1995 (Case Number 41), the Supreme Court disapproves of the Court of Appeal's action in discarding a custom without first hearing from the parties to the case. The Supreme Court's decision is encouraging to this policy recommendation.

Recommendation 2

The second recommendation addresses this question: How can the unofficial and official agencies and institutions for case management among the Igbos work together for improved social control? Several sociologists of social control have asked similar questions (see Black, 1990; Black, ed., 1984; Garland, 1990, 1991; Henry, 1987a, 1987b; Smandych, 1991a, 1991b, 1991c). The meaningful way to address the divide and conflicts between the native Igbo justice system and the English-style justice system is as follows. The official governments should recognize and encourage the nine identified avenues and processes for justice administration (from the *ezi na ụnọ* to the Supreme Court) (figure 5.1). Recognition for the avenues and processes does not necessarily mean that a process in an unofficial avenue must become an official process. The unofficial case management avenues should remain unofficial. But the government should recognize the unofficial avenues and processes as the crucial links that they are in justice administration. The unofficial avenues are presided over by people who are closest to the individuals in the communities. These unofficial judicial personnel are better placed to understand the traditions, customs, and other laws of their communities. On the other hand, the judges of the official courts are far removed from the communities whose laws and customs the judges are called upon to apply.

There is an alternative to officially recognizing all nine avenues in figure 5.1. Official recognition for only some of the nine avenues and processes, if properly implemented, would produce a more efficient and effective justice system than Nigeria's current dependent system. Thus, the channel in figure 5.3 is recommended as a way of restructuring justice processing in Nigeria to make it more native-oriented.

Figure 5.3 includes all the avenues that the data show to be necessary for case management in a synthesized Nigerian justice system. The recommended channel, if properly implemented, would leave the application of traditions, customs, and laws to the people involved in the day-to-day activities of the communities whose lives are affected. A person who is not satisfied with the *ụmụnna*'s decision would have the option to appeal the case to the *obodo*, Customary Court and possibly beyond. Of course, not all cases would go through all six avenues in figure 5.3. Already, unofficially, subject matter jurisdictions at the *ụmụnna* and *obodo* levels extend to all types of issues. An official recognition of this position would allow the Igbos to continue managing the bulk of their cases at some of the most intimate levels of interaction, while only the cases on specialized issues, for example, interpretation of the Nigerian constitution, are reserved for the higher state and federal courts.

As the data show, the official courts are already involved in the management of all kinds of cases, including those based on customs and traditions (see figure 5.1). What is lacking is coordination between the unofficial and official case management organs. The structure recommended in figure 5.3 is expected to supply the necessary coordination if it is implemented as recommended. For this recommendation to be effective, however, it would be necessary to provide on-the-job training on the traditions, customs, and native laws for the official courts' judicial officers. Unofficially, at the local levels, Nigerians who understand the traditions, customs, and native laws well already manage most cases. However, inevitably, cases will be heard and determined officially by persons who may not be very knowledgeable about the Igbo customary laws. This is more likely to occur in appellate proceedings at the higher official courts. Thus, on-the-job training would help the officials to better understand the rules of the native laws, customs and traditions, and ways of life. All official judges in Nigeria are Nigerians. There is no reason why these judges cannot be trained to understand, interpret, and properly apply Nigeria's customary laws, where appropriate. The language issue is also relevant to any on-the-job training. A curriculum on this should aim at helping official court personnel to better appreciate the local languages, particularly those in the court's jurisdiction. It is impossible to fully appreciate a people's traditions, customs, laws, or ways of life without an equal appreciation for their language (Thiong'o, 1993; 1997; Okereafọezeke, 1998a).

Figure 5.3
Hierarchical Representation of the Avenues Recommended for Case Management

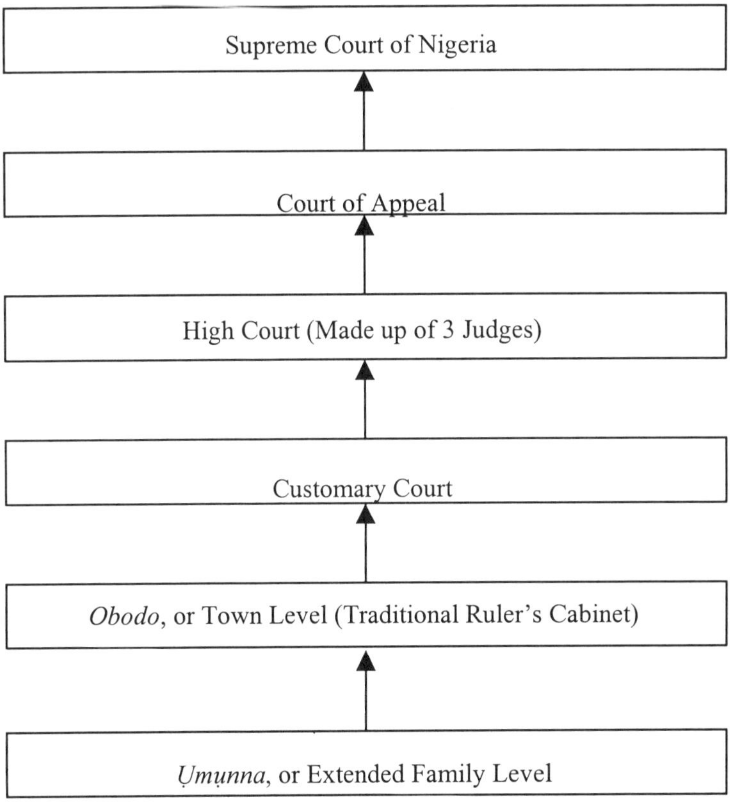

SUMMARY

Justice among the Igbos is plural and hierarchical. It is based partly on the native customs, traditions, and laws and partly on the English laws introduced into Nigeria by the British colonialists. This plurality of justice gives rise to confusion and uncertainty in justice processing. Also, the native Igbo case management organs are subjected to the English-type courts. The following two changes are recommended to redress the situation. First, the official governments and their agencies have to accord more recognition to the Igbo native laws, customs, and traditions. Second, a synthesized justice system is necessary to accommodate the competing native and foreign views of law and justice. The efforts of the official governments, as well as those of the unofficial, customary groups and individuals, would be required to implement these recommendations.

Based on the data, it is expected that implementing the policy recommendations in this chapter would lead to a more coordinated judicial process. It is also expected that implementation of the recommendations would provide the Igbos with a justice system in which the official machinery recognizes the popular practices in the Igbo communities. It would reduce the tendency to impose "customary law" from the top. Instead, the Igbo customary law would develop from popular practices (see Snyder, 1982; Shaidi, 1992). Finally, like the Igbos, non-Igbo communities in Nigeria "face the ambiguity of operating traditional laws under the control of statutory laws" (Iyam, 1995, at p. 162). Therefore, implementation of the recommendations would set the stage for necessary changes to the systems of law and justice in Igbo and the other parts of the country.

NOTES

1. *Mmanwụ* (masquerade) is very important to culture and social control among the Igbos. A masquerade is a masked figure roving the community during certain events. The mask and the manner in which a masquerade is dressed add to the mystery surrounding the culture of masquerading among the Igbos. It is popularly believed that masquerades are the spirits of the dead that have returned to live in other forms among the living. Every person who comes in contact with a masquerade is expected by the community members to respect and defer to the masquerade.

2. Italics added.

3. This is probably in recognition of the entire community's interest in stopping the criminal conduct.

4. These "gifts" are somewhat like the court fees that a plaintiff must pay in an official court. Each of the disputants before the *Eze*-in-Council must make the gifts and pay the required amount of money.

5. Italics added.

6. These time averages do not always hold true. The time lapse varies, depending on the complexity or simplicity of each case.

7. The following main considerations determine the official court that has jurisdiction over a case: In a civil case, the monetary equivalent of the claim is considered. The higher the amount, the more likely it is that the case will be taken directly to the Magistrate Court or even to the High Court. Similarly, in a criminal case, the determining factor is the seriousness of the charge. Most official crimes are tried in the Magistrate Court. However, the more serious crimes arc tried in the High Court.

8. "Formal legal education" means undergoing years of training in law schools, passing the bar examinations, and being licensed to practice law in Nigeria.

9. Lawyer involvement in the High Court proceedings does not produce the awkward situation of a lawyer addressing Customary Court judges who are not attorneys. All the judges in the High Court are experienced attorneys.

10. Italics added.

11. However, unofficial, non-governmental case management avenues beyond the *obodo* exist among some Igbo communities. In such a situation, a group of towns and villages (usually neighbors) form a loose association of autonomous communities,

similar to a confederation, to provide their members with a common avenue for addressing issues among them. Ajallị Town belongs to one such association called *Ndị Eni.*

6

Enforcement of Igbo Judicial Decisions

INTRODUCTION

This chapter is based on a study of the contemporary methods of enforcing judicial decisions in Nigeria's traditional Igbo. In post-colonial Nigeria, the character of Igbo judicial decisions is different in some respects from what it was before the British colonization of Nigeria. Similarly, the techniques and methods for enforcing the decisions have changed in some ways. Some of the differences in character, techniques, and methods are the consequences of the prevailing divide between the native justice systems and the foreign, English-style justice system imposed by the British colonialists. Other differences stem from the societal changes within Nigeria as a result of the passage of time and societal evolution. Thus, with the passage of time, some issues that were not justiceable (subject to the judicial process) in earlier societies, have become justiceable, thereby leading to a new set of judgments to be enforced. Similarly, some issues that were once justiceable are no longer so, with the similar result that the types of judgments to be enforced have changed. The judgments cover crimes and civil wrongs. Also, as in every society, the enforcement of judgment in Nigeria may be official (governmental) or unofficial (non-governmental). The official and unofficial methods of enforcing judgments change with time. This accords with the changing nature of society, generally from simpler to more complex. Prior to colonization, Nigerian societies were relatively simple and close knit. Some remain so (Adeyemi, 1990, July; Anene, 1991), although other Nigerian societies have since colonization become more complex because of the heterogeneous populations presently constituting each society. Thus, there is increased emphasis on officialism in pre- and post-trial law enforcement in Nigeria.

Law enforcement in Nigeria's plural, hierarchical justice systems (Okereafọezeke, 1996; 2000a) may be divided into unofficial and official categories. Unofficial and official agencies and groups play vital roles in law enforcement. The agencies and groups enforce official and unofficial laws. The crucial role of unofficial justice agencies in Nigeria's Igbo is well established (Oli, 1994; Uwazie, 1994; Okereafọezeke, 1996; 2000a). Considering this vital role of unofficialism in Igbo justice, on the particular issue of post-trial law enforcement or enforcement of judicial decisions, it is necessary to understand the dynamics of judicial decision enforcement in contemporary traditional Igbo. The advantage of the study grounding this chapter is that it identifies and examines unofficial, traditional Igbo, post-trial law enforcement techniques used in contemporary Nigeria and how some of the techniques may be borrowed by the official law enforcement agencies or coordinated with the official processes to improve social control in the country.

The following questions guide the research for this chapter: What are the methods and procedures for enforcing judicial decisions in contemporary traditional Igbo? Are judicial decisions in Igbo divided into criminal and civil types? If so, are there differences between the methods and procedures for enforcing judgments on crimes and those for enforcing judgments on civil wrongs? What can be gleaned from the data to offer suggestions on ways to synthesize and improve unofficial and official law enforcement and social control in Nigeria? The last question is based on the theories of several sociologists of social control, including Black (1984; 1990).

ENFORCEMENT OF OFFICIAL COURT JUDGMENTS

Government officials with state authority enforce criminal and civil case judgments by Nigeria's official courts. Thus, state officers enforce the judicial decisions of the Customary Court, the Customary Court of Appeal, the Magistrate Court, the High Court, the Court of Appeal, the Supreme Court, and the other official courts and tribunals. The enforcement procedures are similar to the procedures in other common law countries. The state officers typically enforce these punishments: fines, incarceration, and execution of criminal offenders. There are no provisions for probation or parole in Nigeria. Capital punishment applies in cases of murder, armed robbery, and treason. The state officers typically enforce the following judgments in civil cases: monetary damages awards, prohibitory and mandatory injunctions, and other judicial orders for the successful party.

ENFORCEMENT OF UNOFFICIAL COURT JUDGMENTS – TRADITIONAL IGBO ENFORCEMENT TECHNIQUES

The data reveal that judgment enforcement methods and procedures in unofficial, traditional Igbo vary depending on whether a case is civil or criminal.

Enforcing Judgments in Civil Cases

The data show that Igbo communities rarely take overt steps to enforce judicial decisions in civil cases at the *ezi na ụnọ* (family) level, the *ụmụnna* (extended family) level, the *ọnụma* (village) level, and the *obodo* (town) level. Judgments in civil cases are left to the parties to enforce between themselves. They would do so if they both accept the judgment. The unofficial judicial officials at these levels, however, encourage parties to abide by a decision in their case. In Case Number 19 (1993, a land case heard and determined by the *Eze*-in-Council), the council advises the disputants to cooperate with each other to find a peaceful resolution to the dispute. A disputant may, however, ignore the judgment, although a party that ignores such judgment risks being ostracized because the party would be viewed as having stood against the system.

A disputant who ignores a judicial decision rendered at any of the *ezi na ụnọ*, *ụmụnna*, *ọnụma*, and *obodo* levels may take the case to an official court or refuse the enforcement of the unofficial court decision. Either way, the disputant is viewed as having stood against the unofficial, traditional system. In particular, where a disputant rejects a community judgment and takes the case to an official court, other community members usually react adversely to the disputant. In Case Number 31 (1988, a case of trespass and destruction of property on land), the disputants' relative, who is a witness in the case, expresses disappointment and shame that the disputants have taken their disagreement to the official court rather than have it settled in their family. However, a disputant who disagrees with a judgment at, for example, the *ọnụma* level may take the case to the *obodo* level. Where this is done, the community members view the disputant as exercising an option to complain further on an issue – exercising a right to appeal. Such a disputant would generally not be viewed as having stood against the system, even though the disputant may consequentially enjoy less goodwill among the members of his or her *ọnụma* than among the members of other *ọnụma*s in the town as occurs in Case Number 31 (1988).

The community may react to a member's stand against its traditional system by excluding the defaulting party from the group. In the more serious cases, the exclusion may graduate to ostracism as in Case Number 5 (1989). Also, in Case Number 1 (Record of Proceedings, vol. 1, at p. 24, 1987; on contract to make and sell a new palm oil processing machine), the second disputant does not comply with the terms of the *Eze*-in-Council's judgment. To bring pressure on him to comply, the council resolves as follows: "If [the second disputant] fail[s] to comply, the Cabinet would feel free to support [the first disputant] in whatever legitimate future action he deem[s] fit in pursuance of the case" (at p. 31). "Legitimate future action" should include legal action in an official court. In the event of this, the council members would testify on behalf of the first disputant. If they testified, their testimony would carry a lot of weight in the mind of the official court, particularly if the official court were the Customary Court, whose judges are community leaders. The pressure put on the defaulting party is intended to encourage compliance. The defaulting party has strayed from the community norms and should be brought back in line.

Enforcing Judgments in Criminal Cases

The methods and procedures followed to enforce a judgment on a crime depend on whether the crime is "against public security" or "against public morality." Crimes against public security are the acts and omissions that breach the freedom, property, security, and peaceful co-existence of community members without threatening the moral basis of the community. Crimes against public morality are those that additionally threaten the moral basis of the community. The exact procedure to be followed in enforcing each judgment is determined by the community leaders on a case-by-case basis, but there are common trends in enforcing all judgments in each crime category.

Enforcing Judgments on Crimes against Public Security

Crimes against public security include stealing, assault, battery, public nuisance, *ịda iwu mmanwụ* (violation of the masquerading rules and regulations), street fighting, contempt of a community institution, example *Eze*-in-Council, and destruction of property. Each Igbo community takes overt steps to enforce unofficial judicial decisions in cases dealing with any of these issues. In Ajallị Town, the two main ways of enforcing such decisions are *oriri iwu* (retrieving a fine) (Record of Proceedings, vol. 2, at p. 1) and *ịgba ekpe* (public shaming by humiliating display of convict) (Case Number 12, Record of Proceedings, vol. 2, at p. 4, particularly at p. 6).

Oriri iwu is a common method of enforcing judgments of fines. If an offender has failed to pay a fine, a group of community members is sent to the offender's home. When the group arrives at the home, they give the offender the last opportunity to comply with the terms of the judgment. If the offender fails to do so, the group seizes and removes as much property as they believe would cover the amount of the fine. The particular items of property removed from the offender's home need not belong to the offender personally. The judgment enforcers may legitimately seize and remove any property found in the household where the offender lives, whether or not the property belongs to the offender personally. In the event that the seized property belongs to someone else, the offender must sort it out later with the owner. The offender is given some time, usually a few days, to come to the community leader's home with the fine and recover the seized property. If he or she does not pay the fine, the seized property is sold, and the money realized is used to pay the fine.

In particular, where the offense is a violation of *iwu mmanwụ* (the rules and regulations on masquerading), the judgment is enforced through masquerades. The masquerades, rather than humans, seize the property (Case Number 4, Record of Proceedings, vol. 1, at p. 60, 1988). The masquerades almost always seize goats. A person found guilty of violating *iwu mmanwụ* certainly pays with at least one goat. Depending on the seriousness of the crime, he or she may be fined up to seven goats (Case Number 4, 1988) or more. If masquerades attempt to enforce a judgment but are unable to find goats at the offender's home, they may seize goats from the offender's neighbors. The offender must repay the neighbors for the goats. The goats seized by the masquerades are not returnable. They are killed and shared among the various groups and units in the community. Only men may eat the meat (Case Number 4, 1988, particularly at p. 61).

The data show that *ịgba ekpe* may be applied to any criminal offender, particularly in property crimes such as stealing. The offender is dressed in dirty, torn clothes. He or she is further disguised with palm frond leaves and ashes. The offender is paraded through sections of the community to allow all community members opportunities to witness the offender's humiliation. He or she is treated shamefully, sometimes beaten up in the process. This treatment brings great shame on the offender. At the end of the public display, an offender with the means is likely to leave town for a period of time to get over some of the shame. *Ịgba ekpe* appears to be in less use in Igbo. The data contain only one reference to *ịgba ekpe* (in Case Number 12, Record of Proceedings, vol. 2, at p. 4, 1991). But while growing up in Nigeria, the author witnessed many situations in which criminal offenders were shamed by this means.

Enforcing Judgments on Crimes against Public Morality

Crimes against public morality include incest, *ọchụ* (homicide), and defilement of religious or other important community institutions such as a shrine. Crimes against public morality are more serious than other crimes. Thus, they are known as crimes that pollute the land. They are *arụ*, *alụ*, *nsọ* (taboo, abomination). To expiate evil conduct, the community coerces a person guilty of any of these crimes to offer sacrifices to the land and beg to be forgiven. After the offerings, the offender is expected to leave the community for an extended period of time, probably years. In Case Number 24 (1994), the accused is alleged to have had an incestuous relationship with his daughter aged about twelve years. The community tries and convicts him. In addition to being made to offer specific sacrifices to cleanse the community and *ana* or *ala* (the land), he is forced to leave the town for about seven years.

The data show that some, even if few, criminal offenders resist the judgments imposed on them by refusing to comply with the terms of their punishments. Even for the most serious crimes, an offender is usually given a period of time to comply with the judgment. If the time period expires without the offender's compliance, the community demonstrates the seriousness with which it views the offender's conduct. The offender is usually ostracized (Case Number 24). It is impossible for any community member to survive alone in such a relatively closed community with a fairly common belief (see Adeyemi, 1990, July; Anene, 1991). An offender who defies a community judicial decision and is thus ostracized is not thereby left alone. Few community members who want to prove to the others that the few are the champions of the community's mores may target such an offender. These "vigilante" few may harm the offender to elevate the vigilante group's standing in the community. If the offender is harmed, it is very unlikely that any community member would volunteer information regarding the harm done to the offender, thus leading to the existence of a "conspiracy of silence" among the community members. Even official law enforcement personnel who might enter the community to investigate an official crime would not receive the necessary cooperation of the community members.

FURTHER DISCUSSION

A study of the data gives rise to the following question regarding enforcement of judicial decisions in Nigeria's Igbo: How can unofficial and official enforcement strategies work together to improve social control? The solution is increased coordination and cooperation between the unofficial and official organs, agencies, and strategies (see Black, ed., 1984, 1990; Henry, 1987a; Garland, 1990, 1991; Smandych, 1991a). Thus, the following suggestions are offered to address conflicts between traditional, unofficial, and English-style, official law enforcement and social control strategies in Igbo justice. The official governments should recognize and encourage the nine identified avenues in the administration of justice (from the *ezi na ụnọ* to the Supreme Court) (see figure 5.1). Each of the four traditional case management levels (*ezi na ụnọ*, *ụmụnna*, *ọnụma*, and *obodo*) has its law enforcement methods, including the methods for enforcing judicial decisions as demonstrated by this research. Official recognition of a law enforcement method does not necessarily mean that a traditional, unofficial method must become official. The unofficial processes should remain unofficial. But the official governments, agencies, private groups, and individuals alike should recognize them as the crucial links that they are in justice administration among the Igbos.

People who are closest to the community members preside over and manage the traditional, unofficial case management and law enforcement organs. The members of these organs are thus better positioned to understand the traditions, customs, and laws of their communities, as well as the best ways to enforce judgments on them. On the other hand, the judges of the official courts and the state law enforcement personnel are far removed from the communities whose laws the judges and law enforcement personnel are called upon to enforce. Recognition of this fact would reduce the tendency of Nigerian officials to impose laws and the means of enforcing them from the top (see Snyder, 1982; Shaidi, 1992). Instead, laws and law enforcement practices would be allowed to develop from the communities among individuals whose lives are regulated by the laws. In addition to recognizing the crucial role of traditional methods in justice administration among the Igbos, there is the need for coordination and sharing of ideas and enforcement strategies between unofficial and official law enforcement. These would increase the efficiency levels of the two and lead to improved social control in Nigeria.

SUMMARY

Unofficial law enforcement in Igbo is evolving with the Nigerian society. Colonial and post-colonial changes have necessitated similar changes in native, traditional Igbo law enforcement. With particular regard to post-trial law enforcement or enforcement of judicial decisions, each Igbo community has official (governmental) as well as unofficial (non-governmental) structures for enforcing judgments. The data show that in enforcing judgments in traditional Igbo, a distinction is drawn between civil wrongs and crimes. Crimes are further divided into "crimes against public security" and "crimes against public morality." Judgments on civil wrongs are usually left to the parties to enforce between themselves, although the community or its agency may lend a hand if either party defies the judgment. The entire community, its agency, or a chosen group or individual enforces judgments on crimes. A popular means of enforcing judgments on crimes is *oriri iwu* (retrieving a fine), which may be done by means of masquerades acting on the community's behalf. *Oriri iwu* may, alternatively, be carried out by a group of community members. The community's full authority backs the masquerade or group, as the case may be. A defiance of the masquerade or the group is regarded as a defiance of the entire community. *Oriri iwu*, and *ịgba ekpe* (public shaming by humiliating display of convict) are popular means of enforcing judgments on both crimes against public security and crimes against public morality. However, the community regards crimes against public morality, including *ọchụ* (homicide), incest, and desecration of a religious institution, shrine, or other place of worship, as more serious than crimes against public security. Thus, a person found guilty of incest, for instance, is expected to do more than pay a fine or suffer public shame in atonement. The convict must take further steps to "cleanse" the community of the crime that has polluted it. The cleansing process often includes making offerings to the ancestors and to the land asking for forgiveness. Also, the convict would be required to leave the community for an extended period of time. The period of exile has been as long as seven years for a father's incestuous relationship with his twelve-year-old daughter. The data show that traditional Igbo law enforcement and social control are effective and efficient. What is lacking is a deserved appreciation and recognition of this fact by Nigeria's official justice system (Okereafọezeke, 1996; 2000a). Increased coordination and cooperation between official law enforcement and traditional, unofficial law enforcement that recognizes and incorporates relevant aspects of the traditional law enforcement methods would result in more effective, efficient, and overall improved social control in Nigeria.

Part III

Future of the Native/Foreign Justice Interface in Nigeria

7

Interactions Between Nigeria's Native and Foreign Justice

INTRODUCTION

With particular regard to the Igbo, the research questions addressed in this chapter focus on the policy issues of justice in Nigeria. The questions are: How does the data reflect on the ability of the native Igbo justice system to regulate behavior among the Igbos in contrast to the English-style justice system? What policy statements should be highlighted for future consideration regarding the contemporary status of the Igbo justice system? The research for this chapter is informed by previous studies that have examined the justice systems of these former British colonies in Africa: Zambia (Canter, 1978); Ghana (Lowy, 1978); Malawi and Zambia (Chanock, 1985); Lagos, Nigeria (Mann, 1985; 1991); Kano, Nigeria (Christelow, 1991); Sierra Leone (Thompson, 1996). The studies illustrate the pervasive nature of the contradictions, disagreements, and conflicts between the native African lifestyles and justice systems, and the imposed English system brought about by colonialism. A mixed or plural justice is found in each situation. In most situations, the native judicial bodies are subject to the English-style courts. Whatever the arrangement, each study shows that there is a dual or multi-justice system available to the native, African population. Often, this leads to confusion.

This confusion is illustrated by the "repugnancy test." The repugnancy test in Nigerian justice is a British colonial legacy. Since the policy's creation in 1900, the country's justice officials have used it to subjugate the native justice systems to the imposed English-style justice system. This chapter examines the source of the policy, its historical and contemporary circumstances, and its role in the present Nigerian justice systems. The policy's consequences for the growth of the country's native justice systems are also examined. Does the policy help or hinder the growth of Nigeria's native justice systems? Suggestions are offered for addressing the negative consequences of this policy, if any, to facilitate the growth of Nigeria's native justice systems.

This chapter also highlights how the various military regimes in post-independence Nigeria have influenced law and justice in the country. It seems that the military regimes have subjugated the country's native justice systems to military-imposed law and justice. Considering that the eight military regimes in post-independence Nigeria (1966-1999) have been imposed on the citizens, rather than chosen by them, these regimes could not reasonably be expected to rule according to the popular laws among the citizens. Instead, the military regimes have ruled the country as superiors to the democratic laws of the country, including the native laws and customs. Figure 5.2 illustrates the superior position of the successive military regimes in Nigeria.

COLONIZATION AND PLURAL JUSTICE IN NIGERIA

The initial contacts between the native inhabitants of the River Niger area (Nigeria) and the British took place in the mid-1800s. The British eventually colonized the native Niger area population as well as the other parts of today's Nigeria. The colonization was effectuated through a combined use of slave dealing (Rodney, 1974), warfare (Nair, 1972), and religious evangelism (Ekechi, 1972; Thiong'o, 1986). Ultimately, the British colonizing forces, led by Lord Frederick Lugard, took over the Niger area. The British initially ruled sections of the Niger area independently of one other. Gradually, the different sections were merged without consultation with, or the approval of, the natives. The resulting "Northern Protectorate" and "Southern Protectorate" were similarly merged in 1914 to create "Nigeria."

Prior to the British colonization of Nigeria, respected Igbos ran Igbo community affairs, including the exercise of judicial functions. Such persons were instrumental in holding their communities together. Nigeria's colonization resulted in a destabilization of the lives of the natives. In most instances, the colonialists sought to replace the native structures and ways of life with those of Britain. However, the British lifestyles, as well as their sense of right and wrong were, in many ways, contrary to the lifestyles and collective sense of the Igbos and other Nigerians (Achebe, 1959). The contradictions remain in place.

ENTRENCHING BRITISH COLONIAL POLICIES IN IGBO JUSTICE

Nigeria's colonization allowed the British to infiltrate and, in most cases, usurp the pre-existing native institutions. In the particular areas of justice and law among the Igbos, the British took the following major steps to entrench themselves in local affairs: the setting up of the "native court," the creation of the "warrant chiefs," the adoption of English laws, and the establishment of the "repugnancy test." Each of these phenomena had, and continues to have, far-reaching consequences for the administration of justice in Igbo and other parts of Nigeria.

The Native Court

On conquering the Igbo, the British became aware that the natives had no powerful rulers like their western and northern neighbors (Yorubas and Hausa/Fulanis, respectively). Thus, the British concluded erroneously that the Igbos lived in "ordered anarchy" (Uchendu, 1966, at p. 46) and imposed a system of direct administration on the Igbos. All-purpose "native courts" were created for the Igbos (see *Native Courts Proclamation, 1900*). The Igbos were arbitrarily divided into Native Court areas. Each Native Court area was made up of a number of neighboring towns and villages, which used to be autonomous communities. A Native Court area contained its own administrative machinery. At the head of a Native Court was a British official called the district commissioner (Ekechi, 1972).

About two decades after the creation of Native Court authorities headed by district commissioners, it became clear to Britain that the new system was not working as they had expected. In 1918, the British abolished the office of district commissioner in an attempt to make the courts truly "native" (see *Native Court Ordinance, No. 5, as amended in 1922*). Despite this, the courts and the rest of the colonial government continued to encounter serious problems from the natives who refused to cooperate with the colonial regime (see Achebe, 1959). Later, the British made further changes concerning the Native Courts. The courts lost their jurisdiction as political administrative bodies and thus began to function only as agencies for dispute management. The changes included the substitution of "Customary Court" for "Native Court." But the problem with the British-established all-purpose Native or Customary Court was that, although it was modeled after the English courts, the subject matters over which the Customary Court exercised jurisdiction were often at variance with established English-based laws and practices.

In contemporary Nigeria, a Customary Court is a case management tribunal created and run by a state government. The judges and other officials of a Customary Court are government employees. However, the judges do not have formal training in law. A major criterion for appointment as a Customary Court judge is whether or not the prospective judge sufficiently understands the customary laws and traditions of the communities that make up the jurisdiction of the court and can apply the laws and traditions to the cases that are brought before the court. In northern Nigeria, the Native Court is the equivalent of the south's Customary Court.

Warrant Chiefs

The warrant chief worked closely with the district commissioner of the former Native Court. A warrant chief was a person appointed by the British colonial officers to rule over an Igbo community or group of communities. For the colonial regime, the need to create such an office was based on the belief that an Igbo community had no leadership. Moreover, the colonial officers needed a specific person they could trust to do their bidding among the locals. The persons who were appointed warrant chiefs were often individuals who lacked the respect of the other members of their community. Therefore, the community members resisted such appointments because they were impositions on the natives. Many of the present-day "ruling families" in Igbo communities grew out of the British-created "warrant chiefs."

The Adoption of English Laws

The arrival of the British colonialists in Nigeria marked the beginning of the role of the English customs and traditions (English laws) in Nigerian justice. Initially, the colonialists used English laws to regulate relationships among the British citizens in Nigeria. The laws were soon applied to activities between Nigerians and the British. Gradually, the colonial government adopted the laws of England as the laws of the newly created Nigeria. Colonial Britain adopted the English laws for Nigeria without consulting with, or obtaining the approval of, Nigerians.

The Repugnancy Test

The repugnancy test is the official government's legal requirement that for a customary law or tradition to be enforced, it must not be "repugnant to natural justice, equity, and good conscience, nor contrary to any official law" (*Proclamation No. 6 of 1900*). The legislation, enacted by the colonialists to consolidate their rule over Nigeria, remains a part of Nigerian justice. Today, all states in Nigeria continue to have equivalent provisions as parts of their laws. The repugnancy test, in its various forms, subjugates all Nigeria's native laws, customs, traditions, and practices to the official, English-style laws.

The Repugnancy Test in Post-British Nigeria

An examination of *Proclamation No. 6 of 1900* (and the equivalent provisions in various parts of Nigeria) shows that there are two implications of the repugnancy test. First, a customary law principle will be denied enforcement if it is contrary to any official law (local, state, or federal). Second, a customary law principle, which does not contravene an official law, may nevertheless be denied enforcement if an official court determines that the customary law opposes natural justice, equity, and good conscience. Because of the fluidity of such concepts as "natural justice," "equity," and "good conscience," their interpretations are left to each official court to make.

The data show that the Igbos very often rely on their native, traditional methods of case management. This is consistent with previous findings (see Oli, 1994; Uwazie, 1994; Okereafọezeke, 1996). However, the data also show that the official courts strongly adhere to the colonially imposed and post-colonially sustained repugnancy test. This remains the situation despite the fact that the native, traditional case management avenues play important roles in Igbo justice. This official adherence means that if the locals apply their native laws and customs (for example, through an unofficial tribunal or through the Customary Court) to a given case, an appellate court may declare the native laws and customs repugnant to natural justice, equity, and good conscience, and therefore void (see for instance, *Okonkwo v. Okagbue and 2 Others*, 1994 12 SCNJ 89, Case Number 40).

In *Okonkwo v. Okagbue and 2 Others* (1994), the issue before the Supreme Court is whether or not the first and second defendants (sisters of the plaintiff's late father) could marry a wife for the plaintiff's late father after the father's death. The first and second defendants claim that their custom entitles them to do so. The Supreme Court declares the custom repugnant to natural justice and thus void. The Court further decides that the lower court is entitled to raise the issue of repugnancy on its own. According to the Supreme Court (at p. 101 of the Case Report):

> The question whether a custom is repugnant being a point of law can be raised by counsel in his address to court as was done by the plaintiff's counsel in the High Court. The court itself may raise the point *suo motu* since it is enjoined to take the law into consideration and apply it in determining whether a particular custom is applicable.[1]

By its decision in *Okonkwo's case*, the Supreme Court allows the official courts to bring up the issue of repugnancy, even if the parties to a case do not bring it up. However, the Supreme Court may strike down a lower court pronouncement on the enforceability of a native law or custom without reference to the parties concerned. The Court may conclude that the lower court has followed a wrong procedure (*Ezeanya and Others v. Okeke and Others*, 1995 4 SCNJ 60, Case Number 41).

In the *Ezeanya case*, the issue is whether or not a custom that operates to transform a redeemable pledge of land to an outright disposition of the land is repugnant to natural justice. The Court of Appeal–without reference to the parties to the case–decides that the custom is repugnant to natural justice and therefore void. On appeal to the Supreme Court, the Court holds that the procedure followed by the Court of Appeal (deciding on the issue of repugnancy without reference to the parties) is "grossly erroneous" (at p. 89 of the Case Report). The Supreme Court thus reverses the Court of Appeal's judgment.

The repugnancy test is highlighted mainly in Nigeria's two highest official courts: the Court of Appeal and the Supreme Court. However, this official justice policy affects the country's federal, state, official, and unofficial justice systems. A decision by the Supreme Court on the repugnancy test influences cases before other case management bodies, including the lowest unofficial tribunal. For example, a decision by the Supreme Court affects the judicial proceedings in all the nine identified avenues for case management among the Igbos (*ezi na ụnọ*, *ụmụnna*, *ọnụma*, *obodo*, Customary Court, Magistrate Court, High Court, Court of Appeal, and Supreme Court – see figure 5.1). Supreme Court decisions bind the lower official courts. It is assumed that, where possible and appropriate, the unofficial judicial bodies take relevant Supreme Court decisions into consideration in view of the fact that a case managed unofficially may eventually be heard and determined by the Supreme Court if either party chooses the official justice route.

A seemingly positive aspect of the repugnancy test is that it allows for the monitoring of the operations of Nigeria's native laws and customs as they affect the citizens' fundamental rights. However, the test is open to the official governments and their justice personnel only, even though they are often guilty of curtailing the rights of citizens under the native laws and customs and the Nigerian constitution. The repugnancy test arms the official governments to police the native justice systems and bring them under official control, even when a given customary law accords with the aspirations of the locals. This situation discourages and stultifies the evolution of Nigeria's native justice systems. A set of laws is an embodiment of a people's history, experiences, and aspirations. Their history and experiences are couched as the people's customs and traditions. Changes to those customs and traditions represent the people's aspirations. Such changes should occur only as and when the people determine that changes are necessary. Ideally, therefore, a people's laws should emanate from a broad spectrum of the people, rather than from a few. This is the distinction between "customary law" imposed from the top and that which develops from popular practices (Snyder, 1982; Shaidi, 1992). Laws, which are imposed by a few, cannot become an acceptable means of social control; *a priori* where the imposition is by a foreign power, such as the British did in Nigeria.

The origin, history, contemporary circumstances, and application of the repugnancy test as an official justice policy in Nigeria show that the policy, formulated and promulgated by the British colonialists for Nigerians, is an obstacle to the growth of Nigeria's native justice systems. Measuring the quality of a native law, tradition, or custom on the basis of foreign or alien considerations such as those brought about by British colonial laws or even local official laws made since Nigeria's independence does not augur well for the growth of the native justice systems.

Correcting the Anomaly of the Repugnancy Test

Based on the issues and problems revealed by the data, the following policy changes to justice and law in Nigeria's Igbo are recommended.

First, consistently with earlier recommendations, judicial officers of the official case management avenues (see figure 5.1) should demonstrate increased appreciation and respect for the Igbo customary laws and traditions. The data show that the Igbos follow the native methods of case management widely. The official governments and their agencies should recognize this fact. Moreover, the data shows that the native methods are effective and efficient methods of justice. The official governments should also encourage the native, traditional methods to increase their effectiveness and efficiency levels.

Second, the cooperation of the local, state, and federal governments, as well as private groups and individuals is needed to revise outdated Igbo customary laws and traditions consistently with the dynamic nature of the Igbo society. Such revision should be aimed at making the Igbo native laws and customs conform to the contemporary Igbo ways of life. However, the relevant communities should have the first opportunity and responsibility to revise such laws and traditions since the community members' behaviors are being regulated. The other stakeholders in the revision exercise should contribute their quotas, but the process should begin and emphasize the immediate communities whose members are regulated by the native laws and customs. The official courts should not be too willing to do away with a custom or tradition without proper evaluation (*Ezeanya and Others v. Okeke and Others*, 1995; Okereafọezeke, 2000a).[2]

Third, since the repugnancy test is an officially imposed justice policy, the relevant Nigerian official legislative and executive officials (state and federal legislatures, attorneys-general, governors, president, etc.) should work together to change the policy by repealing the laws that have created and sustained it. The policy has no place in an independent Nigeria. Even if Nigerians now make the official laws to which the native laws and customs are subjected, the point remains that state and federal officials who are far removed from the locals make the official laws, and the official laws are rarely consistent with local traditions, customs, lifestyles, needs, and aspirations. A change in this justice policy would amplify the necessity to avoid official imposition of "customary law" from the top. Instead, the customs, traditions, and laws of each community would be allowed to develop from popular practices within the population (Snyder, 1982; Shaidi, 1992). The Igbos, like non-Igbo Nigerian communities, continue to deal with the dilemma and ambiguity of operating native laws under the control of officially imposed statutory laws (Iyam, 1995). Repeal of the repugnancy test would be a positive step toward restoring the integrity of the Igbo native laws and customs as acknowledged means of social control in Nigeria. Such repeal would also set the stage for needed changes to the justice systems in the other parts of Nigeria.

THE IMPOSITIONS OF MILITARY LAW

The Nigerian military has contributed greatly to destroying or stultifying the growth and advancement of the country's justice systems in its post-colonial history. Nigerian military law, by its very specialized nature, is rightly intended to apply limitedly to a specialized group for the simple reason that the group activities, on which Nigerians depend for the protection of the country from outside threats, cannot be carried out without infringing on some of the rights, regulations, and procedures that apply to the members of the civil society. Thus, Nigerian military law was created to allow the country's armed forces to, as much as necessary, manage their own justice system. However, the eight military regimes in the country since independence have expanded and extended various aspects of the specialized military law and justice to apply to the average Nigerian.

Since the first military intervention in Nigerian politics and government on January 15, 1966, every military regime in the country has taken steps to circumscribe, and in many cases abolish, the basic and fundamental rights of the citizens to stop or prevent the citizens from challenging the illegal militarily imposed regimes. In the context of law and justice, decrees and edicts have been two of the most common weapons that the military regimes have employed to subjugate Nigerians and circumscribe their rights. Specifically, two types of decrees are worthy of note: (1) decrees suspending the previously existing constitutions or parts thereof, and (2) decrees authorizing arrest and detention of persons without reasonable explanation.

The first type of military decrees used to subjugate Nigerians and circumscribe their rights is made up of the decrees promulgated to suspend crucial provisions of the prior existing Nigerian constitution, particularly the provisions that guarantee human rights. It has become fashionable for every military junta in Nigeria to, immediately on seizing power, assemble a band of sycophantic lawyers, which quickly drafts a decree proclaiming that the decree is superior to the constitution, suspending the fundamental rights of citizens and other constitutional provisions, and declaring that anything done or purported to be done under the decree shall not be challenged in court. If any such challenge has already been instituted, it shall abate and become void [see for example, *Constitution (Suspension and Modification) Decree No. 107 of 1993*; *The Federal Military Government (Supremacy and Enforcement of Powers) Decree No. 12 of 1994*]. These decrees thereby oust the courts' jurisdictions. In 1991 (in the thick of General Ibrahim Babangida's fraudulent, despotic tyranny), the then chief justice of Nigeria, Mohammed Bello, gave a paper at the Sixth International Appellate Judges' Conference. The paper expresses the nature of human rights under a military regime:

> Human rights under a military regime may be aberrations. In a democratic government under the rule of law, all judicial powers of the state are vested in the judiciary, under the military regimes, the powers are invariably eroded. The erosion may be creating Military (or Special) Tribunals. It may also be the ouster of the jurisdiction of courts of law (see

Abacha and Others v. Fawehinmi, Appeal No. SC, 45/1997, S.C.N. Reported in *The Guardian* online, May 16, 2000, at p. 6).

The second type of decrees used by successive Nigerian military juntas to subject the citizens to the ruling military and whittle away the citizens' rights is made up of the military laws that authorize the arrest and detention of a person without due process of law. Thus, any person may be identified, arrested, and detained by government agents without legal or reasonable justification [see for example, *State Security (Detention of Persons) Decree, No. 2 of 1984*; *State Security (Detention of Persons) Decree, Cap. 414, Laws of the Federation of Nigeria, 1990*]. The net effect of these obnoxious laws is that any person who is authorized to do so by the Decree may lawfully cause another to be arrested and detained with or without reason, and the official courts are statutorily barred from reviewing the arrest or detention. The ouster clauses also apply to the courts' powers to review the detention of a person and order his or her release on a *habeas corpus* application [see *Lekwot v. Judicial Tribunal*, 1993 2 NWLR (Part 276) 410, at p. 447].

On the issue of ouster clauses, Nigerian judicial officers can learn a few things from their Pakistani counterparts. In October 1999, General Pervez Musharraf and his band of putschists seized the leadership of Pakistan in a *coup d'etat*. Like his Nigerian predecessors, Musharraf suspended the Pakistani constitution and introduced an ouster clause barring the Pakistani judiciary from hearing and determining any legal action challenging the junta's conduct. In January 2000, General Musharraf ordered the country's judges to swear to an oath of loyalty to his military regime; it was to be a fresh oath of office that would require the judges to dispense "justice" according to the wishes of the junta. The chief justice, Siad–UZ Zaman Siddiqui, five other Pakistani Supreme Court judges, and some high court judges took a dignifying position opting to resign rather than legitimize and serve the narrow interests of the military rulers (see "Principles," 2000).

In contrast to the Pakistani judges who challenged General Musharraf's illegal regime, most of Nigeria's official courts and judges have, since Nigeria's first military rule in 1966, consistently honored or deferred to the ouster clauses, which are the wishes of the small military ruling clique in the country, at the expense of the rights and well-being of the overwhelming majority of Nigerians. Examples are legion, but three are cited here. Mohammed Bello, particularly as the chief justice of Nigeria, made several efforts to rationalize the obnoxious, militarily imposed laws, such as the *State Security (Detention of Persons) Decree*. Another example is the then Lagos state chief judge, Ligali Ayorinde, who gave a judgment that the military ruler is a *kabiyesi*, a Yoruba God-like king whose actions and laws are unquestionable (see "Principles," 2000, at p. 2). Thus, many of Nigeria's official courts and judges have adopted a *fait accompli* or fatalistic attitude toward military impositions that allegedly are laws of the land. Many official court judges regard militarily imposed laws as unquestionable as long as the wishes of the military rulers are clear (*Abacha and Others v.*

Fawehinmi, Appeal No. SC, 45/1997, SCN, Judgment on April 28, 2000). In *Okeke v. A-G Anambra State*, 1992 1 NWLR (Part 214) 60, Uwaifo, JCA[3] holds:

> Once the provisions of a Decree of Constitution ousting the jurisdiction of the courts on any specific matters are clear and unambiguous, the courts are bound to observe and apply them. They are not entitled, *even when the ouster has drastic effect on the right of any person*, to approach its interpretation by a false or twisted meaning given to it by unacceptable restricted constructions (at p. 85).[4]

The simple question that comes to mind is: Why should the Nigerian courts and judicial officers become willing partners with a band of military self-serving adventurers, which is pursuing an illegal, criminal enterprise that opposes the fundamental convictions of the Nigerian peoples? It is not sufficient for a judicial officer to plead helplessness because he or she is mandated to *apply* the existing laws and not to *make* new laws. True, a judicial officer's responsibility is to apply existing laws to the facts presented in a case. But it is *not* the judicial officer's duty to facilitate or flatten the way for an illegal, criminal regime to take away the morally and legally guaranteed rights of the citizens. Indeed, it is the judicial officer's duty to take all necessary steps to prevent the erosion, whittling away, or removal of the legally guaranteed rights. If the judicial officer fails to carry out this duty, he or she no longer deserves to be called "the last hope of the common man."

Militarily imposed law and justice in Nigeria do not go away with the imposing military regime. Whenever the military hands over power to an elected civilian government, the military makes sure to foist their wishes on the succeeding government and other Nigerians. Most of the military decrees and edicts remain in force even after the exit of each regime. Each of the military regimes since 1966 that has handed over power to an elected civilian administration has made sure to determine the key provisions of the constitution that regulates life in the post-military regime. Note that neither the constitution nor other law is made with input from average Nigerians. A survey of the *Constitution of the Federal Republic of Nigeria, 1999*, reveals the extent of the military rulers' wishes to continue to influence Nigerian justice in fundamental ways long after handing over power to an elected civilian government. In order to avoid analyses and criticisms of his constitution, General Abdulsalam Abubakar has presided over the emasculation of the overwhelming majority of Nigerians from participation in the creation of the constitution that would regulate them. Thus, his regime kept the *1999 Constitution* from Nigerians until after the elections at the local, state, and federal levels were completed in early 1999, even though the elected officials would govern according to the constitution. The militarily imposed constitution was made available to Nigerians for the first time only days before the new administration was sworn into office on May 29, 1999. Notwithstanding, the constitution falsely and fraudulently proclaims in the preamble as follows:

> We the people of the Federal Republic of Nigeria, having firmly and solemnly resolved to live in unity and harmony as one indivisible and indissoluble sovereign nation under God, dedicated to the promotion of inter-African solidarity, world peace, international co-operation and understanding, and to provide for a Constitution for the purpose of promoting the good government and welfare of all persons in our country, on the principles of freedom, equality and justice, and for the purpose of consolidating the unity of our people, do hereby make, enact and give to ourselves the following Constitution.

In addition to its fraudulent basis, the *1999 Constitution*, like many other militarily imposed laws, includes other provisions with far-reaching consequences for the development of the Nigerian justice systems. *Section 1 (1) of the 1999 Constitution* stipulates that "this Constitution is supreme and its provisions shall have binding force on the authorities and persons throughout the Federal Republic of Nigeria." *Section 1 (3)* states: "If any law is inconsistent with the provisions of this Constitution, this Constitution shall prevail, and that other law shall, to the extent of the inconsistency, be void." On the surface, it seems right to subject Nigeria's diverse traditions, customs, and native laws to the country's constitution. However, the difficulty with accepting this line of reasoning is that the alleged constitution is no more than a symbol of the warped and selfish minds of the military rulers and their few civilian collaborators, who have ruined Nigeria. The overwhelming majority of Nigerians have not been given any opportunity to "make, enact, and give" to themselves the constitution they desire. Further, to preserve their ignoble legacy and hamstring the judiciary, the military has included *Section 6 (6) (d) of the 1999 Constitution*, which provides the following:

> The judicial powers vested in accordance with the foregoing provisions of this section [on Judicial Powers] shall not, as from the date when this section comes into force, extend to any action or proceedings relating to any existing law made on or after 15th January, 1966 [when the military first seized power in Nigeria] for determining any issue or question as to the competence of any authority or person to make any such law.

Thus, Nigerians are effectively denied the right to challenge the actions, programs, laws, and other policies of the erstwhile military rulers even where such actions and programs are at variance with the traditions, customs, and consensual experiences of the overwhelming majority of Nigerians who believe in negotiated, rather than imposed, law and justice.

The stultifying and destructive effects of the military decrees and edicts on the Nigerian justice systems (including the native justice systems) are undeniable. Under such a decree, judicial officials and processes have to satisfy the purpose of the ruling military cabal, which is preservation in office, rather than the ends of justice, which are objective, rational fairness consistent with the history, contemporary circumstances, and aspirations of the majority of Nigerians. Quite apart from the ruling military junta's overt steps to circumvent and neutralize the justice mechanisms, it is mere fantasy to expect the regime to do anything to encourage the development or growth of the native justice systems. Under Nigeria's successive military regimes, the average citizen views militarily enacted laws as necessarily oppressive, since those laws are imposed, rather than negotiated as is customary in most Nigerian communities. Evidence abounds of how, by virtue of the militarily imposed constitutions and other laws, Nigerians live under the military even after the military have handed over political power.

SUMMARY

The "repugnancy test" justice policy in Nigeria stipulates that a native law or custom is not to be given effect if the law or custom is repugnant to natural justice, equity, or good conscience, or contrary to any official law. This is an anomalous provision. It is a British colonial creation and legacy. The successive Nigerian governments since the country's political independence from Britain have, however, sustained it. In both colonial and post-colonial times, this and similar policies subjugate Nigeria's native justice systems to the colonially imposed English-style system. The native justice systems are thereby prevented from growing into more effective, more efficient, and more sophisticated systems of social control. Taking three steps would reverse this situation: (1) the official governments, their judicial and other personnel should recognize the usefulness of the native justice systems, which play crucial roles in social control in the country; (2) the Igbo communities should revise outdated Igbo customary laws and traditions to conform with the contemporary Igbo lifestyles and the official governments and their agencies should facilitate the process by providing some of the necessary human and material resources to achieve this; and (3) the legislators and the executive officers of the official governments should repeal the laws that created the repugnancy test and those that have sustained it. In addition to reversing the repugnancy test policy, the civilian governments at the local, state, and federal levels also owe a duty to abrogate all militarily imposed laws that detract from Nigerians' sense of justice, fairness, and law. Inevitably, attempts at abrogating militarily imposed laws will be thwarted by the current *1999 Constitution*, and constitutional amendment is not a satisfactory means of achieving equity and justice in the country. Thus, the best option is to convene a country-wide Sovereign Conference of All Nigeria's Nations (SCANN) (Okereafọezeke, 2000e) at which every one of Nigeria's nations will have a reasonable opportunity to ensure the preservation, growth, and development of its values and systems, among other things. Such a forum will be an excellent opportunity to do away with the horrible memories of military regimes and military laws in Nigeria and ensure the centrality of the country's native justice systems in the country's affairs.

NOTES

1. Italics added.

2. In addition to this chapter, the need for the official courts to properly evaluate a custom or tradition before deciding on its enforceability is discussed in chapter 8.

3. JCA = Justice of the Court of Appeal.

4. Italics added for emphasis.

8

Criminological Theory Implications of Nigeria's Official Policies, Practices, and Idiosyncrasies on the Native Justice Systems

INTRODUCTION

Nigeria's official governments at the local, state, and federal levels and their agencies make and implement laws and other policies, as well as engage in practices and idiosyncrasies that negatively affect the country's native justice systems, including the Igbo.[1] Some of the relevant policies, practices, and idiosyncrasies involve *do nothing* behavior, which means that the official governments and their agencies fail to do what they should. There are five categories of issues relevant to this topic: (1) the repugnancy test, (2) emphasis on the English-style justice system, (3) conflict in procedures, (4) inaction toward codification, and (5) grossly insufficient teaching. The first, second, fourth, and fifth issues deal mainly with the substantive laws. The third issue deals primarily with the procedural laws. All five issues focus on the different areas in which the official governments have neglected to take necessary steps to ensure the growth of Nigeria's native justice systems.

THE REPUGNANCY TEST REVISITED

The genesis and contemporary circumstances of the repugnancy test in Nigeria deserve to be addressed in this section also in some measure. In relation to traditions, customs, and native laws in Nigeria, the repugnancy test is the official government's legal requirement that a customary law or tradition will not be enforced by the official justice system if the customary law or tradition is repugnant to natural justice, equity, and good conscience. Similarly, a customary law or tradition will not be enforced if it is contrary to an official law. The circumstances of this official imposition go back to 1876, when the British Royal Niger Company took over the Lagos Colony (part of present Nigeria). When the British government took over the control of Nigeria from the Royal Niger Company, the government enacted *Proclamation No. 6 of 1900* as follows:

> Nothing in this Proclamation shall deprive the Supreme Court [of the Colony and Protectorate of Nigeria] of the right to observe and enforce the observance, or shall deprive any persons of the benefit of *any law or custom existing in the Protectorate, such law or custom not being repugnant to natural justice, equity and good conscience.* No party shall be entitled to claim the benefit of any local law or custom, if it shall appear, either from express contract or from the nature of the transactions out of which any suit or question may have arisen, that such party agreed that his obligations in connection with such transactions should be regulated exclusively by English law; and in cases where no express rule is applicable to any matter in controversy, the court shall be governed by the principles of justice, equity, and good conscience.[2]

By this law, Britain consolidated the existing Royal Niger Company's policy of dualizing the Nigerian justice system. One justice system, based on native laws, customs, and traditions, was to address the justice needs of Nigeria's native population. The other justice system, which was a replica of the English justice system, was to protect the British interests in Nigeria. The colonial policies in *Proclamation No. 6 of 1900* did not only dualize justice in Nigeria. They also made the English principles of law and justice dominant over the native principles. In their various forms, the cited provisions of the proclamation are still part of Nigerian justice.

Proclamation No. 6 of 1900, as well as the other provisions based on it, has created a conflict situation in Nigerian justice and law. The conflict is between native laws, customs, and traditions, on the one hand, and English-style law and justice, on the other. Before Nigeria became politically independent of Britain in 1960, many of Nigeria's official court judges were British. As should be expected, the alien judges were often eager to use English notions and standards of justice as litmus tests for issues that arose in Nigeria. Also, the foreign judges generally regarded Nigeria's native laws, customs, and traditions as backward, unrefined, and archaic. In the pre-independence Nigerian case of *Lewis and Others v. Bankole and Others*, 1908 1 NLR 81, chief justice Osborne, an expatriate judge working in Nigeria, states:

> I have during thirteen years experience of West Africa been concerned in one capacity or another with several cases in which native customary law has been the subject of judicial investigation, and in nearly every case I have found that there are general underlying principles not difficult to understand, and obviously based on *the primitive requirements of the community.*[3]

Being so convinced that Nigeria's native systems of justice and law are "primitive," the British have for long viewed their own (English) law and justice system as the means to cleanse and moralize Nigeria's native systems. Thus, the British colonial law, justice, and other social control policies in Nigeria, even as they have survived to date, are geared toward replacing the native systems with the English system. If it is impossible or too difficult to replace a native practice, the practice is to be cleansed partly through the instrumentalities of *Proclamation No. 6 of 1900*.

In post-independence Nigeria, justice officials, particularly judges and justices of the High Courts, Court of Appeal, and the Supreme Court,[4] resort to applications of English laws to determine whether or not a Nigerian customary law or tradition is repugnant to natural justice, equity, or good conscience in a Nigerian circumstance. This means that after the locals apply their native laws and customs, for example, through the *Eze*-in-Council or the Customary Court, an appellate court judge or justice can step in and declare the native laws and customs repugnant to natural justice, equity, and good conscience and, therefore, void [see Case Number 36 (*Nzekwu and Others v. Nzekwu and Others*, 1989); Case Number 40 (*Okonkwo v. Okagbue and 2 Others*, 1994)]. Most of Nigeria's contemporary appellate court judges and justices trained as lawyers in England. Many of these judges and justices are, in reality, no different from the English judges who worked in Nigeria in the colonial days.

With particular reference to the Igbo native laws and customs, the repugnancy test is the most crucial test that a native law, custom, or tradition must pass to be officially recognized and enforced. It is bad enough that this test exists. The way many appellate judges in Nigeria apply it is even worse. With little or no understanding of the relevant native laws and customs, these Nigerian judges often see themselves as the purifiers of the native laws, customs, and traditions of the communities. In Case Number 41 (*Ezeanya and Others v. Okeke and Others*, 1995), where the Court of Appeal unilaterally raises and uses the repugnancy test to strike down an Igbo native law and custom without reference to the parties to the case, the Supreme Court describes the Court of Appeal's action as "grossly erroneous" (at p. 89 of the Case Report):

> The question of whether or not the native law and custom relied upon by the [defendants] is contrary to public policy, equity and good conscience was neither raised as an issue in the pleadings of the parties nor was the matter canvassed by them whether in the [High Court] or before the [Court of Appeal]. Indeed at no time did the [plaintiffs], whether directly or indirectly, suggest, whether in the [High Court] or before the [Court of Appeal] that the said customary law was contrary to public policy, equity and good conscience as propounded by the Court of Appeal. What the [Court of Appeal] did was to raise the point *suo motu* and proceeded to resolve the same in favor of the [plaintiffs] without giving the [defendants] an opportunity to be heard on the point. With profound respect to the Court of Appeal, this procedure was grossly erroneous on the point of law as it was prejudicial to the [defendants] and constituted a breach of their right to fair hearing.[5]

In Case Number 41, the Supreme Court has stepped in and limited the Court of Appeal's moralizing attitude. The Supreme Court does not get opportunities to evaluate the lower courts' decisions in many other cases. Even in Case Number 41, it is important to realize that the concern of the Supreme Court is that the Court of Appeal has acted unilaterally. In essence, as long as an official court allows the parties to address it on the issue of repugnancy or conflict with an official law, it could raise the issue and use it to strike down a native law or custom. In Case Number 40 (*Okonkwo v. Okagbue and 2 Others*, 1994), the Supreme Court holds that whether or not a custom is repugnant is a point of law and thus can be raised by counsel in his address to court. Also, that "the court itself may raise the point *suo motu*" because it is required to consider the law to determine whether or not a particular custom is applicable (at p. 101).[6]

The continued application of the repugnancy test along the lines designed by the British colonialists creates conflict between the principles of Nigeria's native justice and law and their English counterparts. The areas of greatest conflict include land, marriage, and homicide (Salamone, 1980; Ebbe, 1985; see also Jones, 1993). The dilemma in which an average Igbo person finds himself or herself is that the Igbo person understands the Igbo customary laws and traditions and how the laws and traditions govern relationships with others in the society. However, such an Igbo, who conducts himself or herself according to the Igbo native laws and customs may later learn from the official courts that the English law prevails over the native laws and customs. Does this Igbo know or understand his or her rights and obligations under the English law? It is submitted that he or she does not, especially where the person has not been educated on the principles of English law.

In *The Social Reality of Crime*, Quinney (1970, at pp. 15-23) offers six propositions to explain the social circumstances and implications of crime. His Proposition Two states: "Formulating of Criminal Definitions – Criminal definitions describe behaviors that conflict with the interests of the segments of the society that have the power to shape public policy." Although Quinney writes specifically on crimes, in Nigeria conflicts exist in crimes as well as civil issues such as matrimonial causes, inheritance, land ownership, possession, and disposition and contracts. According to Quinney, when the influential segments of a society have formulated the definitions, they go on to diffuse the conceptions in all segments of society by various means of communication (Proposition Five). This happened under the British in colonial Nigeria and has continued under the neo-colonial regimes since Nigeria's political independence in 1960.

During the British colonial rule over Nigeria, "the segments of the society that [had] the power to shape public policy" included the British parliamentarians, the governor-general, the governors, and the judges that worked in Nigeria. In post-independence Nigeria, the country's lawmakers and judges remain in this category. It makes no difference that these lawmakers and judges are Nigerians. They continue this policy even when the illiterate natives do not understand nor believe in the legitimacy and morality of the alien social rules and laws imposed upon them.

In his "Social Bonding Theory," Hirschi (1969) identifies the following four basic elements of the bonding process: *attachment*, *commitment*, *involvement*, and *belief*. Hirschi theorizes that the more an individual is bonded to the four elements, the less likely that he or she will engage in delinquent activity.[7] Also, Hirschi assumes that the more a person is bonded to conventional society by one of the elements, the more likely that the others will bond the person also. The elements may be applied to the Igbos thus:

1. *attachment* to parents, other relatives, peers, and native community leaders.
2. *commitment* to conventional lines of authority, examples *ụmụnna* leadership, *ọnụma* leadership, *Eze* Ajallị, title-holders, and other authority figures.
3. *involvement* in the native community's activities and aspirations.
4. *belief* in the legitimacy and morality of the native community's social rules and laws.

The average Igbo person is *attached*, *committed*, and *involved* in the principles of the Igbo traditions, customs, and native laws, which he or she knows and understands, and with which the Igbo can identify. Most importantly, the Igbo person *believes* in the moral basis and legitimacy of the social rules and norms that he or she understands, rather than the English laws that he or she does not understand.

EMPHASIS ON THE ENGLISH-STYLE JUSTICE SYSTEM

Quite apart from the repugnancy test, Nigeria's official justice system places too much emphasis on the English-style system. Thus, Nweje's (1975) assertion that "'indigenous laws' comprise all the laws in operation in [the Nigerian] society whether based on custom or on some statute" should be rejected. The statement does not get to the root of the problem of justice administration in Nigeria. The point is that the overwhelming majority of the statutes operating in Nigeria are based on foreign cultures, experiences, and aspirations. The British colonialists imported the statutes into Nigeria. The contemporary Nigerian lawmakers and justice officials have continued this policy that subjugates the native principles of justice and law to their foreign counterparts. The circumstances of the *Nigerian Criminal Code* illustrate Nigeria's official emphasis on extra-national legal and justice systems.

Many foreign countries and cultures created the *Nigerian Criminal Code*. The code has little or no relevance to the social and cultural experiences of Nigerians. Sir Samuel Griffiths first drafted what is now the *Nigerian Criminal Code* for Britain in 1880. The British Parliament rejected it. Elements of the code were later included in the *Australian Code* in 1899 with assistance from the *Italian Penal Code* and the *Penal Code of New York*, USA. The British colonialists introduced the code into Nigeria with additional elements borrowed from the then Gold Coast (now Ghana) and the St. Lucia, USA Criminal Codes. The *Nigerian Criminal Code* continues to regulate behaviors among Nigerians. Whenever there is a conflict between a principle of the code and any of Nigeria's traditions, customs, or native laws, the code provision prevails even though the code is based on alien cultures.

The British colonialists adopted the *Nigerian Criminal Code* for Nigeria with little or no regard for the fundamental differences that exist between the Nigerian and foreign societies for which the code had been drawn up. Europeans generally, and the British in particular, lead individualistic lives. On the other hand, the lives of the Igbos, and the other nations of Nigeria, are communal and corporate in nature. The individualistic life would allow a Briton who stole public property to rationalize the conduct by arguing that nobody would miss the property. He would deny injury to the public because he would be concerned about himself alone (see Sykes and Matza, 1957). In traditional Igbo, the common good is the dominant consideration. The Igbo is socialized accordingly in the *ezi na ụnọ*, *ụmụnna*, *ọnụma*, and *obodo* institutions in which he or she is involved while growing up. When, later in life, the official laws dictate otherwise to the Igbo, the result is a confused situation because of the mixed messages from the native and official (foreign) systems. The end result is a condition of anomie or normlessness.

The anomic or normless condition results from confusion as to which norms or rules of conduct govern behavior in a society (Durkheim, 1897/1951). The characteristics of suddenness and unexpectedness in Durkheimean anomie are present in the British imposition of the English-style justice on Nigeria. Although it has been some 100 years since the English law and justice system was imposed on Nigeria, its effects are more apparent now that Nigeria's economic conditions have deteriorated. Given Nigeria's intolerably harsh economic conditions and the present confusion as to which norms regulate behavior, it would be convenient for an Igbo person to rely on an English-style principle of law that affords him or her the opportunity to escape punishment for a crime. The normless condition also makes it easier for Nigerian leaders to cheat, lie, and steal public resources, knowing that they (the leaders) would be able to escape punishment under the English-style justice system. This knowledge is borne out particularly by the fact that the leaders learn the definitions in the Criminal and Penal Codes with a view to determining easier ways to violate the country's official laws and escape punishment (see Sutherland, 1947). Such leaders have replaced fear of the omnipotence of the supernatural with belief in the leaders' abilities to circumvent and corrupt the official, English-style justice system and thus avoid punishment for their crimes (Oli, 1994).

CONFLICT IN PROCEDURES

The differences in procedures between the English-style justice system and the native Igbo justice system demonstrate the elements that facilitate escape from punishment under the English-style system. In the English-style court in Nigeria, a party or witness could easily testify falsely even after he or she has sworn or affirmed to tell the truth. The party or witness would see no reason to tell the truth if he or she does not expect to be caught. This negative attitude transcends the official justice system. The root cause of Nigeria's post-independence problems is religion as much as it is ethnicity. Christianity and Islam, in particular, have corrupted every aspect of the Nigerian being. Nigeria is one country in which an appearance of righteousness (religiosity) equals righteousness. In the native Igbo justice system, a party or witness may not be sworn. None of the disputants and witnesses in the more than twenty-eight case studies in this book tried at the *ụmụnna*, *ọnụma*, and *obodo* levels is sworn or affirmed. But he or she has a reason to tell the truth. The reason is his or her fundamental belief that punishment is inescapable if the party or witness lies in the proceedings. He or she believes in the ability of the supernatural forces to punish the party or witness if he or she lies to the community's symbol of authority. There is no such belief concerning proceedings in an official court.

The native Igbo justice system tries to accommodate the fair trial of an accused person. At the same time, it attempts to ensure that the community does not suffer injustice as a result of the protection given to the accused. The burden of proof is that of the person who makes an assertion. In a civil case, the burden is on the first disputant (or plaintiff) to prove a claim. But the judges focus primarily on peacemaking between the parties. The judges emphasize to the parties the need for them to integrate and cooperate with each other and with the other community members (examples, Case Numbers 2, 12, 16, and 22; see also Quinney, 1988, at p. 74). In a criminal case, the burden is on the accuser to convince the judge, such as the *Eze*-in-Council, that the accused person is guilty (Case Numbers 13 and 18). However, where the crime charged is particularly serious, such as an *arụ* or *alụ* (crime that pollutes the land), the judges recognize that the accused person, if guilty or responsible, should not be allowed to escape punishment, even if he or she has not been proved guilty beyond all reasonable doubts (Case Number 24, 1994, in which the accused father is tried and convicted for incest with his twelve-year-old daughter).

In native Igbo justice, shaming is an important and effective means of social control. A guilty person may be shamed by *ịgba ekpe* as in Case Number 12 (1991). The Igbos believe that shaming would greatly reduce, if not eliminate, the prospects that the offender would commit the same or another crime. According to Becker (1963, at p. 9): "Social groups create deviance by making rules whose infraction constitutes deviance, and by applying those rules to particular people and labeling them as outsides. The deviant is one to whom that label has successfully been applied." Based on this theory, an offender who is shamed through *ịgba ekpe* is thereby given the "criminal" master status. The label denies the person access to the means of legitimate living. The offender therefore gets involved in illegitimate endeavors. But, it seems that this theory does not consider the relativity of the organization or the society concerned. A close and homogenous community like most Igbo communities provides a labeled offender with little opportunity for more deviance. The essence of shaming by means of *ịgba ekpe* is to discourage the shamed offender from further breaches against the other community members. The *ịgba ekpe* procedure helps to protect the community from criminal activities, even if the procedure is not in strict compliance with the Nigerian official constitutional provisions.

LACK OF CODIFICATION

Consistent with their activities as colonizers, the British never made any attempt to codify the Igbo customary laws or traditions, nor those of any other group in Nigeria. Since becoming politically independent of Britain in 1960, the responsibility in this regard has fallen on Nigerian leaders. They have failed woefully. They have done nothing worthy of mention to encourage the growth of Nigeria's native laws and customs. None of the customary laws and traditions applied in the more than forty-two case studies in this book is codified. Nigeria's native laws, customs, and traditions, particularly those of the Igbo, remain fluid and often uncertain. They have been in this form for centuries. That is why a person who intends to rely on a principle of customary law has to establish it by evidence. The fluid and uncertain nature of the Igbo customary law, for example, does not encourage the common trends that exist in this system of justice and law. Rather, the nature of the customary law tends to emphasize those elements that localize, rather than generalize, the justice and law system. The experience of England in the development of their common law should be noted here.

What the world now knows as the common law of England was for a long time masked by an uncertain collection of English tribal customs and traditions. The customs and traditions differed from one English community to another. Indeed, there are still instances of these tribal differences in modern England. However, after the Norman conquest of England in 1066, the Normans took steps to develop a unified system of laws for England. Unlike what the British did in Nigeria, the Normans did not change English customary law by imposing Norman laws. Instead, the Normans granted borough courts the power to administer the customary laws of England. In time, the judges moved around in circuits hearing cases and applying the customs and traditions to the cases with a view to establishing a consistent body of laws. The judges soon began to coordinate their efforts. They were therefore able to create uniformity and consistency in their applications of the customs and traditions. Over time, the result was the common law of England as opposed to the multiplicity of tribal and local norms, customs, and rules of behavior in England. Writing played an important role in the development of the English customs and traditions. As soon as the English judges could, they made sure to reduce their judgments (based on the English customs and traditions) to writing. The written judgments served as guides in future cases and provided a measure of consistency and predictability in the English customary laws and traditions. The growth and expansion of the English system of laws and justice is now well known. Nigerian officials should learn a few lessons from this English experience rather than adopting for Nigeria the common law that was developed for England.

RESEARCH AND TEACHING

The curricula in Nigerian schools either do not contain sufficient consideration of the native justice and legal systems or they contain no such consideration at all. Even areas of study such as law, criminal justice, criminology, sociology, anthropology, and political science emphasize foreign systems and ideas. Rather than channeling efforts toward developing the native ideas and systems through teaching and research, the areas of study concentrate on how to import foreign systems and make them work locally. The relative lack of research on Nigeria's customary laws and traditions is very disturbing. Neither the governments nor the private sector gives deserved resources and attention to research and teaching of Nigeria's native justice and legal systems. The official attitude aimed at standardizing Nigeria's justice and legal systems to foreign systems (particularly the English) has to stop. Especially, Nigerian institutions of higher learning should emphasize the country's native systems of social control. One way to do this is to devote more curricula spaces, time, personnel, and other resources to these systems of justice and law. Also, there is the urgent need to apply for, obtain, and utilize research funds to inquire into various aspects of Nigeria's native justice and legal systems. Such research results would help the development and growth of the native social control systems.

SUMMARY

This chapter examined the criminological implications of some of the key issues identified in chapter 7 in light of this question: How do the justice policies, practices, and idiosyncrasies of the official governments impact on the behavior norms and general social control in Nigeria? One key identified in chapter 7 is the repugnancy test. The test is a major official check on the native justice and legal systems. In both chapters 7 and 8, the retrogressive character of this policy is demonstrated. It was foreign-imposed and designed to subjugate Nigeria's native systems of justice and law to colonial Britain's ideas of law and justice. Unfortunately, Nigerian rulers since independence have either taken no steps at all to reverse this obnoxious and contemptuous British creation, or the government officials have taken steps to reinforce the British imposition even though it has no credible basis in Nigeria. Nigerian government officials emphasize the English-style justice system in Nigeria at the expense of the country's native justice and legal systems. The circumstances that brought about the *Nigerian Criminal Code* illustrate the hollowness of the country's current official efforts at social control. The procedural conflicts between Nigeria's native justice systems and their English counterpart support the need to develop the native systems, which derive from the Nigerian people's histories, experiences, identities, and aspirations. Meaningful steps toward codifying the native laws will help develop the native justice systems. Also, increased research and teaching in this area will strengthen and broaden the native systems. If the recommended steps are taken and sustained, the common features of Nigeria's native justice and legal systems will be brought to light, and with time, the systems will grow toward uniformity.

NOTES

1. The official policies, practices, and idiosyncrasies impact on the Igbo justice system as well as other native systems of justice in Nigeria. However, the Igbo system is used to illustrate the ill-effects of the official policies on the development of the native justice systems.

2. Italics added.

3. Italics added.

4. All judges and justices in contemporary Nigeria are Nigerians.

5. Italics added.

6. Italics added.

7. It is understood that Hirschi's (1969) work is basically about delinquency. However, his theory is used here to illustrate some of the problems that arise from the governments' undue emphasis on the Nigerian official, English-style law and justice system at the expense of the native systems of justice, law, and social control.

9

Future Social Control: Synthesizing Native, Foreign, Unofficial, and Official Controls

INTRODUCTION

At this juncture, it is necessary to ask two key questions: What is the future of social control in Nigeria in light of the country's English-dominated official law and justice? In view of the historical and contemporary circumstances of Nigerians, what major features are necessary in future Nigerian justice and law to ensure more effective and more efficient social control? Some aspects of these questions have been addressed in previous chapters of this book, especially chapters 3-8. Chapters 3-6 specifically provided evidence that Nigeria's native, unofficial institutions of social control continue to work well even after British colonization. However, as chapters 7 and 8 have shown, Nigeria's official governments ignore this crucial role of the native, unofficial institutions in the country's social control. This chapter continues by arguing, based on empirical data, for de-emphasis of the present brand of official law and justice in Nigeria. Finally, an additional case for a synthesis of Nigeria's justice systems is made in the belief that such a step would be a giant stride toward fundamentally curing Nigeria's colonially imposed, dysfunctional official justice system, which alienates the overwhelming majority of Nigerians because of the stark contradictions between the Nigerians' traditions, customs, cultures, and beliefs and the officially imposed system.

THE IMPORTANCE OF NATIVE, UNOFFICIAL INSTITUTIONS IN SOCIAL CONTROL

It is the nature of modern states to emphasize and promote only that system or practice that the state recognizes or with which it identifies. State recognition of a system or practice may be formal or informal. Formal recognition means that the state expressly (in written or spoken words) makes clear that it recognizes a system or practice. Informal recognition is the unwritten, unspoken, attitudinal recognition based on the state's implied acceptance of a system or practice. Whether recognition is formal or informal, it may result in a stronger system or practice based on the considerable economic, legal, and political support it enjoys from the state. The state's power and authority amplify the advantage of a recognized system or practice over its unrecognized counterparts because the state is thus able, willing, and ready to use force to enforce the recognized system or practice, if necessary.

A state may or may not have an objective, stable, ascertainable process for recognizing or withholding recognition for a system or practice. More than an evolving and unstable state, a stable state has definite and objective rules and regulations for deciding whether or not to recognize a system or practice. Whether or not there are explicit and impartial rules and regulations in place, the values, norms, historical experiences, interrelations among the citizens, and collective aspirations should guide the state officers in their decision to recognize or withhold recognition. It is the solemn duty of state officers to honestly and diligently ascertain the citizens' collective wishes (which invariably will reflect the citizens values and norms), and allow those wishes to guide the state officers in their decisions to recognize or refuse recognition for particular systems and practices.

In Nigeria's unstable, chaotic, and dysfunctional official arrangement, rules and regulations for officially recognizing systems and practices, where such rules and regulations exist, are routinely and callously disregarded for the immediate advantages of the people trusted to make the decisions. Nigeria's contemporary official justice system, laws, and practices are little more than remnants of the British colonial rule over Nigeria. The official machinery of justice has changed only minimally since the exit of colonial Britain in 1960. The changes that have occurred are too insignificant to bring about the needed changes in the country's justice and law. As far as can be verified, none of the country's official governments since independence has even contemplated the needed fundamental change to Nigerian law and justice. For avoidance of doubt, the needed fundamental change is the repositioning of Nigeria's native traditions, customs, and laws as the collective basis (*grundnorm*) of justice and law in the country.

Official law and justice in contemporary Nigeria is a British colonial legacy (Okereafọezeke, 2000a). A survey of the three major arms of the official justice system (police, courts, and prisons) shows that Nigeria's official justice system is little more than a copy of the British system of law and justice. In

Nigeria, official laws are made, enforced, applied, and judgments are carried out based on the dictates of the imposed, alien, English-style justice system. Arguably, the native justice systems and personnel process much more civil and criminal cases than the English-style system and its officers. Native justice systems and personnel are routinely relegated and ignored even as they are indispensable in Nigeria's social control efforts. No wonder then that the Anambra State Customary Court of Appeal, although an official court, is yet to be constituted long after it was supposed to be constituted and be in operation.

DE-EMPHASIZING OFFICIALISM

It remains to restate in this and the next section the need to abandon the brand of official emphasis put on the foreign, English-style justice system in Nigeria. It is not suggested to abandon all aspects of Nigeria's foreign, English-style-dominated justice system. It is, however, necessary to fundamentally repair the country's law and justice system to reposition it on the basis of the Nigerian communities' traditions, customs, and native laws. Nigeria's native systems of justice and law must, again, become the basis of the country's justice and legal systems, official as well as unofficial. This would ultimately ensure the establishment of a more relevant, efficient, and effective justice and legal system in the country. With time, and with the proper management and sustained coordination among the different local community systems, the varying systems of justice and law would be merged and synthesized to produce one universal justice system, even if there continue to be some (minor) differences from one local community to another.

A CALL TO SYNTHESIZE NIGERIA'S JUSTICE

There is certainly no sense in advocating for the retention of Nigeria's pre-colonial native justice systems in contemporary Nigeria. For one thing, the pre-colonial native systems have become so diluted by colonial rule and other societal transformations that they cannot be recovered for contemporary use. For another, the pre-colonial systems may no longer be capable of providing effective social control in contemporary Nigeria due to the many changes that have occurred in the ways of life between pre-colonial and contemporary Nigeria. However, it makes a lot of sense to advocate for a justice system in which the elements of the system are drawn from both the native and foreign ideas of justice, law, and social control, provided that the native systems are rightly recognized as the basic, fundamental systems and sources of law for the country. As stated earlier, there are huge advantages to interacting with, and borrowing from, the experiences and ideas of alternative societies and cultures. But any form of interaction or borrowing from a foreign culture that leads to the supplanting–rather than complementing–of Nigeria's native justice systems is unacceptable, hollow, and retrogressive.

This book demonstrates that Nigeria's native justice systems work. Based on the illustrations that the Igbo system provides, Nigeria's native systems are effective and efficient partners in the administration of justice in the country. The greatest obstacles to the native systems' assumption of their deserved and rightful position of primacy in Nigerian justice, law, and social control are negative official policies and attitudes. Since British colonial rule over Nigeria and up to the present post-independence government, there has been no meaningful effort to rescue and indigenize Nigeria's systems of justice and law. In particular, Nigerian post-independence leaders have lacked the nation-building vision, the intelligence, and the political will to reverse the present duplicate judicial path instituted for us by colonial Britain. Are we supposed to ignore or relegate our native and long-practiced systems of justice, social control, and law and continue to play by the rules imposed on us by our defunct colonizer? The British imposition of the English legal and justice system on Nigeria happened by means of political expedience. Thus, the reversal of the obnoxious British policy will involve Nigeria's contemporary political climate and the players.

The recent adoptions and moves to adopt the shari'a legal and justice system by some states in northern Nigeria are relevant. The point of this book is that Nigerian justice and law need to be indigenized to achieve a relevant, an acceptable, and a more efficient and effective justice and social control system. However, the Zamfara state's shari'a system adoption[1] is not the right or proper kind of indigenization in contemporary Nigeria. It is senseless, myopic, and retrogressive to prescribe a particular set of religious principles for an enormously heterogeneous country like Nigeria or any part thereof.

Every justice and law system is based, to some extent, on the principles of a certain religion. In this regard, the shari'a is no exception. What is objectionable and ungodly is to be so dishonest, so immoral, and so narcissistic as to pretentiously inject into a pluralistic society like Nigeria a policy or program that is an insurance for the destruction of human lives or, at the very least, a deliberate means of dehumanizing certain persons whom the policy maker has already concluded belong in the lower echelon of the human ladder. These are the implications of the official adoptions and attempted adoptions of the shari'a in parts of Nigeria. These moves are not intended to control crime or to serve God. They are designed to serve the selfish, narrow, political, and other interests of those who have incompetently, corruptly, and dishonestly ruled the country since independence, thus criminalizing the average Nigerian in the process (Okereafọezeke, 1999a; 2000e). The adoptions and attempted adoptions of the shari'a in parts of Nigeria are in furtherance of the jihadist mentality of some ruling-class Islamic Nigerians in concert with some influential foreigners. The "Nigerians" in name have no interest in the survival or progress of the Nigerian expression unless they continue to hold the stranglehold on the Nigerian space (Abati, 2000a-e; "Shame in Zamfara," 2000).

If the politicians truly intended to blend the shari'a with the other justice systems applicable in northern Nigeria to produce a system consistent with the greater Nigerian ideal, they would accept the *Penal Code of Northern Nigeria*, which has done an acceptable job of balancing the multifaceted interests in the country. The creators of the *Penal Code* appear to have understood the need to respect the traditions, customs, religions, lifestyles, and aspirations of other northern Nigerians–indeed all other Nigerians–who are not Muslim. This remains the only way to ensure peace, harmony, and progress in any part of the country. The *Penal Code* is the result of negotiations, consultations, and exercises of reason. Thus, the *Penal Code* may be offered as an example of an instrument for synthesized justice. The code, to some extent, recognizes the importance of blending the competing needs of a diverse Nigerian polity. It expresses this understanding by marrying the Nigerian diversity and the Islamic faith practiced by some northerners. The *Penal Code* is based on some acceptance that religious-based laws of all kinds must be subjected to secular laws because every society is made up of religious and nonreligious citizens alike. All should, and must, be equally protected. Obu, Anambra State Customary Court judge, states as follows in an interview (2000):

> As much as necessary, the Customary Court adheres to the official laws [*a priori* the Constitutionally guaranteed rights] in that the judges try to ensure that their judgments follow the spirit of the official laws without formally quoting or citing those official laws. Example, if a custom threatens a party's fundamental human right, the Customary Court will not apply the custom.

At the very least, the adoptions and attempted adoptions of the shari'a should be guided by the same reasoning.

It must be pointed out, however, that the *Penal Code* is not without its fundamental flaws. For instance, the code is substantially based on the Islamic faith and practices, whereas the cultures, traditions, and customs of the natives of northern Nigeria are relegated to the background. These native, African animists had lived in the present northern Nigeria, including the so-called far north, for centuries before the contemporary vocal and dominant Fulani tribe occupied it (Abati, 2000a). Even where Native Courts exist in northern Nigeria, there is no question that the shari'a legal and justice system enjoys a primacy of place over and above the traditions, customs, and native laws of the north. This lopsided situation results from the Fulani domination of political power in the north and all of Nigeria for so long.

The flaws attributed to the *Penal Code of Northern Nigeria* may also be ascribed to the *Criminal Code of Southern Nigeria*. The circumstances that led to the enactment of the *Criminal Code* have been described. In a relative sense, the circumstances leading to the *Penal Code* are based on wider consultation than those leading to the *Criminal Code*. However, each of the two codes, unlike the adoptions and attempted adoptions of the shari'a, is predicated on an acceptance of the superiority of the "secular" Nigerian constitution. Thus, each of the codes takes steps to ensure that the procedural and substantive aspects of the code protect the constitutionally guaranteed rights, such as the rights to freedom of association, freedom of movement, freedom of thought, conscience, and religion, and the prohibition against official adoption of any religion as a state religion. In addition to being irresponsible, it is a sure recipe for Nigeria's destruction for any part thereof to seek to impose any set of religious precepts on those who do not subscribe to the faith. That is another way of officially sanctioning a specific religion as superior to all other religions and nonreligions. It is unacceptable. Nigeria's current socio-political circumstances are relevant to the recommended synthesis of the country's justice systems. There is no doubt that the recommended Sovereign Conference of All Nigeria's Nations (SCANN) (Okereafọezeke, 2000e) will provide the desired opportunity to negotiate aspects of the new justice and legal system. Such conference will provide the national consciousness and the necessary mechanism to reverse the present official disregard and negative attitudes to the country's native justice and legal systems. Thus, there would be increased opportunities for more effective and efficient justice and social control in Nigeria.

SUMMARY

The future of social control in Nigeria requires that the competing elements and systems be made to work together to produce a sophisticated, efficient, and effective law and justice body. The resulting justice and legal system will necessarily be rooted in the country's native systems and practices. In other words, the body of Nigeria's native laws, customs, and traditions should constitute the country's *grundnorm* (the basis of the country's justice and legal system). At present, although Nigeria's native, unofficial institutions of social control play a huge role in the country's social control efforts, they are not credited as deserved. The continued low visibility of the native systems is exacerbated by the official governments' action and omission policies that emphasize the British-imposed, English-style legal and justice system. Thus, Nigeria's native justice and legal systems have remained largely hidden from the world. Continued emphasis on the official, English-style justice system will persist in denying focus on the native systems that really work. The time to reverse this undesirable trend is now.

NOTE

1. Many northern states have since followed the Zamfara example, with others at various stages of fully adopting and implementing the shari'a system.

Conclusion

The range of issues in the data for this book is wide. First, some of the issues are criminal, while others are civil. The issue category for one case study is unclear. The crimes in the data include assault, battery, street fighting, *ịda iwu mmanwụ* (violating the rules and regulations on masquerading), public nuisance, contempt of community institutions and officials, incest, homicide, and contempt of official court. Incest and homicide are two of the most serious crimes in traditional Igbo, hence they are described as *arụ*, *alụ*, or *nsọ* (crimes that pollute the land). Some of the civil cases deal with land and land-related disputes, such as disputes over economic trees and destruction of property. The disputes are some of those that the English law calls "torts." Some other cases deal with other issues such as defamation, false accusations, insult and disrespect for an elderly person, and ostracism. The other issues in the cases are those that concern various forms of contract, including business-financing contract, contract to perform services and sell product, validity of marriage, inheritance, and succession to village headship. Thus, the range of issues with which the Igbo native laws and customs deal includes the issues anticipated and managed under the official, English-style justice system. But the native Igbo justice system anticipates and manages a wider range of issues, some of which are not actionable under the English-style justice system.

The great majority of the issues in the data could be processed either unofficially or officially based on the same set of facts. However, some of the issues, for example, ostracism and disrespect, could be processed only unofficially because the official laws do not consider them actionable. Among the Igbos, the social organizational make-up of justice begins with the *ezi na ụnọ* (family). It continues from this lowest unofficial level through the *ụmụnna* (extended family). It goes on to the *ọnụma* (village), *obodo* (town), Customary

Court, Magistrate Court, High Court, Court of Appeal, and the Supreme Court. The Supreme Court is Nigeria's highest official court. At the first four, unofficial levels of case management, the judges are mostly the community leaders and other respected community members working in concert with the entire community. When a decision has been rendered at any of the first four levels, it may or may not be enforced by the community, depending on whether the case is civil or criminal. Decisions in civil cases are usually left to the disputants to enforce between themselves. Decisions in criminal cases are enforced either by the entire community acting together or by a group of people delegated by the other members. In some cases, particularly cases concerning *iwu mmanwụ*, the community's masquerades enforce judicial decisions. The decision as to who will enforce a judgment is that of the community leaders. The official government is not involved in the decisions or enforcement of decisions at any of the first four levels of case management.

Generally, a disputant is at liberty to take a case to any of the first four, unofficial case management avenues to be resolved. There are no strict rules requiring an aggrieved party to take a case to a particular level before it can be appealed to another. Notwithstanding, the opportunity for appeal exists among the first four, unofficial levels. Despite the multiplicity of avenues for case management, a typical Igbo town has a central body or bodies for the management of cases – some sort of "court of last resort" within the town. In the example of Ajallị Town, the central body is the *Eze*'s Cabinet (*Eze*-in-Council). However, depending on whether the subject of a case is a tradition, native law, or custom, on the one hand, or a political issue, on the other, the Ajallị Welfare Union (AWU), rather than the *Eze*-in-Council, may be the proper tribunal to handle the case. Beyond the *obodo* level, case management is in the hands of the official governments and their agencies (Customary Court, Magistrate Court, High Court, Court of Appeal, and Supreme Court). Decisions rendered by any of the official courts are enforced by the state through its law enforcement agents.

In examining the judicial processes in the cases studied, five categories of informality-formality were created to consider the relative informality of the processes: "Very Informal," "Informal," "Semi-Formal," "Formal," and "Very Formal." The processes in the forty-two archived case studies fall in the last four categories, excluding the first category (Very Informal category). None of the processes in the forty-two cases satisfies the conditions for the "Very Informal" category. Most of the cases have passed through two or more of the nine identified levels of case management. Thus, it is often difficult to put a case at one level or the other, or even to describe it as either strictly out-of-court or in-court. However, a consideration of the particular case management level at which each case is *finally disposed of* leads to the following groups of cases. Of the twenty-eight cases that are finally disposed of unofficially at the *obodo* level, twenty-two cases fall in the "Informal" category and six are in the "Semi-Formal" category. Of the fourteen cases that are finally disposed of in the official courts, one case is in the "Semi-Formal" category, twelve fall in the

"Formal" category, and one is in the "Very Formal" category.

The informality or formality of the judicial process in a case is a function of two things: the nature (civil, criminal) of the case and the level or avenue at which the case is managed. The processes used in the criminal and civil cases before the unofficial tribunals are more informal than the processes used in the cases tried before the official courts. At the unofficial tribunals, the relatively minor crimes such as assault are processed more informally than the more serious crimes such as incest. The more serious the crime, the more formal the judicial process becomes. This seems to be in recognition of the severity of the punishment that awaits the accused person should he or she be convicted. Also in the unofficial case management avenues, the processes for civil cases are more formal than those for the relatively minor criminal cases, such as assault and public nuisance. In the official courts, the processes used in the criminal cases are more formal than those in the civil cases. In the Igbo social control structure, the official agencies of law and order, such as the police and the courts, are not involved in the first four, unofficial levels of control (*ezi na ụnọ*, *ụmụnna*, *ọnụma*, and *obodo*). But, once a case goes beyond these levels, it enters the official structure. From that point on, the case could be taken through the structure to the Supreme Court.

The data show that three policy and attitudinal issues, among others, affect justice in Igbo (and the other parts of Nigeria). First, the repugnancy test, which was established over a century ago by the British colonialists, continues to apply to cases on Nigeria's native laws, customs, and traditions. The essence of the repugnancy test is that for any native law or custom to be recognized and enforced by the official system, the native law or custom must be one that is not repugnant to natural justice, equity, and good conscience. Also, the law or custom must not be contrary to an official law. The official courts decide whether or not a native law or custom complies with this standard. The data show that an official court judge may, on the basis of the test, declare a native law or custom void even if the locals to whom the native law or custom applies approve it. It seems more reasonable and progressive that, in applying a form of repugnancy test to a native law or custom, the historical circumstances of the test, as well as the preferences and aspirations of the locals, should be taken into consideration.

The second major attitudinal issue highlighted by the data is the codification of the Igbo native laws and customs. None of the customary laws and traditions applied to the case studies is codified, even though there are several local community attempts to codify different aspects of the Igbo native laws and customs. Because of the generally uncodified character of the Igbo customary law, a party who wishes to rely on a provision of the law must prove its existence. The party has to lead evidence to establish the particular principle of customary law. This situation makes the Igbo customary law uncertain. The situation also discourages parties from relying on the principles of the Igbo customary law. A major way to address the uncertainty in the law and encourage its use is to codify its principles and provisions.

The third main attitudinal issue raised by the data is the publication of decided cases on the Igbo native laws and customs. At present, only a small portion of such cases is published. The published cases are mainly those decided by the Supreme Court and the Court of Appeal. Very few cases decided by the High Court are published. Customary law cases decided by the Customary Court are not published. In addition, none of the customary law cases managed by the unofficial tribunals is published. The insufficient publication of the decided cases contributes to the difficulty in educating the Igbo community members about the customary laws and traditions that apply to them. Further, the insufficient publication makes research in the area of the Igbo customary law more problematic. Relevant records are either nonexistent or inaccessible. This situation hampers research. The policy issues highlighted by the data could be addressed with the assistance of Nigeria's official local, state, and federal governments. Addressing the policy and attitudinal issues would lead to a new direction in Nigeria's social control policies.

As explained in this book, justice in Nigeria's Igbo is a blend of native (mainly unofficial), and foreign (official, English-style) action. Although the official governments' policies often highlight the English-style justice system, the native Igbo justice system plays a crucial role in social control. In criminal proceedings, the native Igbo system accommodates the fair trial of the accused person; it also attempts to ensure that the community does not suffer injustice as a result of the protection of the accused. In this justice system, the burden of proof is that of the person who makes an assertion or accusation. The burden is on the accuser to convince the unofficial, native court judges that the accused person is guilty. However, where the crime charged is particularly serious, the judges recognize that if the accused person is guilty or responsible, he or she should not be allowed to escape punishment, even if not proved guilty beyond all reasonable doubts. In a civil case, the burden is on the party bringing a claim to prove the claim. But the primary focus of the judges is peacemaking for the parties and the larger community. The judges emphasize to the disputants the need for them to integrate and cooperate with each other and with other community members. Despite the crucial role of Nigeria's native justice systems in the country's social control efforts, the native systems continue to be subjected to the alien, English-style justice system. The native systems have the potential to contribute more effectively to Nigeria's social control efforts. However, they must first be recognized as the fundamental systems of justice. The stage is set for underlying changes to Nigerian law and justice.

Appendix A

Data Summary Showing How the Cases Comply with the Predicted Themes and Descriptors

See the "Findings" subsection under the section on "Assessing the Informal and Formal Characteristics of Justice" (in chapter 2) for the guide to reading Appendix A.

	Characteristic/Theme and its Descriptors:	Presence of theme in a particular process:		
		Clearly Identifiable	Somewhat Identifiable	Not Identifiable
1.	[Officialism] Specific descriptors:			
		* * * * * * *	* * * * * * *	* *
		ID #s of Cases Found	ID #s of Cases Found	ID #s of Cases Found
a. *	Process set up by the Constitution or other law, or established by the state	29-42	None	1-28, 31

Theme 1, Appendix A continued

	Characteristic/Theme and its Descriptors:	Presence of theme in a particular process:		
		Clearly Identifiable	Somewhat Identifiable	Not Identifiable
		* * * * * * *	* * * * * * *	* * * * * * * * * * * * * * * * * * * * * * * * * * * *
b. * *	Indication in report showing that dispute was settled in "court" or <u>*unọ ikpe*</u>	29, 30, 32-42	31	1-28, 31
c. * * *	Any reference to *omenala* "custom or tradition"	2-5, 8-10, 12, 14-17, 19, 22, 24, 28-30, 33, 35, 36, 38-41	1, 11, 13, 18, 20, 26, 31, 42	6, 7, 21, 23, 25, 27, 32, 34, 37
d. * * * *	Reliance on the supernatural–any mention of a shrine, cult, etc.	5, 8, 10, 11, 24, 33, 40, 41	4, 16, 41	1-3, 6, 7, 9, 12-15, 17-23, 25-32, 34-39, 42
e. * * * * *	Specific locales of state authority (police stations, court houses, etc.)	29-42	None	1-28, 31
f. *** ***	Authority figures of state	29-42	None	1-28, 31
g. *** *** *	Uniforms/badges or other credentials	29-42	None	1-28, 31

Appendix A continued

	Characteristic/Theme and its Descriptors:	Presence of theme in a particular process:		
		Clearly Identifiable	Somewhat Identifiable	Not Identifiable
2.	[Mediation] Specific descriptors:			
		* * * * * * * * * *	* * * * * * * * *	* * *
a. * *	Reconciliatory–reference(s) to "making amends," "settlement," etc.	1-3, 7-9, 11, 12, 14-17, 19, 22, 25, 27, 28, 30, 31	5, 10, 23, 33, 36	4, 6, 13, 18, 20, 21, 24, 26, 29, 32-42
b. *	Non-adversarial procedure–whether each party states case without being cross-examined	1, 2, 4, 6, 9, 10, 13, 20, 21, 25, 26, 35, 36, 40-42	7, 37, 38	3, 5, 8, 11, 12, 14-19, 22-24, 27-34, 39
c. * * *	Mention of 3rd party ("go-between") involved in resolving the case	1, 9-12, 14, 15, 19, 22, 24, 25, 27-31	16, 33, 41	2-8, 13, 17, 18, 20, 21, 23, 26, 32-42
d. * * * *	Reference to order-maintenance in the community	2-4, 6, 8, 10-15, 17, 19, 20, 22, 24, 25, 30, 40	1, 7, 16, 18, 21, 26, 29, 31, 41	5, 9, 23, 27, 28, 32-39, 41, 42

Appendix A continued

	Characteristic/Theme and its Descriptors:	Presence of theme in a particular process:		
		Clearly Identifiable	Somewhat Identifiable	Not Identifiable
3.	[Lawyer involvement] Specific descriptors			
				*
a. *	Suggestion(s) of need for lawyers	35-42	None	1-34
b. *	Indication of attempt to secure lawyer	35-42	None	1-34
c. *	Involvement of lawyers in case processing	35-42	None	1-34

Appendix A continued

	Characteristic/Theme and its Descriptors:	Presence of theme in a particular process:		
		Clearly Identifiable	Somewhat Identifiable	Not Identifiable
4.	[Litigiousness or Argumentativeness in a legal sense] Involvement of lawyers in:			
				*
a. *	Bickering	35-42	None	1-34
b. *	Debating	35-42	None	1-34
c. *	Contentiousness	35-42	None	1-34
d. *	Disagreement	35-42	None	1-34
e. *	Altercation	35-42	None	1-34
f. *	Challenge	35-42	None	1-34

Appendix A continued

	Characteristic/Theme and its Descriptors:	Presence of theme in a particular process:		
		Clearly Identifiable	Somewhat Identifiable	Not Identifiable
5.	[Punitiveness]			
				* * * * * *
a. * *	Emphasis on guilt	6, 21, 24, 26, 29, 30, 32, 35-42	4, 5, 7, 11, 13, 15, 20, 31, 33, 34	1-3, 8-10, 12, 14, 16, 17-19, 22, 23, 25, 27, 28
b. *	Emphasis on placing blame	6, 20, 21, 24, 26, 29, 30, 32, 33, 35-42	4, 5, 7, 11, 13, 15, 18, 31, 34	1-3, 8-10, 12, 14, 16, 17, 19, 22, 23, 25, 27, 28
c. * * *	Focus on proof	7, 15, 16, 18, 19, 27-42	2, 3, 5, 8, 11-14, 17, 20, 21, 23, 24	1, 4, 6, 9, 10, 22, 25, 26

Appendix A continued

	Characteristic/Theme and its Descriptors:	Presence of theme in a particular process:		
		Clearly Identifiable	Somewhat Identifiable	Not Identifiable
6.	[Stigmatization] Specific descriptors:			
		* * * * * *	* * * * *	* * * * * * * * * * * * * *
a. *	Loss of dignity by a party–any indication that a party has lost the respect of other community members; or any indication that party is no longer to be looked up to; or denying or stripping party of position or honor	4, 6, 13, 18, 20, 21, 24, 26, 31, 40	1, 2, 12, 16, 30, 42	3, 5, 7-11, 14, 15, 17, 19, 22, 23, 25, 27-29, 32-39, 41
b. * *	Loss of autonomy by party–is a party's freedom of movement, freedom of association, or freedom of speech curtailed such as by pre-trial detention or incarceration?	8, 10, 14-17, 30, 39	None	1-7, 9, 11-13, 18-29, 31-38, 40-42
c. * * *	Loss of wealth by a party	14, 16, 29, 32, 33, 36, 39	15, 27, 31, 35, 41	1-13, 17-26, 28, 30, 33, 34, 37, 38, 40, 42

Theme 6, Appendix A continued

	Characteristic/Theme and its Descriptors:	Presence of theme in a particular process:		
		Clearly Identifiable	Somewhat Identifiable	Not Identifiable
d. * * * *	Loss of time by a party in the process	2, 3, 5, 7, 11, 14, 15, 16, 19, 29-31, 33, 35-42	1, 9, 22, 34	4, 6, 8, 10, 12, 13, 17, 18, 20, 21, 23-28, 32
e. * * * * *	Loss of face by party– any indication that a party was shamed or humiliated by members of the community	4, 6, 13, 16, 18, 20, 21, 24, 26, 30	42	1-3, 5, 7-12, 14, 15, 17, 19, 22, 23, 25, 27, 28, 29, 31-41

Appendix A continued

	Characteristic/Theme and its Descriptors:	Presence of theme in a particular process:		
		Clearly Identifiable	Somewhat Identifiable	Not Identifiable
7.	[Individualization] Specific descriptors:			
		* * * *		* *
a. * *	Existence of rules barring an individual holding a position in the process from exercising discretion on an issue	None	None	1-42
b. * * *	Flexible rules and procedures	1-28, 31-33, 35, 36, 38-42	29, 30, 34, 37	None
c. *	Persons holding positions in the process bend rules and procedures to suit individual cases	1-28, 33, 35, 36, 38-42	29, 30, 31, 32, 34, 37	None

Appendix A continued

	Characteristic/Theme and its Descriptors:	Presence of theme in a particular process:		
		Clearly Identifiable	Somewhat Identifiable	Not Identifiable
8.	[Proscriptiveness of norms] Specific descriptor:			
				*
*	Codification of laws, rules, regulations, or customs	32, 36-41	36, 42	1-31, 33-35

Appendix A continued

	Characteristic/Theme and its Descriptors:	Presence of theme in a particular process:		
		Clearly Identifiable	Somewhat Identifiable	Not Identifiable
9.	[Record management] Specific descriptors:			
		*		* * * * * * * * * * * * * * *
a. * *	Sketchy, handwritten files of the proceedings kept	4, 6, 18	None	None
b. * * *	Complete, handwritten files kept	1-3, 5, 7-17, 19-27	None	None
c. * * * *	Complete, typed files kept	28-42	None	None
d. * * * * *	Complete, verbatim transcription of proceedings kept	None	None	None
e. *	Memory only (oral history)	None	None	None

Appendix A continued

	Characteristic/Theme and its Descriptors:	Presence of theme in a particular process:		
		Clearly Identifiable	Somewhat Identifiable	Not Identifiable
10.	[Simplicity of process] Specific descriptors:			
		* * * * * *		
a. *	Procedure for initiating and conducting a case – spoken words may be sufficient	1-25, 27, 28	29	26, 30-42
b. * *	Non-contractual procedure – little or no need for signatures in the process	1-28	None	29-42
c. * * *	An individual holding a given position in the process may play two or more roles in the process	1-3, 6-19, 21-26, 28, 32	4, 5, 20, 27, 29, 30, 31, 33, 34	35-42

Appendix A continued

	Characteristic/Theme and its Descriptors:	Presence of theme in a particular process:		
		Clearly Identifiable	Somewhat Identifiable	Not Identifiable
11.	[Cost of invoking process] Specific descriptors:			
		* * * * * * *		* * * * * * * *
a. *	No cost	4, 6, 13, 18, 20, 21, 24, 25, 26, 28	10, 32	None
b. * *	Minor gifts	1-3, 5, 7-9, 11, 12, 14-17, 19, 22, 23, 25, 27	None	None
c. * * *	Major gifts	None	None	None
d. * * * *	Small amount of money	1-3, 5, 7-9, 11, 12, 14-17, 19, 22	27	None
e. * * * * *	Large amount of money	29, 33-42	30, 31	None

Appendix A continued

	Characteristic/Theme and its Descriptors:	Presence of theme in a particular process:		
		Clearly Identifiable	Somewhat Identifiable	Not Identifiable
12.	[Peacemaking emphasis] Specific descriptors:			
		* * * * * * * * * *	* *	
a. *	Parties encouraged to integrate and cooperate with each other and the others in the community	2, 3, 5-10, 12, 14-17, 19, 20, 22, 25, 31	1, 4, 11, 21, 26, 27, 29, 30	13, 18, 23, 24, 28, 32-42
b. * *	Reference to the community's interest in peace, progress of the community, etc.	2, 3, 5-8, 10, 12, 14, 15, 17-21, 24, 25, 29, 31, 40	1, 4, 9, 11, 13, 16, 22, 26-28, 30	23, 32-39, 41, 42
c. * * *	Presence of altruistic qualities – party does not stand against the system	1-4, 7, 9, 11, 12, 13, 16-20, 22-28, 31, 32	5, 8, 21, 29, 30, 34, 36	6, 10, 14, 15, 33, 35, 37-42
d. * * * *	Absence of self-help – party involves family relations, friends, volunteers, and neighbors in the efforts to resolve the case	1-3, 5-9, 11, 12, 14-17, 19, 21, 22, 24, 25, 27, 28, 30, 31, 33	4, 10, 20, 26, 29	13, 18, 23, 32-42

Appendix B

Application Form for Arbitration

Appendix B is a retyped copy of the original form issued by the *Eze*-in-Council. The form, as presented below, accurately reflects the original in content and appearance. It was necessary to retype the form because it had become difficult to read due to the poor quality of the original document. The reference to "Eze V of Ajalli" leads to the reasonable conclusion that the form was issued before the *Eze* V of Ajallị died in 1978.

ARBITRATION BY THE ADVISORY COUNCIL
OF HIS ROYAL HIGHNESS:

Chief Nwosu Nwafor, Eze V of Ajalli

I, ______________________________ of ___________________________ Ward, Ajalli in Aguata Local Government Area of Anambra State of Nigeria, hereby voluntarily agree that the Chief's Advisory Council should arbitrate in the Civil dispute between______________________ of ______________________ Ward, Ajalli in Aguata Local Government Area and myself.

Signature: _________________________

Date: ______________________________

Appendix C

Marriage in Ajallị – Regulations

Appendix C is a retyped copy of the original legislation. The law, as presented below, accurately reflects the original in content and appearance. Italics are added to distinguish Igbo words from their English counterparts. It was necessary to retype the legislation because it had become difficult to read due to the poor quality of the original document.

MARRIAGE AT AJALLI – REGULATIONS:

1. *MANYA AJIJIJ*: 2 Gallons of Palm Wine

2. *NNETE UNO*:

   i. The would be husband to come with:-
   2 Gallons of Palm Wine, 1 Carton of Beer.

   ii. Duration of *Nnete Uno*: Number of days as agreed by both parties.

   iii. On the expiration of the agreed period:
   The girl would return with assorted gift, 2 gallons of palm wine and some food.

Appendix C continued

3. BRIDAL PRICE:

a. Should not exceed N2,000.00 (Two thousand Naira) N1,500 for the father and N500.00 for the mother irrespective of status. For Non-Indigenes [non-natives], bridal price is limitless or negotiable.

b. Number of people to attend *Ikpa Akirika Nwanyi* should not exceed 5 people from each side.

c. DRINKS FOR *IKPA AKIRIKA NWANYI*:
1. One bottle of Hot Drink.
2. Two Gallons of Palm Wine.
3. One Carton of Beer.

d. FOOD FOR IN-LAWS:
Rich dishes.

4. *IGBA MMANYA NWANYI*:

A. MEN:
Two Cartons of Beer
Two Cartons of Small Stout Beer
Two Crates of Soft Drink
Five Gallons of Palm Wine
Two bottles of hot drink
Two Heads of Tobacco
One Jet Bottle of Snuff
Eight Big Yams
Two big he-goats (*Okiri*)

B. WOMEN – *UMU ADA*:
2 Cartons of Beer
2 Crates of Soft Drink
1 Bottle of Wine
12 Bars of Soap
12 Tablets of Lux toilet Soap
1 Tin of Powder
1 bottle of pomade
1 Head of tobacco
1 Jet bottle of Snuff
1 Gallon of Palm Wine
Ego Ekpere (N10.00)
Presentation of Bride – N20.00

Appendix C continued

C. *IZU OKU*:
1 big he-goat (*Okiri*)
1 50kg bag of rice
2 Gallons of palm Wine

D. *ANUTARA DI*:
1 Carton of Beer
2 Crates of soft Drink
1 Bottle of Wine
8 Bars of soap
12 Tablets of Lux Toilet Soap
1 Head of Tobacco
1 Tin of Powder
1 Jar of Pomade
1 Jet bottle of snuff

E. CLOTHES PRESENTATION:
Father
1 piece of George cloth
1 Dress
1 Hat
1 Walking stick

Mother
1 piece of George cloth
1 Blouse
1 Head Tie

Ada of the Inner Family
1 piece of George cloth

1st Son of the Family
1 Dress

Other Relations of the Bride
Presentations are optional

5. NUMBER OF PEOPLE TO ATTEND FROM EITHER SIDE:
Optional

6. MUSIC: Optional

Appendix C continued

7. ON THE DAY OF *IGBA MMANYA NWANYI:*
The host shall present as follows:- Food and drinks
   a. To the In-Law: Optional
   b. To Towns people: Optional

8. *IKPOBATA OGO UNO:*
   (i) Among Ajallians: Not applicable
   (ii) Ajalli/[Non-]Indigenes: According to the customs of the Non-Indigenes [Non-natives) concerned.

9. CONTRAVENTION: Anybody who contravenes the marriage regulations or part thereof is liable to a penalty of N1000.00 (One thousand Naira).

10. It shall be the duty of the celebrant to inform one or two of the following persons of the family: Chairman, Secretary and the representative of the family in the Cabinet, to witness the Marriage ceremonies. If any of the 3 (three) fails to report the default, the Cabinet shall not view it lightly.

On a reliable information, it shall be the duty of the members of the Cabinet to collect the penalty from the defaulter soonest after the occasion of *Igba Mmanya Nwanyi.* The Cabinet shall arrange a task force to enforce the collection of the penalty from the defaulter/s.

[signed]

Eze C. O Nwosu
(Eze VI of Ajalli)

[signed]

E. U. Okereke
(Cabinet Secretary)

Dated this 30th day of August, 1995.

Appendix D

Death and Burial Ceremonies in Ajallị – Regulations

Appendix D is a retyped copy of the original legislation. The law, as presented below, accurately reflects the original in content and appearance. Italics are added to distinguish Igbo words from their English counterparts. It was necessary to retype the legislation because it had become difficult to read due to the poor quality of the original document.

DEATH AND BURIAL CEREMONIES IN AJALLI - REGULATIONS:

1. If a person dies, the usual method of informing families and relatives, orally and or in writing should continue.

2. SYMPATHY VISITS:
   (a) Until the death of a person is publicly announced no one should visit the place of bereavement.
   (b) Immediate relatives are free to go in for necessary arrangements.

3. *ITU MKPUKPU* AND *IGWU INI*:
   Some kolanuts, 2 (two) gallons of palm wine and a tray of *ncha* or yam are to be served to each of the 2 (two) groups of persons carrying out the assignments.

Appendix D continued

4. ON THE DAY OF BURIAL:
   i. (a) No food or entertainment for Town's people, In-laws are excluded.
      (b) Light refreshments for distant sympathizers, eg. In-laws and co-workers from distant places.
   ii. *IJE MGBARU*: To continue as usual.

5. CHURCH CONDOLENCE VISITS: To be served:- Optional according to regulations of the church concerned.

6. SHOOTING OF GUN: Optional

7. MASQUERADING: (i) For men – yes (ii) For women - no

8. *IHE AGBAGHARA NA OSO*: Things to be served are as follows:-
   (i) *otu Ọru Ewu* or *otu Ọkụkọ*
   (ii) 2 gallons of palm wine
   (iii) 30 lumps of foofoo
   (iv) Kolanuts (4 Igbo Kolanuts)

9. *ONODU*:
   1. *Izu na-ato* and *izu na-asa* may be celebrated by the family concerned.

   Things to be Served:
   A tray of *Ncha*, 5 gallons of palm wine and kolanuts
   ii. Outside *Izu na-ato* and *Izu na-asa*, *ọnọdụ* in general is strictly prohibited
   iii. *Isi Ada* of the Family should take charge of the affairs affecting *Ụmụ-Ọkpụ*

10. ALL SOCIETIES:
Bereaved person shall present:- Food and drinks according to the Rules of the societies concerned.

11. SHADE (*MKPUKPU*) DESTRUCTION: To be destroyed after *Izu na-asa* by the family. Helpers in the destruction of *mkpukpu* are to be served according to custom viz: Kolanuts, 2 gallons of palm wine, 2 yam tubers and 1 (one) cock.

Appendix D continued

12. CONFINEMENT OF A WIDOW: To be confined comfortably, can bathe, SHOULD NOT QUARREL OR SPEAK ALOUD. After 14 days, she can move around within the compound. After 21 days she will be allowed to move out to fend for herself including going to distant market and church.

All forms of mourning by the widow shall end at the expiration of 7 (Seven) months.

13. BRINGING BACK A WIDOW FROM HER FATHER'S HOUSE AFTER THE 7 (SEVEN) MONTHS STIPULATED MOURNING PERIOD:

The late husband's representative to go with 2 gallons of palm wine. The In-laws to reciprocate by serving the late husband's representative with some kolanuts, *Ncha* and 2 gallons of palm wine. This represents the final burial ceremony of the woman's late husband.

14. CASE OF A WIDOWER: Mourning period is 7 months.

15. *ITISU OZU* ON PUBLIC HOLIDAYS:

On Public Occasions namely: Christmas, New Year, Easter, *Otute* and *Ikeji* festivals, *Itisu Ozu* is prohibited as follows:-
4 days before and 4 days after each of the public occasions.

16. MEMORIAL CEREMONY AND *IKWA MADU*:
Optional according to one's capability.

17. *IBU OZU NWANYI*:
This is not our custom and so it is not carried out in Ajalli.

18. *IJA NKWU*: Entirely prohibited.

19. BREACHING OF THE REGULATIONS:
Any breach of the regulations or part thereof is liable to a penalty of N1000.00 (One thousand Naira) payable by the defaulter.

It shall be the duty of the celebrant to inform one or two of the following persons of the family:-
Chairman, Secretary and the Representative of the family in the Cabinet, to witness the burial processes. If any of the 3 (three) fails to report the default, the Eze-in-Council shall not view it lightly.

Appendix D continued

On a reliable information, it shall be the duty of the Cabinet to collect the penalty from the defaulter soonest after the occasion of the Burial ceremonies. The Cabinet shall arrange a task force to enforce the collection of the penalty from the defaulter/s.

[signed]	[signed]
Eze C. O Nwosu (Eze VI of Ajalli)	E. U. Okereke (Cabinet Secretary)

Dated this 30th day of August, 1995.

Glossary

The following key terms and phases are defined to assist the reader in better understanding the contents of this book. The definitions are arranged alphabetically.

Ada First female born of a family.

Ajallị Welfare Union (AWU) Association of all natives of Ajallị Town. It is organized for social, cultural, economic, and political activities. AWU is made up of several organs, many of which are reserved for specific classes of persons. For example, the "Student Union" is made up of the student members of the town, while the "Family Units" are the *ụmụnna*s in the town.

All NLR All Nigeria Law Report.

Anụtara Di All women non-natives that have become part of the Igbo community by marriage to native men.

Chief (or Traditional Ruler) Customary head of an Igbo town or community. Depending on the procedure in each community, the chief may be elected by the community members or may succeed to the position as the surviving eldest descendant of the passing chief. The process of selecting the chief of an Igbo town is a local affair. However, the official government has some role to play in the matter in so far as the government decides whether or not to recognize a community's ruler. The chief or traditional ruler is called by different names in different Igbo communities. In Ajallị, he is known as *Eze*, which literally stands for "King." The chief or traditional ruler is regarded, among other things, as the moral leader of the community. The chief, along with the lieutenants, organizes the community members in their efforts to attain their common aspirations. The aspirations may be social, cultural, religious, economic, or political in nature.

CNN Cable News Network of the United States of America.

Court of Appeal The penultimate court in the Nigerian official justice system. It is a federal institution, although it hears appeals from both federal and state courts.

Ego Ekpere Money given to a group (usually, a women's group) to pray for a person or group of people.

***Eze*'s Cabinet (or *Eze*-in-Council)** Traditional ruling council made up of *Eze* Ajallị, his advisers, and other lieutenants, including a representative from each of the sixteen *ụmụnna*s and a few other persons appointed by him.

Federal High Court (FHC) The official court of first instance for many issues in the Nigerian federal jurisdiction. In particular, the FHC has subject matter jurisdiction over issues of government revenue and admiralty cases.

First Disputant A person who brings a complaint against another in an out-of-court, unofficial judicial setting or tribunal.

Formal Social Control Consists of the methods, means, and procedures for regulating behavior among the Igbos through the local, state, and federal authorities and institutions of Nigeria's official governments, such as the courts, police, and prisons.

FSC Federal Supreme Court. This used to be the name of the present Supreme Court of Nigeria.

High Court A court of each of Nigeria's thirty-six states. It is the highest trial and appellate court of each state. It hears appeals from the state's lower courts, such as the Magistrate Court. An appeal from the High Court usually goes to the federal Court of Appeal.

***Ichi* (or *Ichi ichi*)** Reporting a person's misconduct to another or others, such as parents, guardians, elderly relatives, friends, and age grade society, that have influence over the wrongdoer. A person or group to which such report is made is expected to influence a positive change in the wrongdoer's conduct, which positive change may put an end to a potential conflict or dispute.

Igwu Ini Grave digging.

Ije Mgbaru Paying a condolence visit. The visitor usually gives the bereaved money or other property to demonstrate the visitor's support for the bereaved in the difficult situation. The amount of money or value of property depends on each visitor's financial and material ability as well as status in society.

Ikeji Igbo annual festival in which ***Mmanwụ*** (Masquerades) of different kinds commonly feature.

In-Court Case A grievance, conflict, or dispute that was finally managed in any of the official governments' courts and tribunals, including the Customary Court, Magistrate Court, High Court, Court of Appeal, and the Supreme Court of Nigeria. Additionally, the several military juntas that ruled Nigeria until May 29, 1999, created many official tribunals to hear and determine specific issues.

Informal Social Control Consists of the processes and procedures for regulating behavior in Igbo by means of generally accepted traditions, customs, and norms. The authority of an official government's agency plays no part in this form of social control. Informal social control involves either the disputants negotiating between themselves and reaching a compromise solution or requesting a third, private party to proffer a solution for them.

***Isi Ada* of the Family** The eldest daughter (or surviving daughter) of the family.

Itisu Ozu Honoring a dead person by celebrating a formal occasion. Usually, such a person has been dead for a long time or the body has not been recovered for proper burial even though he or she is known or presumed to be dead. The death could have occurred years earlier. An example is a soldier who does not return home years after a war. Cf. ***Ịkwa Madụ***.

Izu Na-Asaa Seven Igbo weeks, in which each week consists of four days (28 days total).

Izu Na-Atọ Three Igbo weeks, in which a week consists of four days (12 days total).

Ịgba Mmanya Nwanyị Celebration of marriage. The celebration is usually public, but the celebrants may restrict the occasion as they see fit or according to their financial ability. The celebration tends to be expensive.

Ịkpa Akịrịka Nwanyị Bridal price negotiation and payment as a part of the marriage process.

Ịkpọbata Ọgọ Ụnọ An occasion to formally welcome a new wife's close relatives (in-laws) to their daughter's new home.

Ịkwa Madụ Honoring a dead person by a second (final) ceremony that completes his or her proper burial. This usually means that the dead was recovered and properly buried in the first ceremony. Cf. ***Itisu Ozu***.

Ịtụ Mkpukpu Erecting shades, such as by means of palm tree branches and leaves, to protect participants at an occasion, for example, at a burial. See ***Mkpukpu***.

Ịtụnye Mmanya (filing a suit) A procedure for initiating the unofficial judicial process in the native Igbo justice system. In the Ajallị Town example, *ịtụnye mmanya* requires the initiating party to present stipulated gift items and money to the unofficial tribunal to which a case is submitted for adjudication. The responding party (Second Disputant) may also be required to present similar gifts to the tribunal.

Local Government Area (or Local Government Council) Nigeria's lowest official government level. It is the smallest administrative unit of the country recognized by the constitution and other official laws. A Local Government Area is made up of several towns and villages. It may consist of less than ten towns or more than twenty towns. The *1999 Constitution of Nigeria* recognizes more than 700 Local Government Areas, including Abuja's (Federal Capital Territory) six Area Councils. The administrative authority of a Local Government Area is known as the Local Government Authority. Ajallị Town is in the Orumba North Local Government Area.

Magistrate Court A low level official court in each of Nigeria's thirty-six states. The Magistrate Court, which is a state court, is inferior to the High Court.

Manya (Mmanya) Ajụjụ The presentation of wine (usually, palm wine) to the parents and selected elderly relatives of a prospective bride at which occasion the prospective groom and his relatives formally inform the girl's relatives that the prospective groom would like to marry their daughter. Usually, at the end of the occasion, the prospective groom awaits a response from the girl's relatives. If they respond positively, then arrangements would begin toward the marriage celebration.

Mkpukpu Shade, usually erected with palm tree branches and leaves to protect guests at an occasion from the weather. See ***Ịtụ Mkpukpu***.

Mmanwụ (Masquerade) A masked, life-like figure roving an Igbo or other Nigerian community on occasions, such as during cultural and religious events. The mask and the special attire in which a masquerade appears to the public add to the mystery surrounding the Igbo masquerade culture. Masquerades constitute a very important cultural part of the lives of the Igbos. The popular belief is that masquerades are the spirits of the dead that have returned to live in other forms among the living. Every person who comes in contact with a masquerade is expected by the community members to respect and defer to the masquerade. In traditional Igbo, *mmanwụ* plays a crucial role in the maintenance of law and order, and general social control.

Ncha Tapioca. An Igbo cassava food that usually precedes a more formal meal at an occasion.

NLR Nigerian Law Report.

NMLR Nigerian Monthly Law Report.

Nnete Ụnọ A bride's first formal visit to the groom's home to acquaint her with the home and the groom's relatives. The visit, which occurs before marriage as part of the getting-to-know-each-other-well process, usually lasts for about 8 days.

NSCC Nigerian Supreme Court Cases.

NWLR Nigerian Weekly Law Report.

Official Describes an entity, body, activity, or process established, run, or implemented by any of the following: the applicable local government authority, the applicable state government, the government of the Federal Republic of Nigeria, or any of their agencies or agents.

***Omenala* (or *Omenana*)** Consists of all the traditions, customs, norms, ways of life, and laws that are native to the Igbos. Such traditions and customs were in existence before the British occupied Igbo land. *Omenala* includes the traditions and customs as they existed before the occupation and as they exist in contemporary Igbo following the changes that they have undergone.

Otu Ọkụkọ One chicken (live).

Otu Ọrụ Ewu One piece of goat thigh and leg (not separated).

Otute Igbo annual festival celebrating the arrival of new yams. Before *otute*, yams should not be harvested in Igbo. However, on the date the festival begins and for the rest of the year, yams may be customarily harvested.

Out-of-Court Case A grievance, conflict, or dispute that was finally managed in a judicial setting or in an arrangement other than that provided by any of the official governments' courts and tribunals.

Ọnọdụ Keeping wake at the home of a deceased as a way of providing the bereaved relatives company in their mourning period.

Record of Proceedings A handwritten, typed, printed, or otherwise record of the proceedings at which a case was heard and adjudicated upon with a view to managing the case unofficially, for example, at a meeting of Ajallị Town's *Eze*-in-Council (the town's traditional ruler and the council of advisers).

SCNJ Supreme Court of Nigeria Judgments.

Second Disputant A person against whom another brings a complaint in an out-of-court, unofficial judicial arrangement, setting, or tribunal.

State An official administrative unit of Nigeria made up of several Local Government Areas. A state may consist of anywhere between ten and thirty local government areas. Nigeria consists of thirty-six states and the federal capital territory, Abuja. Each state is a creation of the constitution or other laws of the Federal Republic of Nigeria. The administrative authority of a state is the state government. Ajallị Town is in Anambra State.

Supreme Court of Nigeria or **Supreme Court (SCN or SC)** The highest court in Nigeria's official judicial structure. There is only one Supreme Court in the country, and it is the court of last resort. Most judicial decisions by state and federal official courts may be appealed to the Supreme Court.

Unofficial Describes an entity, body, activity, or process that does not fall within the meaning of **Official**. See **Official**.

***Ụmụ Ọkpụ* (or *Ụmụ Ada*)** The daughters of the land. A native daughter is a member of this group even if she is married to a non-native.

Ụmụnna (children of the same father) A group of nuclear families whose members trace their ancestry to a common father. Sometimes, individuals or nuclear families may be permitted to join an *ụmụnna* even though they trace their ancestry through a different paternal lineage. *Ụmụnna* is loosely called "the extended family."

References

Abacha and Others v. Fawehinmi (Appeal No. SC, 45/1997, Supreme Court of Nigeria, Judgment delivered on April 28, 2000). Available from *http:// www.ngrguardiannews.com/law/ln785601.html.*

Abati, Reuben (2000a) "The Second Jihad," in *The Guardian*. Available from *http://www.ngrguardiannews.com/editorial2/en777505.html.*

__________ (2000b) "Obasanjo and the Jihadists," in *The Guardian*. Available from *http://www.ngrguardiannews.com/editorial2/en778202.html.*

__________ (2000c) "The *Sharianisation* of Public Discourse," in *The Guardian*. Available from *http://www.ngrguardiannews.com/ editorial2/ en 77890 2.html.*

__________ (2000d) "Children of the Sharia," in *The Guardian*. Available from *http://www.ngrguardiannews.com/editorial2/en781005.html.*

__________ (2000e) "The Retreat of the Jihadists," in *The Guardian*. Available from *http://www.ngrguardiannews.com/editorial2/en781702.html.*

Abel, R. L., ed. (1982) *The Politics of Informal Justice*. Vol. 1; *The American Experience*. New York, USA: Academic Press.

Achebe, Chinua (1959) *Things Fall Apart*. New York, USA: Fawcett Crest Books.

Adeyemi, A. A. (1990) "Criminology in Contemporary Africa," in *Nigerian Journal of Criminology* 2/1, 1-30.

____________ (1990, July) "Crime and Development in Africa: A Case Study on Nigeria," in Zvekic, U., ed., *Essays on Crime and Development*. Publication Number 36. Rome, Italy: United Nations Interregional Crime and Justice Research Institute (UNICRI).

Afonja v. Aiyelagbe, FSC 317/61 (Federal Supreme Court of Nigeria).

Anambra State Customary Courts Law (Laws of Anambra State of Nigeria).

Anambra State Edict No. 6 of 1984 (Laws of Anambra State of Nigeria).

Anambra State Torts Law (Laws of Anambra State of Nigeria).

Anene, L. O. C. (1991) "A Study of the Rapid Transformation of Ibo Heartland Settlements from Rural to Urban Centers: A Post-Nigerian Civil War Phenomenon." Unpublished Dissertation No. AAC9201061.

Annual Abstract of Statistics, 1990 (Nigeria).

Austin, W. Timothy (1999) *Banana Justice: Field Notes on Philippine Crime and Custom*. Westport, Connecticut, USA: Praeger Publishers.

Becker, Howard S. (1963) *Outsiders: Studies in the Sociology of Deviance*. New York, USA: The Free Press.

Berg, Bruce L. (1998) *Qualitative Research Methods for the Social Sciences*. Boston, USA: Allyn and Bacon.

Black, Donald (1976) *The Behavior of Law*. New York, USA: Academic Press.

___________ (1990) "Elementary Forms of Conflict Management," in *New Directions in the Study of Justice, Law, and Social Control*, School of Justice Studies, Arizona State University. New York, USA: Plenum Press.

___________ (1993) *The Social Structure of Right and Wrong*. San Diego, California, USA: Academic Press.

Black, Donald, ed. (1984) *Toward a General Theory of Social Control*. 2 vols. New York, USA: Academic Press.

Canter, R. S. (1978) "Dispute Settlement and Dispute Processing in Zambia: Individual Choice Versus Societal Constraints," in L. Nader and H. F. Todd, Jr., eds., *The Disputing Process–Law in Ten Societies*. New York, USA: Columbia University Press.

Chanock, M. (1985) *Law, Custom, and Social Order: The Colonial Experience in Malawi and Zambia*. New York, USA: Cambridge University Press.

Christelow, A. (1991) "Theft, Homicide and Oath in Early Twentieth-Century Kano," in K. Mann and R. Roberts, eds., *Law in Colonial Africa*. Portsmouth, New Hampshire, USA: Heinemann.

Constitution of the Federal Republic of Nigeria, 1979.

Constitution of the Federal Republic of Nigeria, 1999 (effective May 29, 1999).

Constitution (Suspension and Modification) Decree No. 107 of 1993 (Laws of Nigeria).

Creel, M. W. (1988) *A Peculiar People: Slave Religion and Community Culture Among the Gullah*. New York, USA: New York University Press.

Criminal Code Law of Anambra State (Laws of Anambra State of Nigeria).

Criminal Code (Laws of Nigeria).

Customary Court Rules of Anambra State, Nigeria.

David, R., and J. E. C. Brierley (1978) *Major Legal Systems in the World Today: An Introduction to the Comparative Study of Law*. New York, USA: The Free Press.

Dickson-Gilmore, J. (1992) "Finding the Ways of the Ancestors: Cultural Change and the Invention of Tradition in the Development of Separate Legal Systems," in *Canadian Journal of Criminology* 34, 479-502.

Durkheim, Emile (1897/1951) *Suicide: A Study in Sociology*. New York, USA: Free Press.

Ebbe, Obi N. I. (1985) "Power and Criminal Law: Criminalization of Conduct Norms in a Colonial Regime," in *International Journal of Comparative and Applied Criminal Justice* 9/2, 113-122.

Eckert, P., and R. Newark (1980) "Central Eskimo Song Duels: A Contextual Analysis of Ritual Ambiguity," in *Ethnology* 19/2: 191-211.

Ekechi, F. K. (1972) *Missionary Enterprise and Rivalry in Igboland 1857-1914*. London, UK: Frank Cass and Co.

Ekpendu v. Erika (1959) 4 Federal Supreme Court 79 (Nigeria).

Elias, Taslim Olawale (1961) *Nigerian Land Law and Custom*. London, UK: Routledge and Kegan Paul.

Evidence Act (Laws of the Federation of Nigeria, 1958).

Ezeanya and Others v. Okeke and Others (1995) 4 Supreme Court of Nigeria Judgments 60.

Ezeokafor v. Otaluka, Suit No. FSC 214/63, (1964) NSCC 234 (Federal Supreme Court of Nigeria).

Fang, Y., M. D. McShane, and F. P. Williams, III (1996) "Concepts and Theories in the Use of Mediation: Shaming Models in American and Chinese Cultures," in C. B. Fields and R. H. Moore, Jr., eds., *Comparative Criminal Justice: Traditional and Nontraditional Systems Law and Control*. Prospect Hills, Illinois, USA: Waveland Press.

The Federal Military Government (Supremacy and Enforcement of Powers) Decree No. 12 of 1994 (Laws of Nigeria).

Garland, D. (1990) *Punishment and Modern Society: A Study in Social Theory*. Chicago, Illinois, USA: University of Chicago Press.

_________ (1991) "Punishment and Culture: The Symbolic Dimension of Criminal Justice," in *Studies in Law, Politics, and Society* 11, 191-222.

Glaser, B., and A. Strauss (1967) *The Discovery of Grounded Theory*. Chicago, Illinois, USA: Aldine Publishing Co.

Gulliver, P. H. (1979) *Disputes and Negotiations: A Cross-Cultural Perspective*. New York, USA: Academic Press.

Hazlehurst, Kayleen M. (1995) "Introduction: Unyielding Domains in the Post-Colonial Relationship," in *Legal Pluralism and the Colonial Legacy: Indigenous Experiences of Justice in Canada, Australia, and New Zealand*. Aldershot, UK: Avebury.

"Headcount" (1990) *The Economist* 315, June 9, 46.

Henry, S. (1987a) "Disciplinary Pluralism: Four Models of Private Justice in the Workplace," in *Sociological Review* 35, 279-319.

Henry, S. (1987b) "The Construction and Deconstruction of Social Control: Thoughts on the Discursive Production of State Law and Private Justice," in J. Lowman, et al., eds., *Transcarceration: Essays in the Sociology of Social Control*. Aldershot, UK: Gower.

Hirchi, Travis (1969) *Causes of Delinquency*. Berkeley, California, USA: University of California Press.

Iroegbu (For himself and as representing the Chiefs and people of Avonkwu Ibeku) v. Okwordu and Nwubani (For themselves and as representing the Chiefs and people of Eruete Ibeku) (1995) 4 Supreme Court of Nigeria Judgments 7.

Iyam, D. Uru (1995) *The Broken Hoe: Cultural Reconfiguration in Biase Southeast Nigeria*. Chicago, Illinois, USA: University of Chicago Press.

Jones, M. (1993) "Nigerian Crime Networks in the United States," in *International Journal of Offender Therapy and Comparative Criminology* 37/1, 59-73.

Land Use Act, 1978 (Laws of Nigeria).

Lekwot v. Judicial Tribunal (1993) 2 Nigerian Weekly Law Report (Part 276) 410.

Levi's case, in *Miramichi Weekend* 31/38, Friday, July 12, 1996. Miramichi, New Brunswick, Canada.

Lewis and Others v. Bankole and Others (1908) 1 Nigerian Law Report 81.

Lowy, M. J. (1978) "A Good Name Is Worth More Than Money: Strategies of Court Use in Urban Ghana," in L. Nader and H. F. Todd, Jr., eds., *The Disputing Process–Law in Ten Societies*. New York, USA: Columbia University Press.

Mann, Kristin (1985) *Marrying Well: Marriage, Status, and Social Change among the Educated Elite in Colonial Lagos*. New York, USA: Cambridge University Press.

____________ (1991) "Law, Accumulation, and Mobility in Early Colonial Lagos," in K. Mann and R. Roberts, eds., *Law in Colonial Africa*. Portsmouth, New Hampshire, USA: Heinemann.

Meribe v. Egwu (1976) 3 Supreme Court 23 (Nigeria).

Merton, Robert K. (1957) *Social Theory and Social Structure*. New York, USA: The Free Press.

"The Missing 20 Million" (1992). *The Economist* 322, March 28, 37.

Nader, L., and H. F. Todd, Jr., eds. (1978) *The Disputing Process–Law in Ten Societies*. New York, USA: Columbia University Press.

Nair, K. K. (1972) *Politics and Society in Southeastern Nigeria 1841–1906*. London, UK: Frank Cass.

Native Court Ordinance (No. 5, as amended in 1922) (Laws of Nigeria).

Native Courts Proclamation, 1900 (Laws of Nigeria).

Nettheim, G. (1995) "Mabo and Legal Pluralism: The Australian Aboriginal Justice Experience," in K. M. Hazlehurst, ed., *Legal Pluralism and the Colonial Legacy: Indigenous Experiences of Justice in Canada, Australia, and New Zealand*. Aldershot, UK: Avebury.

Nezianya v. Okagbue (1963) 1 All Nigeria Law Report 352.

Nigerian Criminal Code (Laws of Nigeria).

"Nigeria's Population Tops 108 Million," CNN, October 23, 1998. Available from *http://cnn.com/WORLD/africa/9810/23/RB000959.reut.html*.

Nweje, M. O. (1975) "In Search of Justice," in T. O. Elias, et al., eds., *African Indigenous Laws: Proceedings of Workshop (7-9 August, 1974)*. Enugu, Nigeria: The Government Printer.

Nwomeji and Others v. Nwegbe, Suit No. AB/27CCA/88, Decided in July 1993 (Anambra State, Nigeria, Customary Court).

Nzekwu and Others v. Nzekwu and Others (1989) 2 Nigerian Weekly Law Report 373.

Obi, S. N. C. (1963) *The Ibo Law of Property*. London, UK: Butterworths.

Ochomma v. Unosi (1965) Nigerian Monthly Law Report 321.

Ogbalu, F. (1979) *Igbo Institutions and Customs*. Onitsha, Nigeria: University Publishing Co.

________ (1981) *Omenala Igbo*. Onitsha, Nigeria: University Publishing Co.

Okafor, F. (1978) *Africa at the Crossroads*. New York, USA: Vintage Press.

Okeke v. A-G Anambra State (1992) 1 Nigerian Weekly Law Report (Part 214) 60.

Okereafọezeke, Nọnso (1996) *The Relationship Between Informal and Formal Strategies of Social Control: An Analysis of the Contemporary Methods of Dispute Processing Among the Igbos of Nigeria*. UMI Number 9638581. Ann Arbor, Michigan, USA: University Microfilms.

________________ (1998a) "*Isi N'Ezi Ama Mma*; Anomic Conditions in the Management and Utilization of Africa's Human and Natural Resources." Paper presented at the Phi Beta Delta Honor Society for International Scholars' symposium on Africa in the 21st Century: A Look at the Potential of the Continent's Natural and Human Resources, Western Carolina University, Cullowhee, North Carolina, USA, December 3, 1998.

________________ (1998b) "Qualitative Versus Quantitative Approaches to Teaching Criminological and Criminal Justice Research Methods: An Unholy Rivalry?" Paper presented at the American Society of Criminology Conference, Washington, D.C., USA, November 11-14, 1998.

________________ (1999a) "Analysis of the Criminalizing Policies, Programs, and Idiosyncrasies of the Nigerian Governments in the Country's Darkest Age, 1985-1999." Paper presented at the Southeast Regional Seminar on African Studies Conference, Armstrong Atlantic State University, Savannah, Georgia, USA, October 15-16, 1999 (see *http://www.ecu.edu/african/sersas/programf99.htm*).

________________ (1999b) "Socio-Cultural Variables in the Interpretation and Application of Criminal Laws in the 21st Century U. S. A." Paper presented at the American Society of Criminology Conference, Toronto, Canada, November 17-20, 1999.

________________ (2000a) "Igbo Justice" as a British Colonial Legacy in Nigeria (unpublished).

Okereafọezeke, Nọnso (2000b) "Still Rooted in British Colonialism: On Fashioning an Acceptable Justice System for a Federal, Democratic Nigeria." Paper presented at the Southeast Regional Seminar on African Studies Conference, Western Carolina University, Cullowhee, North Carolina, USA, April 14-15, 2000 (see *http://www.ecu.edu/african/sersas/program400.htm*).

____________________ (2000c) "The Immigrant Offender and the Dynamics of Socio-Cultural Defenses to Crimes in the United States of America," in *Phi Beta Delta International Review* 10, Spring, 173-189.

____________________ (2000d) "Methodological and Procedural Issues in 'Archiving at a Distance': From Nigeria to the United States of America." Paper presented at the Southeast Regional Seminar on African Studies Conference, University of Tennessee, Knoxville, Tennessee, USA, October 27-28, 2000 (see *http://www.ecu.edu/african/sersas/Fall2000Program.htm*).

____________________ (2000e) "Government in Nigeria: the Criminalization of a Nation," in *The Journal of African Policy Studies*, in press.

Okereafọezeke, Nọnso, and W. Timothy Austin (1996) "A Qualitative Measure of the Relative Informality of a Judicial Process." Paper presented at the American Society of Criminology Conference, Chicago, Illinois, USA, November 20-23, 1996.

Okonkwo v. Okagbue and 2 Others (1994) 12 Supreme Court of Nigeria Judgments 89.

Oli, S. I. (1994) "A Dichotomization: Crime and Criminality Among Traditional and Christianized Igbo," in A. T. Sulton, ed., *African-American Perspectives On: Crime Causation, Criminal Justice Administration and Crime Prevention*. Englewood, Colorado, USA: Sulton Books.

Ome and 14 Others v. Ugeze, Suit No. AB/CC/3A/92, Decided in May 1993 (Anambra State, Nigeria, Customary Court).

Onyechi, N. M. (1975) "A Problem of Assimilation or Dominance," in T. O. Elias, et al., eds., *African Indigenous Laws: Proceedings of Workshop (7-9 August, 1974)*. Enugu, Nigeria: The Government Printer.

Osu v. Igiri (1988) 1 Nigerian Weekly Law Report (Part 69) 221.

Penal Code (Laws of Northern Nigeria).

Porter, G. (1992) "The Nigerian Census Surprise," *Geography*, 77, October, 371-374.

Pratt, J. (1995) "Aboriginal Justice and the 'Good Citizen': An Essay on Population Management," in K. M. Hazlehurst, ed., *Legal Pluralism and the Colonial Legacy: Indigenous Experiences of Justice in Canada, Australia, and New Zealand*. Aldershot, United Kingdom: Avebury.

"Principles Distinguish Pakistani and Nigerian Judges," *Vanguard*, February 3, 2000. Available from *http://www.afbis.com/vanguard/VC203020.htm*.

Proclamation No. 6 of 1900 (Laws of Nigeria).

Quinney, Richard (1970) *The Social Reality of Crime*. Boston, Massachusetts, USA: Little, Brown.

Quinney, Richard (1988) "Crime, Suffering, Service: Toward a Criminology of Peacemaking," in *The Quest*, Winter, 66-75.

Record of Proceedings of the Ajallị Town's *Eze*-in-Council deliberations (Record of Proceedings), volumes 1-3, 1987-1995.

Rodney, Walter (1974) *How Europe Underdeveloped AFRICA*. Washington, D.C., USA: Howard University Press.

Ross, R. (1992) *Dancing with a Ghost: Exploring Indian Reality*. Toronto, Canada: Octopus Publishing Co.

Salamone, F. A. (1980) "Continuity, Change and Conflict in Gbagyi Law," in *Research in Law and Sociology* 3, 221-253.

Shaidi, L. P. (1992) "Traditional, Colonial and Present-Day Administration of Criminal Justice," in *Criminology in Africa*. Publication No. 47. Rome, Italy: United Nations Interregional Crime and Justice Research Institute.

"Shame in Zamfara" (Editorial) *The Guardian*, March 31, 2000. Available from *http://www.ngrguardiannews.com/editorial2/en781001.html.*

Smandych, R. C. (1991a) "Tory Paternalism and the Politics of Penal Reform in Upper Canada, 1830-1834: A 'Neo-Revisionist' Account of the Kingston Penitentiary," in *Criminal Justice History: An International Annual* 12, 57-83.

____________ (1991b) "Rethinking 'the Master Principle of Administering Relief' in Upper Canada: A Response to Allan Irving," in *Canadian Review of Social Policy* 27, 81-86.

____________ (1991c) "Upper Canadian Considerations About Rejecting the English Poor Law, 1817-1837: A Comparative Study of the Reception of Law," in *Canadian Legal History Project Working Paper Series*. Faculty of Law, University of Manitoba, Canada.

Snyder, F. G. (1982) "Colonialism and Legal Form: The Creation of Customary Law in Senegal," in C. Sumner, ed., *Crime, Justice and Underdevelopment*. London, UK: Heinemann.

Stafford, C. (1995) "Colonialism, Indigenous Peoples, and the Criminal Justice Systems of Australia and Canada: Some Comparisons," in K. M. Hazlehurst, ed., *Legal Pluralism and the Colonial Legacy: Indigenous Experiences of Justice in Canada, Australia, and New Zealand*. Aldershot, UK: Avebury.

State Security (Detention of Persons) Decree, Cap. 414, Laws of the Federation of Nigeria, 1990.

State Security (Detention of Persons) Decree, No. 2 of 1984 (Laws of Nigeria).

Sutherland, Edwin H. (1947) *Principles of Criminology*. Philadelphia, Pennsylvania, USA: J. B. Lippincott Co.

Sykes, Gresham M., and David Matza (1957) "Techniques of Neutralization: A Theory of Delinquency," in *American Sociological Review* 22, 664-670.

Thiong'o, wa Ngugi (1986) *Decolonising the Mind: The Politics of Language in African Literature*. London, United Kingdom: James Currey.

Thiong'o, wa Ngugi (1993) *Moving the Centre: The Struggle for Cultural Freedoms*. London, UK: James Currey.

_______________ (1997) *Writers in Politics: A Re-Engagement with Issues of Literature and Society*. Oxford, England: James Currey.

Thompson, R. B. (1996) "Due Process and Legal Pluralism in Sierra Leone: The Challenge of Reconciling Contradictions in the Laws and Cultures of a Developing Nation," in C. B. Fields and R. H. Moore, Jr., eds., *Comparative Criminal Justice: Traditional and Nontraditional Systems of Law and Control*. Prospect Heights, Illinois, USA: Waveland Press.

Todd, H. F. (1978) "Litigious Marginals: Character and Disputing in a Bavarian Village," in L. Nader and H. F. Todd, Jr., eds., *The Disputing Process – Law in Ten Societies*. New York, USA: Columbia University Press.

Uchendu, V. C. (1966) *The Igbo of Southeast Nigeria*. New York, USA: Holt, Rinehart and Winston.

Uwazie, E. E. (1994) "Modes of Indigenous Disputing and Legal Interactions Among the Ibos of Eastern Nigeria," in *Journal of Legal Pluralism and Unofficial Law* 34, 87-103.

Weisheit, R. A., D. N. Falcone, and L. E. Wells (1996) *Crime and Policing in Rural and Small-Town America*. Prospect Heights, Illinois, USA: Waveland Press.

INTERVIEWS

Nwankwo, Jerry, Local Government Councilor, Treasurer-General, Ajallị Welfare Union (AWU); *Ụmụnna Ụmụabịama* Secretary, 1984-1988; *Ụmụnna Ụmụabịama* Welfare Association Treasurer; interview at his residence, Ajallị, Anambra State, Nigeria, August 3, 2000.

Nwosu, C. O. *Eze* VI of Ajallị; interview at *Eze*'s Palace, Ajallị, Anambra State, Nigeria, July 18, 2000.

Obu, Noel, Justice of the Peace, Customary Court Judge; interview at Obu's residence, Ajallị, Anambra State, Nigeria, July 22, 2000.

Okereke, Mgborie; interview at her residence, Ajallị, Anambra State, Nigeria, July 23, 2000.

Index

About the Author

NỌNSO OKEREAFỌEZEKE is an Assistant Professor of Criminal Justice at Western Carolina University. He studied and practiced law in Nigeria before beginning graduate studies in the United States. In addition to his legal training, he holds an M.A. in Criminal Justice and a Ph.D. in Criminology. His research interests include the role of unofficial, non-governmental groups and structures in social control, and the challenge of fashioning a relevant, acceptable justice system for post-British Nigeria.